The Campaigns of Field-Marshal Blücher

FIELD-MARSHAL PRINCE BLÜCHER OF WAHLSTATT

The Campaigns of Field-Marshal Blücher
During the Seven Years War, the Revolutionary War and the Napoleonic Wars, 1758-1815

ILLUSTRATED WITH 49 PICTURES AND MAPS

August Gneisenau

The Campaigns of Field-Marshal Blücher
During the Seven Years War, the Revolutionary War and the Napoleonic Wars, 1758-1815
by August Gneisenau

ILLUSTRATED WITH 49 PICTURES AND MAPS

First published under the title
The Life and Campaigns of Field-Marshal Prince Blücher of Wahlstatt

Leonaur is an imprint of Oakpast Ltd
Copyright in this form © 2022 Oakpast Ltd

ISBN: 978-1-915234-48-3 (hardcover)
ISBN: 978-1-915234-49-0 (softcover)

http://www.leonaur.com

Publisher's Notes

The views expressed in this book are not necessarily those of the publisher.

Contents

Letter to His Majesty the King of Prussia	7
Preface	9
A List of Napoleon's Marshals and Civil Officers	11
Enters into the Swedish Service	13
Colonel Blücher's Campaigns on the Rhine in 1793 and 1794	24
General Blücher's Campaign in 1806	33
Opening of the Campaign by General von Blücher	42
Battle of Lützen	64
Blücher's Ambuscade at Haynau	92
Blücher's Victory on the Katzbach	115
Blücher Crosses the Elbe	143
Battle of Leipsic	179
Blücher passes the Rhine	212
Battles of Brienne and La Rothière	242
Blücher Marches His Army on Paris	258
Victory of Laon	270
The Congress at Vienna	288
Napoleon Buonaparte's Escape from Elba	295

Letter to His Majesty the King of Prussia

Sire,

In presenting the following pages to Your Majesty, I perform a duty at once pleasing to myself and useful to the world. To me it is a feeling of unmixed delight, that I am thus enabled to record the illustrious deeds of your great general; and that delight is augmented by the hope, that this faithful history of them will obtain Your Majesty's approbation; while to the world it must ever afford a useful example, to behold the career of a successful conqueror, fighting in the cause of liberty, of virtue, and of honour, and nobly rewarded by his sovereign for the achievement of his renowned deeds.

Your Majesty must have experienced no common sentiment of exultation and felicity, in the brilliant termination of that contest in which you so promptly engaged when the auspicious moment presented itself for a wise and efficient co-operation; nor can Your Majesty recall the series of warlike triumphs by which that success was obtained, without finding the name of Blücher visibly stamped on all. It would be difficult to determine whether it be more glorious to have conquered in such a cause, or with such a general.

But while we thus pay the tribute of our gratitude and admiration to the virtues of Your Majesty, and the transcendent exploits of the venerable hero, let us not forget the patriotism, the ardour, the intrepidity, and the fortitude of the people: they seconded with a noble zeal, worthy of themselves and their ancestors, the efforts of their sovereign. The cry of battle rang in their ears; the love of independence was in their hearts. They remembered the deeds of their forefathers, and, as if animated by one soul, they arose in the fulness of their strength, buckled on their shield, and marched to victory or death.

The descendants of Hermann were not slow to chase the foul invader from their fields: they sprang to arms—they fought—they conquered. They carried their avenging swords to the doors of their oppressors, and there they sheathed them; thus exhibiting to the world the affecting and sublime spectacle, of an insulted but magnanimous nation, proudly shaking off the fetters that tyranny and fraud had imposed, and generously disdaining to retaliate upon the vanquished the evils they had suffered.

Such, Sire, is the picture which the following volume displays; and in the various groups of which it is composed, Blücher, the idol of his army, the favourite of his sovereign, and the benefactor of mankind, stands pre-eminently conspicuous.

With feelings of the most profound respect, permit me to subscribe myself,

    Sire, Your Majesty's most faithful.
        And most devoted Servant,
                            James Edward Marston.

Hamburg,
August 1815.

Preface

It is the duty of the biographer to detail every trait of character, to portray every feature, whether stamped with the image of virtue or of vice. Each page is to present something to praise or admire, or to display a portrait that may create disgust and contempt. But when he fortunately has for his subject one of the most valiant, skilful, and prosperous commanders of his time, his only aim must then be to render the theme of his memoirs interesting as well as useful. The limits of such an undertaking cannot be strictly defined. Contrast is the soul of narration; and in noticing the illustrious actions, greatness, and military genius of our hero, we ought surely not only to embrace the mention of those gallant soldiers, who may with justice be ranked in the line of his equals, but also those who have disgraced humanity, though the recollection of their deeds must ever create both horror and detestation.

This is the system upon which the present volume has been formed, and our exertions have been principally directed to the procuring and collecting every information, that could be derived from original and authentic sources; we are therefore willing to hope, that no material occurrence has escaped our diligent and extensive search, as every sketch that has appeared in the German language of Blücher's life, and the events of the late war, particularly what has been written by General Count Gneisenau, and General Müffling, has been carefully examined and faithfully translated.

It is a grateful task which we have taken upon ourselves, to single out an individual as an example of heroism, and uncommon resources of mind, and to render him more distinguished, who is already so universally and deservedly known and admired. We feel conscious not only of the utility of our attempt, but of the delight arising from it. In opening the domestic tent of our veteran warrior, we bring forward the private actions of one of the bravest and noblest generals the world ever produced, and we find every personal qualification that can dignify man, supported by a military reputation which valour and discretion, when united, never fail to beget.

The public are well aware that anecdotes and biographical incidents are more apt to be the production, of some fertile brain than founded on fact; we can, however, with truth assure our readers, that no one anecdote is introduced into this work, which has not been obtained either from the most undoubted authority, from eyewitnesses themselves, or from our own personal connexions.

Might we be permitted to boast of success in any part of our undertaking, the execution of the plans of the several battles would tempt us to become our own panegyrists. They are facsimile copies of drawings taken on the spot, and owe their particular and uncommon correctness to those Prussian engineers, whose office it has been to lay them down upon paper. We flatter ourselves, therefore, that the military reader will find every wish gratified, on their near and detailed inspection.

A List of Napoleon's Marshals and Civil Officers

Arrighi, Marshal—Duke of Padua.

Augereau, Marshal—Duke of Castiglione.

Bernadotte, Marshal—Prince of Ponte-Corvo, Crown Prince of Sweden,

Berthier, Marshal—Prince of Neufchatel and Wagram,

Bessières, Marshal—Duke of Istria,

Cambacères—Duke of Parma, Arch-Chancellor of the Empire.

D'Avoust, Marshal—Duke of Auerstädt, Prince of Eckmühl.

Duroc, Marshal—Duke of Frioul, Grand Marshal of the Palace.

Fouché—Duke of Otranto, Governor of Rome.

Kellerman, Marshal—Duke of Valmy.

Lefebvre, Marshal—Duke of Dantzic.

Macdonald, Marshal—Duke of Tarentum.

Marmont, Marshal—Duke of Ragusa.

Mortier, Marshal—Duke of Treviso.

Ney, Marshal—Duke of Elchingen.

Oudinot, Marshal—Duke of Reggio.

Savary—Duke of Rovigo.

Talleyrand de Perigord—Prince of Benevento, Vice-Chancellor of State.

Victor, Marshal—Duke of Belluno.

CHAPTER 1

Enters into the Swedish Service

Posterity, as well as the present age, will doubtless be curious to know something of the biography of that consummate warrior, Field-Marshal Prince Blücher of Wahlstatt, (see note following), one of the greatest captains of his time, and whose reputation in military exploits can scarcely be equalled in any period of ancient or modern history.

★★★★★★

Knight of the grand order of the Black Eagle, of the Red Eagle, of that of the Iron Cross, and of the order of Merit of Prussia; of those of St. Alexander Newsky, of St. Anne, and of St. George, of the first class, of Russia; Knight of the order of St. Charles of Spain; and Grand Cross of the order of Maria Theresa of Austria.

★★★★★★

His character is marked by a combination of rare qualities, great frankness of manner, and a popular freedom of speech, which have gained him the unbounded confidence and love of his soldiers, whom, on all occasions, he calls his children, and who never speak of him, but by the appellation of father. A firmness and decision in the hour of danger, rank him with the first commanders in the world. In the heat of battle, in the tumult of an important onset, when leading his troops to an attack, his courage, intrepidity, and presence of mind, are most conspicuous. His voice always cheers the resolute, and his example animates the wavering and tardy.

But nothing concurred so much to raise our hero to that pinnacle of glory which he has attained, as that singularly intuitive penetration and foresight which he displays, in counteracting the deep-laid designs and manoeuvres of the enemy in the field. No movement of his adversary seems to escape his eagle-eyed precaution, and his determination is at all times as rapidly formed, as his consequent orders are executed. No distance seems too great, no impediments insurmountable, for his military genius, and the devotedness, discipline, and resolution of his troops. His discretion, prudence, and calmness, even in the hour of victory, are so happily blended with vigorous measures, that, from their combination, the happiest results are derived on all occasions, so as to preserve his conquests, and secure the full harvest of the heroic deeds of his gallant army. After the lapse of centuries, our veteran's character will, no doubt, still afford a constant theme of admiration, and be held up as a perfect model for imitation.

The illustrious subject of these memoirs, Gebhardt Leberecht von Blücher, is a descendant of a very ancient and noble family, whose barony is situated in the dutchy of Mecklenburg-Schwerin. He was born at Rostock, in that dutchy, on the 16th of December, 1742, being the youngest of six brothers. His father was a captain of dragoons, in the service of the Elector of Hessen-Cassel.

During the memorable war carried on by, and against, Frederick the Great of Prussia, known throughout Germany by the name of the seven years' war, his parents (then residing at Rastow, in Mecklenburg-Schwerin), who were fearful of his safety amid the scenes of plunder and devastation that daily occurred, sent him with an elder brother, Ulrich Siegfried Blücher, to their son-in-law, Captain von Krackwitz, in the island of Rügen, near Stralsund, as a place less exposed to the horrors of war. He was at this period about twelve years of age. Four of his brothers were already serving in the Prussian, Russian, and Danish armies.

******

A son of the brother who entered the Danish service, is now. (1815), Grand President of the city of Altona, in Denmark; a gentleman, whose liberality of sentiment, and philanthropy, have won him the hearts of the whole of the inhabitants. When the peaceful citizens of Hamburgh were driven from their homes by the cruelties of Davoust, the President, von Blücher, waved every consideration, to relieve *individual distress*.

******

The Swedish Hussars, quartered in the island, attracted his notice so powerfully, and gave such a bias to his youthful inclinations, that his mind became dazzled with military glory, and, notwithstanding the earnest remonstrances of his sister and brother-in-law, to whom he expressed his desire of entering as cadet into the Swedish regiment of Hussars, he soon after secretly left their house, and offered himself to the captain of a squadron, then in quarters in the neighbourhood. This officer, however, happened to know von Krackwitz, and he sent him notice of his brother-in-law's intentions; young Blücher was accordingly summoned home again, and every argument was employed to persuade him to wait at least a few years before he executed his project; but all was in vain:" he would pursue his favourite propensity, he would become an officer of hussars," he said, "and the sooner he entered the service, the less time would be lost."

In consequence, he commenced his military career, as cadet, in the present Swedish regiment of Mörner Hussars, and he first drew his sword upon an enemy, in combating that very Prussian regiment of Black or Death's Head Hussars which he was afterwards destined to command. Gebhardt Leberecht von Blücher, in his second campaign as cadet in the Mörner Hussars, being with his regiment at the outposts, was sent by the commanding officer with a detachment of ten men, to occupy ah advanced post, with express orders, should he be menaced by an attack from the Black Hussars of the enemy, to fall back; but, that he might depend upon having a squadron ready at hand to support him, if necessary.

Twenty-four hours elapsed without any enemy showing himself. By break of day, however, a *vedette* reported to the Cadet von Blücher, that some movements of the enemy were observable in the woods opposite his post, and that he presumed an attack was meditated. Our young officer rode forwards at the head of his men, to have a nearer view of the wood, which he scarcely had in sights before an enemy's troop rushed at full gallop out of it.

Blücher was too weak to attempt any opposition, and, therefore, obliged to make good his retreat, and, if possible, to join the support which had been promised him, or at least to fall in with his own troop, from which he had been detached; but that had already retreated, as well as the support. He was briskly pursued by the enemy, and, after having had his horse shot under him, he fell into the hands of the Prussian Black Hussars; a private of which corps, Martin Krauze by name, having ridden up to him, when fallen with his horse, and taken him prisoner.

The skirmish of the day having terminated to the advantage of the Prussians under Colonel von Belling, and the squadrons that had been in action having been called over, the prisoners and booty were collected, and the former brought before the colonel. The very juvenile appearance of Blücher particularly struck Colonel von Belling: he asked him his name, who was his father, how long he had served, and other questions of the like import. The frank and ingenuous answers of Blücher excited the admiration and wonder of the by-standers, and quite won the heart of the colonel, who from that moment sought to gain the confidence and friendship of his youthful prisoner.

His first step was to keep him about his person, previously accepting his proffered word of honour, not to leave him, on any pretence whatever, until he was regularly exchanged. A year nearly elapsed in this manner, during which time Blücher was often persuaded to enter the Prussian service; but he always replied to every overture made to him:

> I have taken my oath of allegiance to serve the King of Sweden, and I cannot on any terms forego that oath. My father, I know full well, has a high sense of the honour of an officer, and I should never dare to appear again before him, if I should now enter the Prussian service, without my being first officially dismissed the Swedish.

The remonstrances which his father at this period made to him, did not a little tend to strengthen him in his resolution. A veteran captain of the hussars, likewise, took some pains to instil into the mind of young Blücher those principles of honour which are the brightest ornament to the character of an officer. In fine, everyone that saw him with Colonel Belling felt interested in his welfare; and his affability insensibly procured him the goodwill and friendship of all around him. In the course of the campaign, the Death's Head Hussars, commanded by Colonel von Belling, took a Swedish officer prisoner, that had, in a former part of the campaign, deserted from the Prussians; and the Swedish general, on hearing of his capture, made great interest to have him exchanged.

Colonel von Belling had determined to have him hanged as a traitor; but, on being much importuned to release him, he made an offer to the Swedish general, that if he could procure Blücher's formal dismission from the Swedish service, he would send his prisoner back to headquarters. To this proposal the Swedish commander-in-chief consented, and soon afterwards transmitted Blücher's discharge. It happened, that, on the very day this arrived at Colonel Belling's quarters, Lieutenant Helmholdt, of the Black Hussars, had been killed in action, upon which, the colonel proposed our cadet to fill the vacant lieutenancy: it was granted; and, that no impediment might intervene to prevent him from commencing his military career in the Prussian service with every advantage and honour to himself, he generously purchased for him Helmholdt's equipage, made him a present of it, and kept him near his person, by appointing him one of his adjutants during the remainder of the campaign.

Colonel von Belling continued to act towards Blücher as an indulgent father, and was often heard to say:

> My young adjutant will one day become the ornament of the Prussian Army, if his natural qualities and talents are blended with a well-digested ground-work of military tactics." Blücher himself often mentions, that to the attentions and directions of his patron, and the veteran Captain von Pulscharbi, his early knowledge of the theory of military affairs is wholly owing. His gratitude towards; his benefactor raided in his heart such an unbounded love and affection for him, that, upon some unpleasant differences breaking out subsequently in the regiment amongst the officers, he, on all occasions, warmly defended Colonel von Belling from the malicious aspersions of his enemies.

He had, about this time, been promoted to a company in the regiment; soon after which, Colonel von Belling, upon some occasion or other, at the end of the Polish campaign, fell under the displeasure of the king, was obliged to retire, and lost his regiment. The command of it was then given to Colonel von Lossow, a bitter antagonist of Belling, in all those unfortunate differences between the officers, which eventually deprived him of the favour of his sovereign.

The major of the regiment, von Merseberg, having died a few months after these occurrences, Captain Blücher, as senior officer, ought to have been promoted to the vacant majority; but Lossow, knowing his attachment for Belling, and disliking him on that account, proposed Captain von Jägerfeld for the vacancy, with such a brilliant display of his merits, that he obtained the majority, to the disadvantage and vexation of Blücher.

Colonel Lossow, it seems, entertained a rooted antipathy to him, because of the steady friendship with which he defended the character of his benefactor in all the attacks that were secretly made against it under the connivance of Lossow. Blücher did not hesitate to inform Frederick of the injury which had been done him; but his memorials had no effect, and his petitions were rejected. On finding that all further application was entirely useless, he at last wrote a letter to the king, in the following terms:

Permit me, with all due submission, to apprise Your Majesty how insupportable it is for me to see myself superseded by an officer, who has no other essential merit whatever to boast of, than being the son of the Margrave of Swedt.

Your Majesty will therefore be graciously pleased to permit me to resign, sooner than expose myself to the most acute sensations during every hour of my life,

Blücher.'

To this letter, Frederick wrote the following laconic and characteristic note, addressed to Major von Schulenberg, (Schulenburg), *commandant* of the regiment:

Captain von Blücher has leave to resign, and—may go to the devil as soon as he pleases

Frederick.

Blücher's disappointment was doubly painful because he was at this period paying his addresses to the daughter of Colonel von Mehling, in the Saxon service, then residing in Poland. He had himself but little fortune; and the amiable young lady could boast, perhaps, of almost every good quality but that of wealth; yet, our honest Blücher, scorning to retract, married her soon after, leaving the Prussian Army, farmed an estate under his father-in-law, and became a country gentleman, devoting his leisure hours to the simple occupations of husbandry, and after the lapse of a few years, by his own personal exertions and diligence, became possessed of considerable landed property in Pomerania.

He was afterwards chosen High Bailiff of the province. To the honour of Frederick the Great, many of whose actions bear the marks of a whimsical eccentricity, it must be mentioned, that Blücher, in his agricultural pursuits, received much pecuniary assistance from him, to enable him to purchase advantageously, and improve his estates. His purse was open to him, whenever he wanted it. Upon the death of Frederick the Great, which happened fifteen years after Blücher had quitted a military life, he was again restored to the Prussian Army, by his successor, who appointed him major of the second battalion of his former regiment of Black Hussars.

He soon rose to the rank of lieutenant-colonel, and within the year to that of colonel. In 1789 he was invested with the order "*Pour le Merite.*"

Blücher is a soldier to the full extent of the expression. The field of battle has formed him for a commander. On that theatre of heroic action, his energetic soul found scope for development. The cavalry of the Prussian forces loved him to an excess of enthusiasm; and, soon after this period, his popularity amongst the troops began to show itself on several memorable occasions. But, before we enter into details, we will, close this portion of his biography with the following authentic sketch of the memoirs of his family, and an epitome of his own life, up to the present moment.

Death having deprived Colonel von Blücher of his first lady, he afterwards married the daughter of Mr. von Colomb, Counsellor of the Finances, and sister to Major von Colomb, in the Prussian service. By his former marriage he had three children; two sons, Francis and Gebhardt, and one daughter; who are all still living, (1815.) Count Francis von Blücher is, at present (1815) colonel-*commandant* of the Brown Hussars, and, distinguished himself, in the most eminent manner, during the campaigns of 1813 and 1814.

✶✶✶✶✶✶

1. Major von Blücher, with a detachment of Prussian hussars, from the army of his father at Altenburg, succeeded in surprising General Souham's advanced guard on the 19th of April 1813, drove it sword in hand through Weimar, and made a great number of prisoners. General Souham having pushed forward a numerous support, the major was obliged to retire, after having first caused the troops of the Confederacy of the Rhine, belonging to Weimar, Gotha, Coburg, and Hilburghausen, to surrender at discretion; and who now, with eager hearts, assembled under the banners of Prussia, unfurled by the hand of victory, to avenge the disgrace that had sullied the German name.

2. Lieutenant-Colonel Francis von Blücher, being with the rear-guard of General von Kleist's corps, when reconnoitring the enemy near Nollendorf, on the 14th of September 1813, had the misfortune, after an obstinate affair, to be unhorsed by the lance of a Polish hussar, to whom he surrendered himself prisoner, after having received seven wounds. He was, without delay, sent to the rear of the first French corps. The Pole, on hearing his name, hastened to announce his prize to Napoleon, who immediately ordered him into his presence, although bleeding from every wound, and in the most exhausted state. Napoleon began with his usual hasty manner of questioning; "What's your name?" "What's your rank?" "How many troops

has the King of Prussia?" "How many can he bring into the field?" The son of our veteran hero collected strength enough to answer this last question with the coolness and brevity worthy of his father:

"My beloved monarch. Sire, has as many soldiers as he has loyal subjects!"—"Your answer is very haughty," rejoined Napoleon, in the hollow tone of displeasure so natural to him; and then dismissed him. The lieutenant-colonel was conveyed to Dresden, treated with respect and attention, and obtained his liberty by the capitulation of Dresden in the October following. An eye-witness to this conference, from whom we have the anecdote, corroborated by the count himself, here adds,—that when the lieutenant-colonel had left Napoleon's presence, the Pole, who had taken him prisoner, stood erect, in military attitude, before his emperor, and being unacquainted with the French language, attempted by signs to give Napoleon to understand, that he had deserved the decoration of the Legion of Honour. The former seemed inclined, at first, to pretend ignorance of what he meant; but as the Pole would not stir from the spot. Napoleon suddenly exclaimed, in a tone of vexation: "He shall have it." But many of the bystanders confessed, that the gallant prisoner had acquired more honour, by his answer, than the Pole did by his acquisition of the cross of the Legion of Honour.

******

The second son, Count Gebhardt von Blücher, served as captain, in his father's regiment; but, having resigned, now (1815) resides on the family estates in Pomerania. The daughter married Count von Schulenberg, became a widow, and, in 1814, was united to Baron von der Asseberg.

Our hero's path of glory commenced during the campaign on the Rhine in 1793. It was at the head of the Black, or "von Golz's" Hussars, that those talents for enterprise, so conspicuous in his following campaigns, first began to expand themselves. In the formation of his plans, he evinced, a certain cool circumspection, a dexterously concealed caution, and an irresistible energy in their pursuit, which, with his peculiar talent of making his arrangements in the presence of the enemy, imperceptibly procured him, though only at the head of a corps of partisans, a considerable reputation in the army He acquired the entire confidence of his troops also, because he was known to provide for their wants with an indefatigable care, which overlooked, at times, both limits and restraints. The young officers were particularly attached to him, it being his custom to live on terms of intimacy with them, that at once, flattered their pride and gained their esteem. The hours devoted to the table were enlivened by a conviviality on his side, which, however prominent, never. On any occasion, derogated from the dignity attached to a superior officer.

When galloping down the front of his regiment, either on parade or before the enemy, his heroic figure, his eye full of fire and energy, an inspiring voice, and a gallant chivalrous management of his horse, attract the notice of the files, fix their attention, make an indelible impression on the spectators, and seem to pledge success to the heart of every soldier, if led on by such a commander.

In the campaign of 1794, the regiment of Black, or Death's Head Hussars, was given him, as a reward for his important services; and on the 4th of June of the same year, he was promoted to the rank of major-general, and made a Knight of the Grand Order of the Red Eagle. He published, at this period, a small but interesting work on a war of posts and skirmishes, with remarks on ambuscades, that may be accounted the most excellent of its kind.

Major-General Blücher was made a lieutenant-general in 1801, took possession of Erfurth and Mühlhausen in the name of the king in 1802, and was afterwards appointed Governor of Münster. Blücher's campaign of 1806, his brave and persevering defence of Lübeck, and his very honourable capitulation at Ratkau, near that place, will be the subject of one of the following chapters. General Blücher was exchanged for the French General Victor, and on his passing through Finkenetein, in East Prussia, on the road to the headquarters of his sovereign, was received by Napoleon with marked distinction.

After the peace of Tilsit, His Majesty the King of Prussia intrusted him with the care of the military affairs of Pomerania, one of the three military governments newly created. At the opening of the campaign of 1813, his royal master gave him the chief command of the Silesian Army, that army whose deeds have immortalised the name of Blücher and of Prussia, and dispersed those lowering clouds which had so long overcast the former resplendency of the Prussian arms. His unparalleled marches, the prudence of his masterly manoeuvres, his unceasing activity, that overthrew, in so many instances, the mighty preparations of the most experienced chief—his bloody and obstinate battles, his splendid victories in this and the following campaign and the rapidity that accompanied the execution of his deeply-concerted plans, have excited the astonishment, admiration, and unfeigned eulogiums of his contemporaries, and indeed of all Europe.

After the stupendous victory of Leipsic, our veteran was promoted to the rank of general field-marshal (see first note following); and a few days previously to his landing on Albion's sea-girt shores, he was raised to the dignity of Prince Blücher of Wahlstatt, by the most grateful, the most magnanimous, and the best of monarchs, (see second note following).

******

1. Which mark of distinction was announced to him by the following letter:

General Blücher, Your repeated victories increase the services rendered your country, so rapidly, that I find myself deprived of the power of following you with proofs of my gratitude.
Accept of a fresh mark of it, by my naming you General Field-Marshal; and may you enjoy this dignity for many years, to the satisfaction of the country, and as an example to the army, which you have so often led to victory and glory.

Frederick William.

Leipsic, October 20th, 1813.

2. His Prussian Majesty wrote Blücher the following lines on this occasion:

You have happily and gloriously closed the struggle for the honour and welfare of your native country; but the gratitude which the State owes you still continues; and, as a proof of it, I hereby raise you to the dimity of Prince Blücher of Wahlstatt, and your heirs to peers of the realm, as Counts Blücher of Wahlstatt, It will forthwith be my first care, in showing my due sense of your heroic services, to grant to yourself, and your descendants, such domains as may be best suited to support your rank.

Frederick William.

Headquarters, Paris, June 3rd, 1814.

The name of Wahlstatt is derived from the cloister and village of Wahlstatt, near Liegnitz, on the River Katzbach. This cloister and village are famous for having been built on the spot where a great battle was fought between the Tartars and Henry II. Duke of Silesia, in 1241; the duke lost his life and the battle;

and, in commemoration of this unfortunate event, the cloister was built by his mother, and, to this day, (1815), a description of the battle is annually read from the pulpit, on the 9th of April, being the anniversary of that on which the battle was fought. The word Wahlstatt has, besides, a double signification in the German language, as it likewise implies, "a field of battle;" so that Blücher's title has the significant meaning—Prince of the Field of Battles.

✶✶✶✶✶✶

His visit to England, so fresh in the memory of everyone, resembled more the triumph of an adored hero, than the presence of a general accompanying his sovereign. Blücher's name became the watchword of exultation with all ranks in the metropolis; and, wherever he appeared, he seemed to inspire everyone with love and veneration towards him.

As a new war may break out, and rage with equal fury, and the enemy of mankind, alike ambitious, whether as sovereign prince of an island, or as emperor of a kingdom, may renew the contest for universal dominion, and the downfall of social order, morality, and religion, it is but natural to suppose, that our veteran hero is anxious to add fresh laurels to those which already grace his brow, and that he is eagerly bent on meeting his deadly foe once more, on those plains which have already witnessed his noble exploits.

CHAPTER 2

Colonel Blücher's Campaigns on the Rhine in 1793 and 1794

Blücher as Colonel of the Death's Head Hussars, was attached to the *corps d'armée* of General Prince von Hohenlohe, destined to open the campaign on the Rhine, in 1793, against the French; and he here gave such proofs of his valour and discretion, that he was soon noticed by the commander-in-chief.

The camp of the Prussians, near Eisoing, having been often disturbed just before break of day, by the riflemen of the enemy, who, under cover of hedges and bushes, frequently succeeded in killing off the outposts, Colonel von Blücher was ordered to place an ambuscade, to check this petty warfare. An opportunity offered itself, with every prospect of success, on the 25th of July. Blücher having received authentic information that the French intended to lie in ambush, near Orchies, for the purpose of surprising one of the Prussian patrols on the morning of that day, he determined to counteract this design, by anticipating them; and, accordingly, about three o'clock in the morning, when the French were seen on their march, carefully watching all the outlets as they moved onwards, a few Prussian hussars pushed into the high road, and galloped away as if retreating, while others seemed on patrol, and to withdraw on seeing superior numbers.

The enemy were completely deceived by this manoeuvre: they eagerly pursued, flushed with the hopes of booty; and the Prussians, bursting from their ambush, cut down all that opposed them, taking about a hundred prisoners, with much baggage and a number of horses. To Blücher's success in this enterprise the camp was indebted, for a comparative state of tranquillity till it broke up. In September 1793, the Prussians fixed their camp near Luxemburg, soon after the

Austrians had left it.

The French, in the vicinity, had accustomed themselves, almost daily, to plunder the nearest villages without mercy, and seemed still inclined to continue their predatory excursions; but the vigilance of Colonel Blücher and his hussars soon checked their audacity. He surprised one of the enemy's principal detachments, killed and wounded a considerable number, and took fifty-seven prisoners. To enter into a detail, however, of all the reconnoitring excursions which Blücher made in the rear and flanks of the enemy, and the numberless skirmishes in which his brave troops came off victorious, would, from their wearisome uniformity, afford but little entertainment to the reader, and be of no importance to the historian. In fact, by a rare combination of skill, caution, and valour, he drew the eyes of the army upon him, and paved the way to that renown which has placed him on an equal footing with a Caesar or a Marlborough.

On the opening of the campaign of 1794, Colonel Blücher had again an opportunity of acquiring the unaffected praises and congratulations of his companions in arms. He formed the plan of surprising Morsheim, a village on this side of Kirchheim Polanden, (Kirchheimbolanden) and of driving the enemy, who were strongly posted there, out of it. A battalion of infantry under Captain Trützschler, a detachment of sixty riflemen, and two guns of the horse-artillery, were ordered to march from Alzei, and to post themselves near Oppenheim at half past twelve at night.

In the meantime, to cut off the enemy's retreat, if possible, from Morsheim, Colonel Blücher caused Major von Lorenz to put himself in march with two squadrons of hussars, by the route of Pichenheim, detaching an hundred infantry and sixty riflemen through the wood to the right of Oppenheim, to get into the rear of a detachment of the enemy unobserved, who were posted on the verge of the wood; to the left, on the road to Kirchheim, a body of two hundred infantry were ordered to march straight forwards towards the wood, at the same time that a hundred picked men proceeded to the right, across the Sionshut.

Colonel von Blücher drew up the remainder of his regiment on the high road to Morsheim. It was previously arranged, that all the other detachments were first to await the signal of Captain Trützschler having commenced his attack on the small body of the enemy in the wood, and then to press forwards, with all the rapidity in their power, to the different points. Captain Trützschler was so far successful as to turn the enemy unobserved, and to salute him with a volley before he was prepared. The French detachment was thus thrown into confusion, and being unable to retreat along the wood, it was obliged to debouch into the plain, which gave Colonel Blücher an opportunity to charge upon them, and, in spite of its heavy fire, he succeeded in either killing or wounding, or taking prisoners, the whole detachment.

Captain von Planitz, at the head of a squadron of Black Hussars, and supported by infantry and sharpshooters, proceeded to the village of Morsheim; and although they were received with a warm fire of musketry, and the entrance into the village was blocked up with waggons, he soon overcame every obstacle, cleared a passage, pursued the enemy pell-mell into the village, and completely drove them out of it at the point of the bayonet. The enemy's cavalry, which hardly had time to form, were furiously charged and dispersed with heavy loss. Major von Lorenz had already penetrated to the village, notwithstanding an abattis, across the road out of the wood, presented some hindrance to the celerity of his march.

Colonel von Lestocq, who turned the village to the left, about the same time that Major von Lorenz had turned it to the right, now succeeded in cutting off the enemy entirely, and the few that escaped were indebted for their safety to the ground being so much intersected with hedges and ditches. The fugitives that reached Kirchheim spread a universal alarm; the whole expedition succeeded to the wishes of the most sanguine, and stamped the character of Blücher as the first partisan chief of the age. His military reputation now rose progressively, while the brilliant affairs that followed on the 23rd of May, and 18th September, served to fix it more firmly.

The Prince von Hohenlohe, General of the Prussian Army, having ordered an attack to be made on the French on the 23rd of May 1794, Colonel von Blücher headed the column of the right wing, and its operations were intrusted wholly to him. Accordingly, he put himself in march, on the evening of the 22nd of May, with five squadrons of his own hussars, three battalions of infantry, and three companies of sharpshooters, towards Schorleberg; and early on the morning of 23rd continued his march to the other side of Frankenstein, that he might be able to reach the Neustädter road before break of day; by which means he cut off all communication between Kaiserslautern and Neustädt. Major von Coring was likewise detached from Schorleberg with a battalion of grenadiers, a company of sharpshooters, and two squadrons of hussars, towards Ritterhof, on the road between Hochspeier and Frankenstein.

The high road towards Furkheim was found broken up, and a deep entrenchment dug across it by the French, behind which a considerable body of the enemy's infantry had posted themselves. Colonel von Blücher lost no time in harassing them with a galling fire of sharpshooters, which forced them to retreat into Frankenstein. The place itself being found of too great natural strength to be taken by assault, our prudent colonel resolved to continue his march across the high road, to which step he was the more inclined, as he heard the cannonade of Prince von Hohenlohe's army to the left, evidently on the advance, and, as the enemy had broken up: the roads, little danger was to be apprehended to the right of Frankenstein.

In order, however, to secure his rear, he left a strong detachment posted on the Steige. On entering the woods his difficulties increased. The enemy, who was very numerous both in cavalry and infantry, obstinately defended every foot of ground, and the number of abattis thrown across the roads materially contributed to render the contest very sanguinary, as they were obliged to storm them one after the other. Our gallant colonel, at last, succeeded in clearing the woods and strong grounds, of the French, and forced them to fall back on Weidenthal, whence they were at last driven by the riflemen and sharpshooters. He now took a position on the heights near Weidenthal, close to the high road to Neustädt, his left flank being continually harassed by the enemy's *tirailleurs*.

The enemy, in the meantime, drew up their troops, and halted on the other side of Reidenfels. It was impossible to pursue him thither, from the circumstance of Frankenstein being still occupied by the enemy. In the course of an hour, the outposts reported to the colonel, that the enemy were on the advance; it was the French General Cisée, with two battalions, two guns, and about a hundred horse, who, finding his retreat cut off to Lautern, by Major von Coring's detachment, had the hardihood to attempt forcing a passage with the bayonet through Blücher's corps. Dearly would he have purchased success in this enterprise, if the colonel had not been, at that moment, hard pressed on his left flank by the reiterated attacks of the enemy's columns.

Our resolute commander found himself suddenly placed between two fires; the French were more than treble in number; and to resist such a superiority required no little share of intrepidity, as well as the most skilful dispositions. By bringing some of his guns to bear on the high road to Neustädt, and the others towards that of Frankenstein, he kept the impetuosity of the enemy in check, and rendered their junction a matter of great difficulty. Here Blüchers presence of mind availed him much. He rode with a flag of truce towards the French General Cisée, and called out to him to surrender, as he was cut off, and defence was useless.

A general discharge of musketry was the only answer returned, and the enemy's line immediately pressed forwards to assault the heights on which Blücher stood with his brave troops, and they partly succeeded in forcing back the detachments in advance. He did not pause a moment in this critical juncture, but putting himself at the head of von Müffling's battalion, furiously charged the enemy with the bayonet. The effort was crowned with success; the impetuous French were repulsed with heavy loss, entirely broken, and those that did not escape into the woods, were cut in pieces by the hussars.

A considerable number of prisoners were taken, and two pieces of artillery. Major von Coring then occupied Frankenstein, and Colonel von Blücher kept his position on the heights of Weidenthal. A less vigorous and resolute conduct would have caused the total destruction of Blücher's corps, instead of the discomfiture of the enemy. It was the first time our gallant chief had scope of action to display his military talents, and the issue gave fair promise of future greatness.

A commander at the outposts of an army, when adored by his troops, when endowed with skill and courage, and the rare talent of drawing advantage from the occurrences of the passing hour, may be said to be capable of executing wonders, even with a handful of men. No instance more striking can be given of the justness of this remark, than the conduct of our enterprising colonel on the 28th of May 1794, near Kirrweiler, in the Pfalz.

The French had advanced with two large bodies of cavalry, supported by infantry and artillery, by the way of Fenningen and Edighofen, towards Kirrweiler and Maikammer, while another of their detachments took post between Friesbach and Freimersheim, keeping, by this movement, the regiment of Prussian hussars stationed near Gemsheim and Duttweiler in check. The Prussian outposts at Maikammer and Kirrweiler were forced back on the main body, and the enemy established two batteries towards Diedesfels., Blücher's regiment of Black Hussars were drawn up in front of Diedesfels, facing Kirrweiler.

A battalion of infantry, and two companies of sharpshooters, were in possession of the heights. Another battalion of infantry, with half a battery of horse-artillery, covered the road to Neustädt and Winzengen, by being posted on the high ground before Hambach. General

SINGLE FIGHT BETWEEN A MAGYAR AND A FRENCH HUSSAR

von Wolfrath, with two battalions and five guns, had likewise taken up a position between Duttweiler and Kirrweiler. The enemy, with a strong force, pushed on through Kirrweiler, and their sharpshooters spread themselves to the right and left in the cornfields, favouring, by their incessant fire, the approach of their horse-artillery.

Colonel von Blücher at this critical moment rode forwards, to reconnoitre the enemy's dispositions. He plainly perceived that it was their intention to take up a position on this side Kirrweiler, preceded by a heavy cannonade; and, as he had only light artillery with his corps, he could not prudently accept of a contest with this arm, on such unequal terms, which would ultimately have led to the evacuation of the posts of Maikammer and Kirrweiler, to regain which, would have cost a number of brave men, if he wished to maintain his present position, or have it afterwards in his power to advance.

As soon as this conviction flashed across his mind, his bold and vigorous spirit formed the resolution of immediately attacking the advancing enemy. He estimated their numbers at about six thousand, which, though far superior to himself, did not weigh much in the scale of his calculations. Orders were issued to withdraw the flanking troops, so as to entice the enemy's sharp-shooters into the open ground, pretending at the same time to retreat with a part of his hussars, by defiling behind some heights, unperceived by the enemy. All his outposts were called in, and lay quietly in ambuscade, and our daring chief watched the approach of the favourable moment, when the ground, and intermission of vigilance on the part of the enemy, offered every advantage to his premeditated blow, and then, suddenly issuing from his ambush, he furiously fell upon the flank of the enemy's column, before the gates of Kirrweiler.

The French riflemen, on perceiving the Prussian hussars, endeavoured to regain the town, but were most of them cut in pieces in making the attempt. Blücher succeeded in breaking and dispersing the first column of the French with such vigour and celerity, that their artillery was taken by Lieutenant von Arnim, before they could fire a round of grape-shot. A part of the head of the column tried to enter the town, and the troops in the place were equally eager to get out of it, to support their comrades; in short, the confusion and disorder amongst the French were so great at the moment, that no orders could be obeyed, or were listened to. Our gallant colonel, accustomed to pursue his acquired advantages to the utmost, did not hesitate about pushing through the place, at the head of his brave hussars, dispersing, wounding, and taking prisoners, every troop of the enemy that came in their way: two more guns were added to the trophies of the affair, and, advancing to Fischlingen, the remainder of his light troops followed him.

Some part of the success, of the day might be attributed to the enemy having placed their artillery in line of battery, to cannonade General Wolfrath. The enemy's second column had retreated, and only two regiments of heavy dragoons stood their ground in front of Edesheim. Colonel von Blücher, from an eminence near Fischlingen, having got a view of their position, instantly collected the whole of his horse, and proceeded without delay to throw himself on their right flank, and, if possible, to take them by surprise; he had, indeed, penetrated within thirty yards of their, flank, as one of the enemy's regiments wheeled round with rapidity and order, and showed an imposing and tremendous front, that might be compared to a lofty, impenetrable wall. Dragoons, six feet high, with horses in proportion, presenting their long straight swords, like so many pikes, formed a singular contrast to the small lively animals, and agile evolutions, of Blücher's hussars.

The suddenness of the enemy's movement checked the impetuosity of the Prussians, who for a moment stood wavering; but Blücher, ever ready at expedients, suddenly called out, Halt! and ordered detached parties to gallop down the enemy's line, where the ground admitted of this manoeuvre, to skirmish at a distance with the enemy, and, by a constant firing of their pistols at the horses of the French, to cause a confusion and disorder in their files. He accomplished his design. The commanding officer of the enemy's dragoons found, as he thought, his position too much exposed to the teasing attacks of the Prussian light troops, and commanded his soldiers to wheel in column, and to march off the ground.

This was the moment for Blücher: a strong compact body of hussars, kept in reserve, now rushed with the swiftness of arrows upon the open lines as they were forming, and instantly broke the regiment. More than two hundred were cut in pieces, the colonel-*commandant* and a hundred men were taken prisoners, and two standards fell into the hands of the victors. During this, the second battalion of von Golz's hussars had attacked the enemy in front, and happily succeeded in dispersing the remainder of the two regiments. Our indefatigable victor pursued the enemy through Edesheim, following them up, till they got under cover of the batteries belonging to the main body.

This brilliant affair, and gallant enterprise, cost the enemy fifteen officers, and five hundred rank and file, as prisoners. General Ferrino escaped by hiding himself in a field of corn. The French left six hundred wounded behind them, and four hundred horses proved an acceptable booty to Blücher's intrepid troops. No Prussian officer was either killed or wounded, although they all charged at the head of their men.

These splendid proofs of a bold unwearied perseverance, united with skill and foresight, met with the most gracious acknowledgment from His Majesty the King of Prussia; and the renowned Colonel Blücher was promoted soon after, to the rank of major-general in the Prussian Army. Thus elevated, he did not fail to distinguish himself whenever opportunity offered. An attack upon Edesheim, on the second of July, in which the Prussian horse-artillery, in following his dispositions, did wonderful execution, and his hussars again broke and dispersed the enemy's columns, served but to enhance his character in the eyes of all military men.

The Prince von Hohenlohe, as commander-in-chief, makes particular and honourable mention, in his bulletin of the 19th September, of the brave Major-General von Blücher, ascribing the success of the enterprise carried into execution on the 18th, solely to his judgment. Blücher's orders were, to advance with his brigade of hussars, by the way of Mohrlautern, as soon as he should receive a report, that the attack near Hockspeier had succeeded: but our vigilant Blücher here again acted from the spur of the moment. He had advanced; but to have waited for reports, he found, would give the enemy too much time, and, with his usual energy of action, he detached two of his squadrons to the Kaisersburg, to turn the flank of the flying French, marching with his other squadrons, and a regiment of light horse, straight towards Honek: he dispersed the enemy's light troops on all sides of him, and brought in 600 prisoners.

Blücher's own regiment of Death's Head Hussars took 9 pieces of artillery, 2 howitzers, and 5 pair of colours from the enemy, and made 1 lieutenant-general (Labossiere), 137 officers, 3,327 rank and file prisoners; sharing a booty of 1,341 horses, during the campaigns of 1793 and 1794. The regiment never lost more than six men, as prisoners, in the whole period.

After this campaign, Major-General von Blücher received a command in the Army of Observation stationed on the Rhine, which proved barren of any military occurrences worthy recording.

Major-General von Blücher was made a lieutenant-general in 1801; and sometime after this, previously to the campaign of 1806, he was appointed Governor of Münster.

CHAPTER 3

General Blücher's Campaign in 1806

This campaign forms an unfortunate epoch in the military history of Prussia. It was not a campaign for conquest, or to avenge trivial injuries and transgressions, but a contention for those rights and privileges, in the enjoyment of which, nations that have a regard for social order and sound morality, place their most substantial happiness. The gigantic ambition of one man involved Prussia in misfortunes the most bitter for her sovereign to support, and cast a foul blot upon her military character, which our intrepid hero was ordained by the wise dispensations of Providence to obliterate for ever. Blücher was not backward in assisting his royal master with salutary advice, and encountered the greatest difficulties, and braved the greatest dangers, in protecting the Prussian name from ignominy. It was *he alone* of all the Prussian generals, that scorned to yield, as long as a charge or a ball was left, to fire upon the enemy.

This short but eventful struggle produced effects that shook the Prussian monarchy to its foundations. Her army took the field, powerful, well appointed, full of confidence, and flushed with the recollection of past deeds in arms, both glorious and immortal. It returned, dispirited, nay, almost annihilated: a certain fatality, an unaccountable concurrence of unpropitious events, seemed to accompany, and to be inseparable from, every step of the government. But the villainous projects of the arch-tyrant of Europe were not at that time appreciated. The Prussian people had not then felt his rod of iron: oppression had not yet roused them to a sense of what they owed to themselves as Germans, and to their king as devoted subjects.

A few years of the most painful humiliation paved the way to their acquiring, at the point of the sword, that noble independence, so worthy of themselves. Prussia's blazing star of victory shone forth once more in the distant horizon, ascending with majestic effulgence to its meridian, cheering the surrounding nations with its warmth, while prostrate Germany blessed the hour of its deliverance.

When the Prussian Grand Army opened the campaign in 1806, under the immediate command of its adored monarch, General Blücher was intrusted with the right wing. At the commencement of the Battle of Jena, he was ordered by the king to take upon him the command of the advanced guard of cavalry, consisting of three regiments of dragoons, twenty-five squadrons of light cavalry, and a battery of horse-artillery; The general, having advanced in front of the Grand Army, to reconnoitre the enemy's movements, was prevented by a heavy fog from ascertaining their several positions.

Some reports made by his outposts and skirmishers, induced him to proceed towards Kosen, in hopes of surprising or meeting detachments of the enemy. Between Poppel and Tauchwitz, Blücher encountered the French division Gaudin, which he attacked with vigour and intrepidity, making a terrible slaughter among the enemy, and pursuing them sword in hand to the other side of Hassenhausen. The Queen's Own regiment of Dragoons, the finest in the Prussian service, had here an opportunity of distinguishing itself most conspicuously. The enemy seemed to make a stand, as if they had fallen in with their support, and the Prussian artillery being brought up, began to thunder against their supposed position, the fog still continuing so dense, that it scarcely allowed a distance of fifty yards to be distinctly seen.

The French answered this cannonade briskly, and with heavier metal, from their battery, for about half an hour; and it appeared by their dispositions that a large body of troops was debouching in line. General Blücher in consequence drew off his artillery, and formed his cavalry in columns. The infantry meant for his support, were not yet arrived, and the fog prevented the gaining any authentic intelligence of the actual force of the enemy. In this state of things Blücher was obliged to remain a considerable time inactive. It was the Duke of Brunswick's wish, that the whole army should be drawn up in close order of battle, and no important step taken until the fog had sufficiently dispersed, so that the position and manoeuvres of the enemy could be, in some degree, ascertained.

The cautious advice of the veteran was not followed. Field-Marshal Möllendorf insisted that no time ought to be lost, that a rapid march forwards, must disconcert the enemy's plans, whatever they might be, as their corps were now all in motion, and in a probable state of dislocation. Vigorous measures, we grant, could alone baffle the enemy; but vigour without foresight, is at all times dangerous. Möllendorf's opinion gained the ascendancy, and the army was ordered to march in advance, incommoded by a mist that prevented the soldiers seeing objects within twenty yards of them.

General von Blücher did not, however, renew his attack with the advanced guard, until this mist had dispersed itself, opening to his view a large body and extended line of French infantry. His old manoeuvres, of indirect charges following each other in succession, and skirmishing on all sides, first throwing the files into disorder, and then, by a heavy unexpected charge, to break through, were here found of no avail. The new tactics of Napoleon, of drawing up his infantry in alternate squares, flanked by light artillery, and connected by troops in line, frustrated all Blücher's desperate attempts to make an impression. He felt himself foiled. On making his last charge, he had his horse killed under him. He then drew back his cavalry in good order towards Eckartsburg, and passed through Auerstädt.

It has been confidently asserted by many, that General Blücher, in pressing too hastily forwards, brought the army under the necessity of fighting, and that his conduct deserved censure. But, in answer to this reproach, we have only to remark, that if blame ought to attach anywhere, it could only fall upon Marshal Möllendorf, who turned a deaf ear to the suggestions of the old, experienced Duke of Brunswick, and thus evidently precipitated the army, not upon a disorganised, but upon a prepared enemy, and that, too, under peculiar disadvantages. Möllendorf's greatest misfortune was that of being short-sighted, which is extremely dangerous for a general.

After the Battle of Jena, General Blücher was ordered by his sovereign to take the command of the Prince of Würtemberg's corps, and to conduct it across the Oder; but, in consequence of the capitulation of Prenzlau and Pasewalk, no other course was left him but to direct his march towards the Lower Elbe, and, by forming a junction with the corps of Weimar and Lestoçq, at least to relieve Magdeburg, if not, present an imposing force to the enemy in that quarter. This plan was the best which human foresight could have adopted, as it tended to divide, not only the attention, but the forces of the enemy, and served to prevent the whole mass of the French Army from penetrating into the heart of Prussia, without any impediment in their rear or flanks; but the vastly superior numbers of Napoleon's forces, added to the unusual celerity of their movements, frustrated any good effects which the execution of the plan might have produced, and General von Blücher saw himself under the necessity of fighting his way to Lübeck, instead of crossing the Elbe, or keeping it on his flanks. He was constantly assailed by the enemy on this retrograde march, from all sides.

On the 16th of October, near Greussen, he fell in with the French light troops, under General Klein. To avoid an engagement, in the position his troops were then in, was absolutely necessary, if he would render practicable the accomplishment of his design, to reach the Lower Elbe. Blücher's presence of mind, ever fertile of expedients on the spur of the moment, assisted him most essentially in this dilemma. On the first appearance of the enemy, he rode on towards them, accompanied by a few of his staff-officers, desiring to be conducted to the French general as a flag of truce. He immediately gave the general to understand, that he had received advices from the King of Prussia, that peace had been already concluded, calling upon Colonel von Massenbach, who was present, as a witness, who had read Napoleon's letter to the king, in which he had offered him peace.

The French general greedily swallowed the bait, as did likewise General Lasalle, who followed with two regiments. (*Lasalle—the Hussar General: the Life & Times of Napoleon's Finest Commander of Light Cavalry, 1775-1809* by John H. Lewis is also available from Leonaur.)

Blücher's corps was permitted to pass unmolested; and, by a forced march, placed themselves out of all danger from that quarter. Buonaparte particularly mentions the occurrence in one of his bulletins, accompanied by a severe reprimand on the conduct of the two generals. General Kalkreuth attempted to practise the same deception upon Marshal Soult, soon afterwards, but without success.

The troops under Blücher's command, in high spirits at having deceived their wily foe, and full of confidence in their chief, now pursued their march with vigorous alacrity. They came up with a body of French, on the 27th, near Fürstenburg, and, by a gallant and well-ordered attack, succeeded in forcing through them; and, on the following day, near Lychen, they were no less successful. It was our general's intention to proceed to Prenzlow; but it being reported to him, that Prince Hohenlohe's corps had been entirely dispersed, that step became quite impossible.

He therefore turned to his left towards Strelitz, being sanguine enough to hope, that, after effecting a junction with Winning's corps, he should be able to force his way to Magdeburg; or, by throwing himself across the Elbe, gain time for the fortresses of Magdeburg and

Hameln to be provisioned for a siege: and then to operate, according to circumstances, in the rear of Napoleon's Grand Army.

Engineer officers were sent to Lauenburg, to prepare materials for throwing a bridge over the Elbe at that point. At this juncture advices were received by Blücher, that Marshal Soult, at the head of a considerable force, had already passed the Elbe, and was directing his march towards him. Nothing appalled our gallant general; he continued his route towards the Elbe, firmly determined to fight his way, being flushed with his former successes, and possessing the entire devotion of his troops. A continuation of attacks now followed in rapid succession. The Prussian cavalry performed prodigies of valour, and roughly handled the enemy's horse, whenever they ventured a charge with them.

The Prince of Ponte-Corvo, commanding a strong corps of the enemy, sent a flag of truce, on the 1st of November, to General von Blücher, with a summons to capitulate, stating at the same time, that, as he was nearly surrounded by three corps of the French Grand Army, there was no retreat in his power. The general assured the prince, that he never should capitulate as long as he had a cartridge left: adding:

> He, for his own part, knew not the man that should prevent his marching to Berlin, or relieving Magdeburg.

In the interim he was reinforced by Colonel von Osten, who joined, with four squadrons of his own regiment, a battalion of infantry, and a company of sharpshooters.

Amidst daily skirmishing, and simultaneous attacks, Blücher reached the neighbourhood of Schwerin, on the 3rd of November. A very warm affair with the advanced guard, took place near the village of Krimitz, which continued till the evening. The Prussians beat the enemy completely out of the field, taking a considerable number of prisoners, amongst whom was a colonel, and an adjutant of the Prince of Ponte-Corvo. Partial as the advantages certainly were, that could be derived from these bloody rencontres, they were not without ultimate benefit to the Prussian service; the soldier became convinced that, upon equal terms, his strong and vigorous arm was ever an overmatch for Gallic agility.

A second summons from the Prince of Ponte-Corvo, to capitulate, was treated with the same disdain as the former, and Blücher notified his wish of declining to listen to any further overtures of the like nature.

Blücher's intended march upon Magdeburg, which, but a few days before, he had defied any one to prevent, was acknowledged, by himself as well as his staff, to have now met with obstacles that appeared but too evidently insurmountable. A continuation of forced marches had fatigued the troops to an inconceivable degree. All stragglers fell into the hands of the French. Ammunition, in particular, began to fail, and there were no magazines within their reach. These considerations, maturely weighed, induced the general to alter his plan, and to throw himself into some city of note, by which step he could procure his brave followers that rest they stood so much in need of, gain time to supply them with necessaries, and to replenish his ammunition.

To avoid a pitched battle was, however, his first and principal care. As long as he could keep the field, or employ the French Army by his marches and manoeuvres, he held Napoleon in check from approaching the Oder, delayed his march on that river, and thus gave time for the Prussian forces to assemble and form themselves in East Prussia: these manoeuvres, also enabled the Russians, who were actually in march, to reach the frontiers early enough for their assistance to be of important benefit to the kingdom.

On the evening of the 3rd of November, after reports from the outposts had been made to Blücher, there was every reason to suppose that Murat was marching on his left flank, Soult on his right, and the Prince of Ponte-Corvo very near him in front. Thus situated, by break of day on the 4th, no other alternative was left him, but either to fight desperately against superior numbers, with little or no chance of success, or to throw himself into Lübeck or Hamburgh. In one or the other of these cities the general hoped to maintain himself for some considerable time. Lübeck appeared the most proper for his purpose, as it still had remains of old fortifications. Some Swedish troops were already in it, who, he flattered himself, might be persuaded to make a common cause with him.

If Blücher's retreat had been crowned with success, no doubt, it would have been compared with that of Moreau. Every attendant circumstance was well reflected upon: it was undertaken with wisdom and foresight, and the heroic valour of a handful of men, whose names deserve to be recorded on the brazen tablets of history, accomplished it. What difficulties had our general not to encounter! On his right the Baltic, and on his left a neutral territory, was a situation not among the least of them.

A toilsome forced march of thirty-six hours brought Blücher and his army before the walls of Lübeck, on the evening of the 5th of November. The Senate refused him and his brave followers admittance.

Prussians, that have since secured the independence of this city for ever, and saved the German name from eternal disgrace, had the gates shut in their faces! But the times of sluggish grovelling inactivity are over! Entreaties and representations proved useless, and Blücher ordered the gates to be forced. The general proceeded to the Senate-house, and demanded bread and quarters for his troops. His application was formally protested against. The urgency of the moment constrained him to declare, that if his simple demands were not immediately complied with, he should feel himself obliged to adopt coercive measures.

The Senate reluctantly consented to provide for his exhausted troops. Quarters were appointed them, and refreshments distributed with a liberal hand. A few hours of rest only prepared the way for a more busy scene, and the temporary calm was followed by a storm. Blücher's desperate defence of Lübeck gave his name a celebrity throughout the north of Germany, and procured him a popularity, which had lost none of its vigour, when he again took the field, seven years afterwards. He there fought, as every son of Germania ought to fight, as long as a grain of powder was in his cartridge-box. If his fame had not been established, this intrepid conduct would have fixed it on the firmest foundations.

General Blücher, on the following day, drew up his little army of heroes on the Trave, leaning his right on Lübeck, and his left on the village of Travemünde. A corps of Danes, under General von Ewald, were posted on their frontiers, nearly touching Blücher's right wing. The two generals exchanged civilities, and the former hastened to announce, that his orders were to defend the frontiers against the aggressions of either party, but to take no decided part whatever in their operations.

At an early hour of the morning, Lübeck was invested on all sides, by three corps of the French Grand Army, under the Prince of Ponte-Corvo, Murat, and Soult. They made preparations to take the place by assault, and a most sanguinary conflict ensued. After the brave Prussians had expended the whole of their ammunition, and their artillery was rendered useless, from the want of powder and balls, the French, perceiving the slackening fire of our valiant general, proceeded to storm the Burg-gate of the city, at the point of the bayonet: the most dreadful slaughter ensued: the Prussians were but a handful of men, not exceeding 6000 capable of bearing arms; the French had more than 40,000 men before the place, and by dint of pouring in fresh troops through the gate, forced their way at last into the town, over the dead bodies of their comrades, that lay, by thousands, in the gateway. To withstand so great a superiority was impossible; our gallant general was obliged to yield. The French got possession of the place, and the remains of the Prussian Army passed the night in their position on the Trave. Early the next morning, the Prince of Ponte-Corvo again offered General Blücher a capitulation; which, after the preliminaries were settled, was accepted by him.

General Blücher, in drawing up the terms of the capitulation, began it in the following words:

> As a capitulation has been offered me by the Prince of Ponte-Corvo, and having accepted it, for want of every kind of ammunition, I, &c.

Objections being made to this by the French officer, who declared that it was unusual to mention the reasons of a capitulation, in stating the terms, Blücher answered abruptly:

> By G—, I'll capitulate on no other conditions whatever, let what will come of it.

It was afterwards arranged, that Blücher should be allowed to state his reason for capitulating, above and below his signature to the capitulation; and which he actually did.

Those acts of savage barbarity, those scenes of rapine, plunder, and devastation, which have always marked the bloodstained path of the followers of Napoleon, and which now took place in Lübeck, can neither be conceived nor described. Horror herself would shrink aghast at the sight, and the pen of the historian falls from his hand. The virtuous citizens of Lübeck, that venerable sister of the Hanse League, have a remembrance left them of French atrocity, that will ever rouse them to a just sense of the duties they owe to the common cause of Germany.

******

> A corps of French troops, headed by Marshal Murat, in marching through the territories of the Prince of Lippe-Schaumburg, had stripped his stud of every horse; amongst them was a favourite animal, whose peculiar fate and extraordinary sagacity had rendered him an object of particular regard and estimation to the prince and his family. This horse had formerly belonged to an uncle of the illustrious house, and had been ridden by him when colonel of a regiment, during the campaign in Flanders, in the course of which, their relative was killed in action, and

the body never found; but, before the afflicting news reached them, to their great surprise and astonishment, the horse returned alone, wounded in the neck, from the field of battle to the castle stables, a distance of at least a hundred miles. That the animal was much caressed, and a great value set upon him, no one can doubt, from the singularity of the circumstance.

Every kind of application was made, and every exchange offered to the French marshal, that this charger in particular might be restored, but without effect; a deaf ear was turned to all their entreaties, remonstrances, and representations of the causes that rendered him so great a favourite of the family. They never saw him more. Another instance of the vile principles, and selfish turpitude of sentiment, that influenced the conduct of some of the Satraps of the most execrable of tyrants. (Related by the prince to the editor himself.)

★★★★★★

The excesses of the French soldiery lasted three days.

General Blücher, after performing the most painful of all tasks for a warrior, that of seeing his brave men lay down their arms, wrote the following letter to His Majesty the King of Prussia:

> It is with a heart deeply wounded that I have to report to Your Majesty the gradual destruction, and fate of the corps of troops under my command, which I have had the misfortune to head, under circumstances which permitted no other alternative. The troops have, throughout, evinced a steadiness and bravery which have exceeded my expectations, and which, in any other situation, would have immortalised them. They have shown a patience under intolerable privations, and a love of discipline, that reflect eternal honour upon them. The sense of having faithfully discharged my duties to my country, affords me the only consolation I can feel, in this hour of bitter sorrow.
>
> Your Majesty's devoted servant,
>
> Von Blücher.

Our distinguished general was afterwards exchanged for General Victor, and joined his king in East-Prussia.

After the peace of Tilsit, he was appointed to the military government of Pomerania.

Chapter 4

Opening of the Campaign by General von Blücher

The tide of victory, like an irresistible torrent, in pursuing her tumultuous course, from the walls of Moscow to the shores of the Niemen, had burst asunder those ponderous chains of iron with which the tyranny of a despotic conqueror, to promote his ambitious views, had held the Teutonic nation, enthralled. The high behests of Heaven having miraculously ordained, that Germania's sons, should never again drag his triumphal car, nor do homage at his feet; it must have doubly redounded to their shame, when rescued from further disgrace, and delivered from their hated shackles, to have followed their enslaver, and, full of obsequious submission and humility, spontaneously to have offered their obedient necks, once more, to his galling and perfidious yoke.

Amongst the meanest race of animals, no traces are to be found of willing slavery; and vile must be that heart, which is capable of estimating man below the brute creation.

The little Prussian Army, under General von York, deserted and neglected by the flying French, proceeded with order and firmness through the snows and woods of Courland towards their native soil, there to devote itself to the future service and will of its revered master, its only fit and honourable destination. A Russian corps had already hemmed in its line of march to the frontiers of Prussia. The commanders, on both sides, soon came to a good understanding with each other. The Prussians had been driven into Russia by force, and no other rights bound them, but those of the stronger party. By an idle abuse of his power, Napoleon had himself destroyed the means of constraining others, and these self-created rights had now evaporated into nothing.

Standing thus alone, and unbiassed, the Prussians could no longer consider themselves as enemies to the Russians; for they had never been such in reality; and honour forbade them to acknowledge any commands, or fulfil any other destination, but what the immediate orders of their lawful sovereign might contain. The Russians, trusting to approaching alliances with all states recovering their freedom, derived no little advantage from permitting the effects of the enforced coalition between Prussia and France quietly to subside, thus smoothing the way to a subsequent close confederacy in the common cause of all. Avowing their mutual independence, and not as enemies or Allies, the two corps separated, and the Prussians took up their neutral quarters within their own territories.

This reduced corps had but just shaken off Napoleon's trammels; and no sooner had the people beheld these arrogant vainglorious conquerors, returning like troops of miserable mendicants, in a state of contemptible wretchedness (the conqueror must be ever fortunate, or else he is justly contemptible), than they felt themselves as if led back, by the invisible hand of Fate, to an independent existence, and to the urgent indispensable duty of putting forth every individual energy to maintain this independence, in a more laudable and vigorous manner than in the year 1806. The loud and unanimous voice of the people, and their national feelings, were listened to, and cherished, by the monarch and his ministers. They confessed the necessity of supporting the nation with all the influence of legal authority, of improving the probable short period of free action, to bring forward her physical strength, and then to begin the struggle anew, for liberty and an honourable station amongst the continental powers.

The truly unfortunate days of Jena and Auerstädt had tarnished the long-enjoyed splendour of the arms of Prussia, and blasted her name with scorn and dishonour. The army, on its retreat after these defeats, had disbanded itself entirely; the fortresses and strongholds of the monarchy fell most disgracefully one after the other; the kingdom was conquered; and, after the expiration of only four weeks, insignificant were the wrecks of either, that were left for a beloved sovereign to mourn over. The few bands of faithful warriors that afterwards joined the Russian forces, in the Upper Prussian provinces, were too weak, and the means of filling up their ranks too inefficient, to attempt the recovery, at that moment, of what had been lost.

This evil was rendered greater by the peace of Tilsit, in which, disgraceful bounds were set to the augmentation of the Prussian Army, its strength being limited to 42,000 men; and even the proportion of

FLIGHT OF THE PRUSSIAN ARMY AFTER JENA

RECEIVING NEWS OF THE DECLARATION OF WAR IN THE PRUSSIAN CAMP

its arms to each other was prescribed and dictated by their haughty, inflexible, and wily enemy. In the course of a year, that brilliant and splendid military character of Prussia, so much the admiration of every friend to warlike and glorious achievements, and held up as an example to all Europe, disappeared. Reproaches from all sides followed, instead of admiration, and humiliations supplied the place of homage.

The army was dispirited, the past afforded no satisfaction, futurity opened no heartening prospects. A well-placed confidence in any single commander, that might have kept alive their ardour, was nowhere to be found; the war of 1806, had been too short to give anyone an opportunity of raising himself to a post of eminence, and the few that did distinguish themselves, shared the divided approbation of popular opinion,

Owing to this spiritless situation of the army, the diminished opulence of the state, the embarrassed finances, the reduction commanded by a foreign power, and a party of lukewarm patriots at home, that opposed every energetic measure whatever, it was extremely difficult to attain those objects still kept in view. The army was to be reorganised entirely, its courage revived, its spirit re-inspired, all abuses rooted out; and besides the formation and completion of the number fixed in the treaty, the foundation of a new and great military power was to be imperceptibly laid, which, at some future period, might, at a decisive moment, suddenly arise for self-defence, and retrieve the honour of the Prussian name.

The few years of peace, from 1808 to 1811, were, with unwearied solicitude, devoted to the accomplishment of these intentions.

According to the treaty with France, the army should consist of

24,000 men, infantry;
 6,000 " cavalry;
 6,000 " artillery;
 6,000 " guards.

42,000

These were divided into six corps of all arms, called brigades, each brigade consisting of from 6,000 to 7,000 men. Three military governments were created; namely, the Prussian, the Silesian, and the Mark, including Pomerania. Few difficulties occurred in completing the army to 42,000 men; but its new formation, and particularly the regenerative spirit to be inspired, found a thousand prejudices to struggle against, together with the ill-will and self-interest of individuals, deep-rooted habits, an obstinate sluggishness, and an imaginary desponding helplessness; but, in spite of all these obstacles, seeming to present insurmountable barriers, advances were fortunately made, and the impediments insensibly and gradually removed.

In the year 1809, the army was completely reformed, had new laws and regulations, a new exercise; and, we may say, felt itself invigorated throughout. It was brought nearer the people, and hopes were entertained that it might become a school for the future formation of a military national character, refined from all impure particles. Those obstructions met with, in the attempt to enlarge unnoticed, the new foundation laid for the whole military power of Prussia, were now happily overcome, and it would be but tedious to name them, in rehearsing the means that were resorted to. We must be satisfied with remarking, that only unremitting exertions in employing and bringing into effect well-digested measures, as local circumstances permitted, could lead to the desired consummation of Prussia's dearest wishes.

The principal objects were:

1. To be able rapidly to reinforce the army, by the continual exercising of recruits for a certain time, and then to disband them to make room for others; by which method, in less than three years, more than 150,000 men had passed the routine of military exercise and evolutions.

2. To establish workshops for the manufacturing of arms. The Berlin manufactory produced 1,000 stand of arms every month; an entire new manufactory was erected and arranged at Neisse, in Silesia; and a considerable number of arms were bought up in Austria.

3. To form parks of artillery. As the whole of the field artillery was lost, it was necessary to replenish the loss out of the eight fortresses still in possession, by refounding all the heavy brass ordnance in them, and mounting iron ones in their stead. Foundries and laboratories were built at convenient places, and, in three years, the army had again complete parks of artillery for 120,000 men.

4. To arm, and furnish with supplies, the eight fortresses: as they were to be looked upon as the pillars and props of the Prussian monarchy, whose geographical situation rendering the open country so easy to be overrun by an enemy, they, stood like rocks

SCHILL.

ONE OF SCHILL'S FOLLOWERS.

DEATH OF SCHILL IN THE MARKET-PLACE AT STRALSUND.

in the sea, unmoved by the passing storm. In them, the warlike strength of Prussia could be collected and preserved, in case of such an event. On which account, entrenched camps were thrown up near Pillau and Colberg, and in Silesia. Besides the extended lines of Neisse, a fortified camp marked out near Glatz, was intended to receive troops and military stores. The rough and unformed means of defence and warfare, both in men and materials, could be collected in them, and be there modelled and formed, even during the inroads of an invading enemy.

In 1812, these camps were all completed. Such unwearied exertions, and a wise economy in the application of those means, formerly so little attended to, had placed the Prussian Army on a footing, in the course of four years, that, from 42,000 men, of which it actually consisted, it could, in a few months, be increased to 120,000 or 150,000 men.

Officers, both civil and military, well versed in the duties of their different stations, and in the prime of-life, stood at the head of the several departments.

The injurious consequences arising from a too strict attention to seniority by promotions, were averted, and the useful man, who had distinguished himself in battle, or made great sacrifices to the state, was patronized and brought forward; and thus, by degrees, a regard for the new order of things, a renewed confidence in themselves and in their innate value, were instilled into, and diffused throughout the whole.

To finish the work of this new creation, the idea of a national defence, by an organised militia and levy *en masse*, seemed naturally to present itself. By the former, if war broke out, the army could be doubled in its numbers; and by the latter, the defence of this little kingdom could receive some degree of stability. Yet those very means that tended to reinforce the standing army with the utmost celerity, encroached on the embodying of the militia; if, by the increase of the army, all the arms in store, and the exercised and trained men, were brought into service, and none were then left to compose an efficient groundwork for the militia.

But the treaty of alliance with France, in 1812, put a stop at once to all these wise and provident preparations for erecting a firm national defence against any foreign subjugation that might be attempted. By it, the little army was robbed of half its numbers, to be employed for purposes very opposite to its original destination; and, in consequence, all attempts to attain the end proposed were paralysed; indeed, by the uncertainty how the means produced might be made use of, it would have been the extreme of folly to continue them in any shape whatever; Therefore, not only no progress was made during the year 1812, but the hope of any, seemed to be extinguished. The auxiliary corps returned at the end of the campaign into Russia, with a loss of 10,000 men, and the flower of the army was weakened, by at least a fourth.

This loss, severe as it was, might perhaps be outweighed by the military experience this little corps had acquired, by the confidence they had gained in themselves and their new formation, by the esteem with which they inspired both their Allies and opponents; and, above all, by the inveterate and renewed hatred imbibed against the tyrant and oppressor of legal liberty and civic freedom.

★★★★★★

The Emperor Alexander, a short time previously to the inroad of Napoleon into Russia, in 1812, with the view of averting the spilling of so much human blood, sent General Balaschoff to the headquarters of Napoleon.

He was received in Napoleon's antechamber by General Duroc, who, with a feigned graciousness, entreated him to excuse the delay, but that the emperor was breakfasting at the moment.

The door of the adjoining apartment was at length opened; the general perceived Napoleon as if just rising from his breakfast; near him were standing the King of Naples, the King of Westphalia, and the Viceroy of Italy. Upon General Balaschoff's entering the room, the emperor called out to the *grand personages* that surrounded him, "*Allez vous en!*"

The conference lasted several hours, in the course of which, Napoleon brought forward every specious and wily argument to prove, that Russia would act the wisest part in submitting to his demands, as there was no possible chance of her being able to withstand the combined strength of France and her Allies. Amongst many singular reasons adduced by Napoleon, in defence of his assertion, and to confirm it, the following may be worthy recording, as it proves what was actually the degree of estimation in which he held the German nation: "Taking for granted," he proceeded to say, " that the power of your emperor is equal to mine, yet, you ought to reflect, that when your monarch loses five men, they are five Russians; whereas, I can only lose, in this campaign, one Frenchman and four hogs:" (*Je ne perds qu'un Français et quatre cochons.*) Meaning by *cochons*, his Allies the Germans!

General Balaschoff's mission, it need hardly be added, was ineffectual.

******

The military force of Prussia was thus situated at that epoch, when the rapid floods of discomfiture burst on the French Grand Army, and scattered and impelled its feeble remains, like the fragments of a shipwreck, over the plains of Germany.

The decisive moment was now arrived in which those numerous and digested plans, that had so long and anxiously occupied the Prussian Government, could ripen to perfection. Although there was no possibility of attaining the desideratum of having the country defended by 250,000 men, well trained and skilled in evolutions, and it must eventually suffer some curtailment, while it is in the nature of things attempted by man to fall short of the object in view; yet, in the execution, much depended on energy, vigour, and activity, to reach the goal at a greater or less distance. The sequel has proved that this was by no means an extravagant scheme, for a few months realised the hopes cherished with so much solicitude.

To complete the regiments, and to form new corps, recruits were drawn together in Prussia, early in January 1813, about the time that France began to raise her new levies, by a rigorous enforcement of the conscription-laws.

Within a period of rather more than two months, that is, at the end of March, the army in Silesia amounted to 25,000 men, fully equipped and well disciplined, exclusive of the garrisons, and about 20,000 men, whose formation was not yet complete. The corps of General von York arrived in the Mark, out of Prussia, about 15,000 men strong (but had more than 6,000 sick). In the Mark and in Pomerania there were nearly 10,000 men, well exercised, without reckoning the garrisons, and 15,000 recruits, in an approximate state of organisation.

The Prussian forces might consequently, at this time, be estimated as follows:

1. Well-disciplined, exclusive of garrisons	50,000
2. In a state of organisation	35,000
3. The sick	10,000
4. Garrisons in the eight fortresses	15,000
	110,000

The army was therefore recruited to almost four times its former numbers. The troops were all completely disciplined towards the end of April, when hostilities commenced; but the recruits were not able as yet, to join the theatre of the war in Saxony. At the beginning of May, about the time of the Battle of Lützen, the Prussian Army might be placed under the following heads;

In active service, before the enemy, 70,000 men; *viz.*

In Saxony, at the Battle of Lützen	35,000
Under General Kleist, at Halle	4,000
Detached	1,000
On the Elbe, and before the fortresses of Spandau, Stettin, Glogau, Wittenberg, &c.	30,000

Not before the enemy, 40,000; *viz.*

Reserves marching to the army	15,000
Garrisons	15,000
Sick	10,000
	110,000

The militia were at this time only forming; but, according to the plan of embodying them, they were to be 150,000 men strong.

The best spirit animated all the disciplined troops; and their being divided into small brigades of 7,000 to 8,000 men, of all arms, well provided with every equipment, was one of the best formations which troops could receive.

The commanders of the several corps were:

First Corps.

General von Blücher, General of the cavalry.
First brigade, Colonel von Klüx.
Second brigade, General von Ziethen.
Reserve brigade of infantry (guards), General von Röder.
Cavalry reserve, Colonel von Dölfs,

Second Corps.

General von York,
First brigade, Lieutenant-General von Kleist,
Second brigade, Colonel von Horn.
Third brigade, General von Hünerbein.
The series of operations in which this latter corps was engaged, since the campaign in Courland, had so changed its former

organisation, that at the Battle of Lützen very little traces were discernible. General von York (Yorck) was present at the battle with 8,000 men, and under him General von Hünerbein, and Colonel von Horn. General von Kleist, with a detachment of the corps, and some regiments of Russians, about 5,000 men, was before Leipsic. The remainder were left to invest Spandau and Wittenberg.

Third Corps.
General von Bülow.
Under him, General von Borstel commanded all the corps before the fortresses of Magdeburg, Wittenberg, and on the Elbe,

Fourth Corps.
Lieutenant-General von Tauenzien commanded the troops blockading Stettin; General von Schulen, those before Glogau; and General von Thümen invested Spandau.

This was the state of the Prussian Army, when operations commenced on the right bank of the Elbe.

Imperious circumstances unavoidably caused a dispersion and derangement of the forces, which are usually but little taken into consideration by him, who, distant from the seat of war, attempts to calculate and weigh military occurrences in his armchair. Two very sufficient reasons may, however, be assigned for this dispersion: first, because a considerable number of fortified places, both of the enemy and our own, were in the rear of the line of operations: secondly, Prussia had begun the formation of her military power in the distant provinces of her dismembered monarchy, at a time when the enemy was actually occupying them; and the celerity of the movements made, would not admit of the places being relieved by the Russians, so that the whole of her active force could gradually converge to, and be concentrated at one point.

General von Blücher marched out of Silesia towards the end of March 1813, at the head of a gallant army of 25,000 men, well-disciplined and equipped; and, on the 3rd of April, passed the Elbe at Dresden. The Russian General Winzingerode, with 13,000 Russians, was placed under him, and formed his corps in advance.

★★★★★★

General Winzingerode being taken prisoner by accident, in October 1812, near Moscow, was brought under a guard into the presence of Napoleon, at the little town of Wereja, not far from Mojaisk. Napoleon, with a countenance inflamed with rage and passion, received him with a volley of abusive words and indecorous expressions, ending at last with:

"I find you everywhere. You are a subject of the King of Westphalia, are you not? He shall punish you as a traitor."

Winzingerode replied with dignity; "I am born a free knight of the free German empire, and have no master to honour but Germania's emperor. A King of Westphalia is unknown to me. When I lived in Westphalia, neither a king nor a kingdom were even thought of."

Napoleon became enraged, and hastily exclaimed, "Away with him! His doom is fixed!"

The general was given to understand that the King of Westphalia would have him shot, as a traitor, when arrived in his territories. But happily, on being transported, accompanied by his adjutant Prince Noischkin, towards the rear of the French Army, as a prisoner of war, his escort was surprised by a party of Cossacks, belonging to Czernischeff's corps, near Minsk, in Polish Lithuania; and he regained his liberty a short time previous to the famous passage of the Beresina.

******

Count Wittgenstein, General von York, and General von Borstel, with their united corps of 25,000 men, were on the right bank of the Elbe, blockading Magdeburg. The Russian detachments under Tettenborn, Dörenberg, and Czernischeff, of 6,000 to 7,000 men altogether, had penetrated below Magdeburg, on both banks of the Elbe.

******

On the 12th of March 1813, the French garrison, under the command of General Carra St. Cyr, left the city of Hamburgh, and, on the 18th, Colonel Tettenborn entered it, at the head of 2,000 Russians, amidst the loud and unfeigned acclamations of the whole population. The march of the Russian detachments into the city may be compared to the triumphal entry of conquering heroes. More than a thousand citizens, and inhabitants of the neighbourhood, far and near, led the cavalcade on horseback. An enthusiasm, bordering on adoration, burst forth throughout all ranks, who tumultuously pressed forward to hail their deliverers, as angels sent from heaven, with flaming swords to consume and devour their galling yokes of bitter servitude and intolerable slavery.

THE DEMAND FOR THE SURRENDER OF COLBERG

NETTELBECK AND GNEISENAU ON THE RAMPARTS AT COLBERG

And Hamburgh, the good city of Hamburgh, set the first glorious and bright example to the rest of suffering Germany, of an exalted spirit of independence, faithful to its country, and honouring her name. Her indignant youth, eager for revenge, panting to enter the paths of glory, formed of themselves, in a few days, a corps of volunteers, nearly 4,000 strong, consisting of infantry, a regiment of light horse, and artillery, under the appellation of the Hanseatic Legion. Voluntary subscriptions, for its equipment, flowed in from all sides, and considerable were the sacrifices of gold and silver ornaments, and the little hoards of domestic thrift, offered on the shrine of Liberty, by the fair sex of all ranks. In short, no one shrunk from disclosing his sense of loyalty and patriotism.

The Hanseatic Legion, fired with the hopes of retaliation, and animated with the prospect of avenging the sufferings of their native city, were so far advanced in their discipline, by their own individual efforts, as to be able to take the field against the common enemy on the 7th of May, on which day they particularly distinguished themselves, in the affair at Wilhelmsburg, bringing in a number of prisoners. Their subsequent actions with the French and Danes, at Dannenberg, Hohen-Vicheln, Zarantin, Mustin, and in Möllenerwalde, have covered them with glory, and the far-famed character of the old Hanse Towns was maintained with undiminished splendour.

★★★★★★

The principal army of the Russians, consisting of 30,000 men, and whose advanced guard was commanded by General Miloradowitsch, stood in the neighbourhood of Kalisch, in Poland, and towards the borders of Silesia.

The fortresses in the rear, namely, Dantsic, Thorn, Modelin, Zamocz, Stettin, Cüstrin, Glogau, and Spandau, were either formally besieged, or blockaded and invested.

Prince Poniatowsky's corps, occupying a part of Poland, was kept in check and narrowly watched by a corps of Russians.

From the frontiers of Bohemia, to the mouth of the Elbe, the aggregate force of the Allies could be estimated at 70,000 men in the field. They were in possession of no tenable point on the Elbe, as unfortified Dresden could not be considered as such, and all the bridges over the Elbe, by Dresden, Meissen, Mühlberg, and Roslau, were as yet undefended by any intrenchments or works. On the other hand, the

French kept strong garrisons in Magdeburg and Wittenberg, on the same river; and in case of any misfortune, Torgau was to be considered as if held by the enemy. On the Upper Elbe the French had no troops, and Würtzburg was become the centre to which the march of all their new levies and reinforcements was directed.

The Viceroy of Italy was stationed on the Middle Elbe, with a force of 50,000 men, including the garrison of Magdeburg, and the troops under d'Avoust. Towards the Lower Elbe, the French had two weak detachments under Vandamme and Morand, with which our troops in that quarter were nearly upon an equal footing.

Such was the exact situation of the hostile armies when the campaign opened by General Wittgenstein's passing the Elbe, besieging Wittenberg, and removing the seat of war to the Lower Saale.

At this period it was strongly believed, and the prejudice seemed to gain ground in public, that much negligence and tardiness were shown in not pushing on with the Grand Army into Thuringia and Franconia, to anticipate the enemy, and, by attacking and destroying his crude and hasty assemblage of troops in and about Würtzburg, at once to baffle and frustrate his unripe designs. But a calm retrospective view and unprepossessed comparison of the forces of the belligerent powers will offer incontrovertible proofs that it was absolutely impossible.

Even if the 43,000 men under Blücher, Winzingerode, and Wittgenstein, on the Upper Elbe, had been marched forwards to Würtzburg, the enemy could not have been brought to battle before the 20th of April, and it was very improbable, according to advices and accounts from all sides, that he should not have previously collected a much superior force at that place; and the result has fully justified the foresight of the Allies, and the correctness of their intelligence.

For, towards the latter end of April, from 70,000 to 80,000 troops arrived on the Saale out of Franconia, and which they would consequently have had so much the sooner to encounter in Franconia itself. On the whole line of the Elbe, they did not occupy a single stronghold, to serve as a rallying point: these were all in the hands of the enemy; and the viceroy was found to be more than equal in strength to Count Wittgenstein, as the attack by Möckern could by no means make the Allies easy concerning the preponderance of these two armies; and if Count Wittgenstein should eventually be unfortunate, the Grand Army in advance from the Elbe had not only a victorious army and a river occupied by the foe in the rear, but likewise a very superior army of the enemy in front, being, in fact, separated from all other armies and corps, and without any communication with its magazines and resources.

The history of former military events clearly proves, that to stand in such a situation before Napoleon, would inevitably have led to results the most pernicious for the good cause, and perhaps to complete defeat; and who could have vindicated it to himself or to others, to have rested the hopes of Europe upon the doubtful issue of such an imprudent and short-sighted expedition? Be that as it may, the plan of letting the grand Russian Army effect a junction with General Wittgenstein on the Upper Elbe, for the purpose of forcing the viceroy to abandon the Elbe entirely, might more readily have found its advocates; but even on that point, some previous matters required arrangement.

The field could not be taken against the viceroy before the middle of April, Count Wittgenstein not being ready with his bridge over the Elbe, nor General von Blücher able to arrive on the Lower Saale before that time. It was about the middle of April, that the greater part of the enemy's force appeared in Thüringia, and the whole line of the Upper Elbe was then to be left uncovered, with all the bridges, and the army obliged to confine itself to the solitary bridge at Roslau, situated between two fortresses, garrisoned by the foe. This was certainly no very favourable circumstance, yet the Allies might have exposed themselves to the chance of such a critical position, if they could thus hope to gain and insure a decisive advantage over the viceroy.

But the substance of every intelligence obtained, clearly evinced the intention of the viceroy's leaving the Saale and withdrawing into Thüringia, the moment he found himself pressed and harassed by a superior force; so that in all probability he would not have accepted battle, and the whole operation would have attained no other object than having changed the theatre of war, by forced marches.

The army of Blücher and Wittgenstein would then have had the Middle Elbe in their rear, and the straight and nearest road to the Upper Elbe left open to the inroads of the enemy. Such a transference of position was a self-evident loss, and an impairment of the moral strength of the Allies. The shortest lines of communication with their supplies and resources were to be given up, the enemy permitted to place himself between them and the Russian Grand Army on the confines of Silesia, and they reduced to no other alternative but to take up a position with two of the enemy's fortresses, Magdeburg and Wittenberg, at their backs, or to recross the Elbe.

To entangle themselves in complex operations, upon whose favourable issue no dependence could be securely placed, out of mere vanity and restlessness of inaction, would certainly have shown a high want of reflection.

In maturely weighing these considerations, we are imperceptibly led to the conviction, that, until the arrival of the main body of the Russian Army on the Elbe, by which the line of that river could be secured, and *têtes de pont* thrown up to defend and protect the bridges across it, no further offensive operations ought to have been undertaken.

The Russian Grand Army reached the Elbe on the 26th of April, and the Battle of Lützen was fought on the 2nd of May. As soon as this army arrived on the line of operations, the army of Blücher and Winzingerode being placed under the immediate orders of the commander-in-chief, their determinations, as was before possible, could have no influence on the whole, either one way or the other.

It has been our wish, by these representations and arguments, to convince our brother-soldiers in arms, that no reprehensible forgetfulness of what they were destined to fulfil, ever for a moment crept into the councils of the army of the Allies; and that their commanders have never neglected, through indolence and irresolution, to embrace each favourable moment of bringing up the disciplined valour and energy of the Prussian nation against the unprepared foe, whenever they presented themselves. The opinion that such a moment had occurred in the spring of 1813, was at the time generally adopted, but never combined with a clear conviction of its existence, and, as we have already proved, was both delusive and groundless.

The mighty power that gained those victories on the Moskwa and Beresina, had exhausted itself on the Elbe. The Russian Army, weakened by gigantic operations till now unheard of in history, in pursuit of the beaten and discomfited enemy, and by the numerous fortresses which it had to besiege, blockade, or invest, on its glorious career, had been utterly incapable of reaching the Elbe, if it had not found in the martial strength of Prussia a most powerful ally. But even when this ally was likewise capable of bringing the Russian armies (whose operations, in the nature of things, must have ended on the Vistula), through all the fortresses that impeded their way, to the banks of the Elbe, yet the Confederate forces were hardly sufficient to remove the seat of war 200 miles further in advance to the Maine; and it proves a want of common sense and understanding to forget for an instant, that the power of the enemy, the nearer he approached his resources, must increase in the same ratio as that of the Allies decreased.

The months of January, February, and March afforded Napoleon time enough to draw together a force in Thüringia and on the Lower Saale, which was almost double to that of the Allied Army under Blücher and Wittgenstein on the Elbe, at the latter end of April. This fact was not to be controverted; nor could it be denied, whatever turn and direction might be given to the future operations of the Allies, that, with such a superiority, there was no prospect of defeating Napoleon, how disproportionate soever the armies might be in other respects.

The month of April elapsed on the Upper Elbe, in a state of inaction by no means optional. General von Blücher's army occupied Saxony, to profit by the resources of the country, in case of necessity to support General Wittgenstein, and at the same time endeavour to harass the enemy on his flanks and in his rear, by detachments of light cavalry and partisans.

Count Wittgenstein carried on the war against the Viceroy, with as many advantages as the superior force of the latter would allow. By gaining the Battle of Möckern, he protected Berlin and the Mark from an invasion, with which they were threatened by an enemy's army, 40,000 strong, who (according to the intercepted reports of the enemy himself) were actually repulsed by only 17,000 men of General Wittgenstein's army. An irresolute timid conduct, attended with some blunders, on the side of the enemy, and the most inflexible courage and undaunted military spirit on the part of the Allied troops, rendered it alone possible for the skill and intrepidity of the count to gain this hard-fought and honourable victory. Prussians! you had your share of the glory of this day!—Count Wittgenstein has himself eminently distinguished you in his dispatches.

The detachments on the Lower Elbe opened the campaign with some success. General Doraberg took the French General Morand, prisoner, with his whole division; and you, Prussians, again bore a considerable part in the glory of the contest! Six hundred Prussians bravely defended a gate and a bridge at Lüneburgh for several hours against the whole division of the enemy. The expeditions of the light troops of the Allies into the forests of Thüringia were likewise equally glorious to their arms. Major Hellwig, at the head of 120 horse, surprised a Bavarian regiment of infantry, 1300 men strong, dispersed it, and took from it five field-pieces.

It was these acts of an exalted bravery, performed, as it were, before

Stendal
Spandau
BERLIN
Charlottenburg
Brandenburg
Potsdam
Teltow
Gross Beeren
Belitz
Mockern
MAGDEBURG
Leibnitz
Belzig
Treuenbrietzen
B R A N D E
Leitzkau
Rabenstein
Dennewitz
Juterbock
Zerbst
Zahna
Roslau
Coswig
Wittenberg
Dessau
Seyda
Dahme
Jessen
Luckau
P R U
Kothen
Wartenburg
R. Elbe
Herzberg
Zorbig
Bitterfeld
Duben
Torgau
Landsberg
Delitzsch
Halle
Eilenburg
Schilda
Muhlberg
Elsterwerda
Taucha
Leipzig
Merseburg
Lutzen
Grossenhain
Konigsbruck
Weissenfels
Grimma
Meissen
Naumburg
DRESDEN
Borna
Colditz
Plauen
Zeitz
Altenburg
Nossen
Penig
Freyberg
Dippoldiswalde
Konigstein
Chemnitz
Oderan
WEIMAR
Neustadt
Marienberg
Teplitz
Culm
Schleiz
Auerbach
Schwarzenberg
Erz Gebirge
Plauen

Enlarged Map
OF
SAXONY, PART OF PRUSSIA &c
Forming part of
PRUSSIA AND POLAND
Plate 34
Zellin
Wartha
Custrin
Oder
Cunnersdorf
Posen
B U R G
P O S E N
S I L E S I A
Bober
Glogau
Sprottau
Oder
Liegnitz
BRESLAU
Gorlitz
Zittau
Riesen Gebirge

the eyes of the whole army, that nourished a growing confidence in itself, and proved a kind of touchstone, upon which, on trial, they discovered the sterling metal of their own prowess, while at the same time it contributed rapidly to increase the natural and real strength of the Allies. Without any marks of pride and arrogance, this confidence in themselves, and in the sacredness of the cause of their dear country, bleeding under the scourge of oppression, was conspicuous throughout the ranks, and never was an army inspired with a higher spirit.

A few days afterwards, this spirit strikingly displayed itself before all Europe on the bloody plains of Lützen.

PRUSSIAN VOLUNTEERS LEAVING BERLIN

Chapter 5

Battle of Lützen

As the French troops accumulated in the forests of Thüringia, and those coming front Italy approached the frontiers of Saxony, Count Wittgenstein marched from the Lower Saale towards Leipsic, and General von Blücher, who could not as yet venture to leave the high road by the way of Chemnitz to Dresden, being the shortest communication from Franconia to the Elbe, took position at Altenburg; so that, by a quick movement on his right, he could easily form a junction with Count Wittgenstein.

★★★★★★

General von Blücher issued from his headquarters at this, place, the following proclamation to his brave army:

Soldiers of my army!

Your exemplary conduct has undergone no change whatever, since you have left your native provinces, and entered the territory of Saxony. You have hitherto made no distinction between the two countries, but have held yourselves bound in duty to observe the same excellent discipline. I thank you for this proof of your noble forbearance. Such a conduct evinces the true spirit of warriors, and is best fitting us, fighting, as we are, for the most honourable and costly of all earthly possessions—our country and our freedom!

Prove to the inhabitants of the German provinces, by the moderation of your demands, and the mildness of your treatment, that we are come, not as their oppressors, but as their brethren and preservers. Continue to act with this excellent spirit of subordination, and should the fame of your exalted behaviour have preceded you far and near, you will be received with blessings.

and open arms, wherever you show yourselves, and fate may lead you.

Altenburg, April 24, 1813.

★★★★★★

The numbers of, the French Army had been carefully estimated. The several corps in march from Würtzburg to the forests of Thüringia might be calculated at from 60,000 to 70,000 men. The Italian divisions under General Bertrand might be 30,000 strong. It was, however, a matter of uncertainty, whether the whole would be brought up, as, according to an earlier destination, two of them were to halt on the Danube. But the strength of the viceroy's army was better known and appreciated; for, besides the garrisons of Magdeburg and Wittenberg, and including d'Avoust's corps, it amounted to 38,000 men, of which d'Avoust had 12,000 with him. It was, therefore, justly calculated that the viceroy would form part of the left wing of the French Grand Army, with about 20,000 men; the whole constituting an aggregate force of nearly 120;000 combatants.

The armies of General von Blücher and Count Wittgenstein might be estimated at 55,000 men, after having left the necessary troops on the Lower Saale, before Wittenberg, and in the *tête de pont* of the bridge at Dessau; the Russian Grand Army at 30,000 men: in the whole, 85,000 well-disciplined warriors. It was, therefore, impossible, as before stated, to oppose even an equal force to the enemy in Saxony.

There was here no other alternative but either to evacuate Saxony without striking a blow, to take up a position behind the Elbe, and to defend that river, or instantly to attack the enemy as soon as he had crossed the Saale.

In defending the Elbe, the Allies could not be very sanguine in their expectations of keeping the foe long in check, he having Wittenberg, and, in case of the Allies retreating over the Elbe, most probably Torgau in his possession, and the crossing of so narrow and placid a stream, presented no very insurmountable obstacles.

★★★★★★

General Thielman was appointed Governor of Torgau on the 22nd of February. The king having left Saxony, and the political state of affairs assuming a very changeable aspect, from the uncertainty of the nature of those steps His Majesty might eventually take, the general determined to observe the strictest neutrality! Marshal d'Avoust, as well as the Viceroy of Italy, were urgent in their requests, that the general might send the garrison to defend Meissen, and line the ramparts of Wittenberg with his artillery. The former even demanded permission to send French troops to garrison Torgau, but which was firmly resisted; a conduct that, at the time, met the most unreserved approbation of the Saxon monarch.

On the 5th of May Marshal Ney appeared before the gates of Torgau, and demanded entrance. General Thielman stated his want of instructions, and would not open them. On the 8th, the marshal again presented himself before the fortress, and repeated the same pretension, which proved equally unavailing. On the 9th, a member of the intermediate commission arrived from Dresden in Torgau, demanding the opening of the gates in the name of Napoleon.

The general remained firm to his adopted neutrality till the 11th, when, at the express command of the king, he delivered up the place to the French. He now quitted the service of Saxony, and entered that of the Emperor of Russia, being well convinced that, as long as French influence governed the king, the unfading laurels of honour and glory could never grace his brow, nor the smiles of fortune ever crown his efforts.

★★★★★★

There was, besides, every appearance that the Allies would thus entangle themselves in a dangerous defensive operation; for nothing could be clearer, than that it was impossible to gain sufficient time for the Austrians to be ready to assist them in the general cause of so large a portion of Europe; and to continue their retrograde movement into Lusatia and Silesia, merely to enable the Imperialists to take the field, was evidently as little practicable, it requiring no great foresight to calculate that such a step would have led them to the frontiers of Poland, and perhaps farther.

An attempt must, therefore, be made, to give the enemy battle, and it certainly appeared more advantageous, not voluntarily to submit to the evil impression which a retreat in form would make upon Germany and the army altogether, but rather boldly and daringly to fall unawares upon the enemy, than to accept the battle he might offer; or force upon the Allies; in any well-chosen defensive position in the rear. Many weighty and collateral reasons concurred also to render it possible that the event might prove important and decisive, both from the character of Buonaparte as a general, and the superiority of numbers which he possessed.

It still remained doubtful whether Napoleon could bring into action his 120,000 men on the day of battle, if the Allies hastened to attack him directly on his crossing the Saale; for he would then have the steep valley of that river in his rear, and must debouch in a plain forming a fine glacis very favourable to the Allied troops, as they had 25,000 cavalry with their army, and the enemy only 5,000.

★★★★★★

It has been since ascertained, that Napoleon had brought up all his corps into the field of battle, except the 12th corps, under Marshal Oudinot, which was a few marches in the rear, and did not come into action at all, on this side of the Elbe.

★★★★★★

The infantry of the Allies were indisputably better in moral value than his. Perhaps he might not expect so daring an attack; and as Napoleon and his host had never been brought to battle entirely on the defensive, there was every reason to expect, that the hostile army would be taken by surprise, and thus deprived of their usual confidence of success. In blending all these arguments together, hopes of victory, and of overthrowing at one blow Napoleon's delirious plans of conquest, might certainly be cherished, without yielding too much to illusive conjectures.

Napoleon made good his passage over the Saale at Weissenfels, on the 30th of April, with a considerable force; by which movement his supposed intention of proceeding to the plains of Leipsic was confirmed. The Allied Army broke up, to meet the foe without loss of time, on the plain of Lützen, to form in front of the high road to Leipsic, and, in case of beating the enemy, to force him from Weissenfels and Naumburg, by driving him towards the morasses and swampy grounds at the junction of the Elster with the Pleisse.

The Prussian Army was collected at Borne on the 31st of April, and on the 1st of May at Röthe; Count Wittgenstein with the Russians at Zweckau: during which, General Winzingerode observed and kept the enemy on the alert near the Flossgraben. In the night of the 1st of May the Prussian Army put itself in march; and both armies united, crossed the Elster at Zweckau and Pegau.

General Miloradowitsch had taken upon him to watch the enemy on the road from Chemnitz, as the Prussians began to move to the right; and when it was ascertained that no enemy appeared from that quarter, he marched off towards Zeitz, to cover the road from Naumburg and Camberg, it being impossible, on the 1st of May, to be certain that the enemy would not push on from this point with from 20,000 to 30,000 men, and thus get into the rear of the army without impediment. The remaining part of the Russian Grand Army, consisting of guards, grenadiers, and *cuirassiers*. From 15,000 to 20,000 strong, had marched from Dresden, by the way of Röchlitz, to the Elster, and took position on the morning of the 2nd of May in the rear of Wittgenstein and Blücher as Reserves.

General Count Wittgenstein was commander-in-chief of all the Allied troops. The Emperor of Russia and the King of Prussia arrived on the field of battle with the reserves.

It was evident that this intrepid determination of the Allies confounded Napoleon, and took him by surprise. He was marching at this period towards Leipsic, in hopes of pushing forward from thence to Dresden, and by this rapid movement to strike a decisive and irretrievable blow at the liberties of Germany. His own bulletins express as much. He probably expected to encounter General Wittgenstein's army before his junction with General von Blücher, whom he still supposed to be at Altenburg; or he had the intention, before he attacked them, to cut them off from all communication with the Elbe, if they were united in the direction of that place.

But in these "sublime manoeuvres," as the French papers termed them, he received a check; the Allied Army having; at the most critical moment, fallen on his rear, and arrested his confident and impetuous career on the plains of Lützen, where Nature had poured forth her riches in unbounded profusion, but which the horrors of this terrible conflict, have now covered with ruin and desolation.

The corps of Marshal Marmont formed Napoleon's rear-guard, and occupied the villages of Rahno, Gross-Görschen, and Klein-Görschen. to cover the march. He had to bear the brunt of the first shock; Napoleon immediately caused his army to halt, and the columns already near Leipsic were recalled.

Here it was manifest that the right point had been chosen, both in time and place, so openly confessed by Napoleon himself; and if we add the important and valuable consequences that must ensue, supposing the battle to be successful, we may assert, without fear of contradiction, that the bold attempt forms one of the finest military combinations to be met with in the annals of any war.

In entering into the minutiae of the battle itself, the author begs the particular indulgence of the reader to this very superficial sketch. Although the Confederate warriors, for whom these sheets are more immediately intended, must feel themselves much interested in seeing noticed, clearly and succinctly, all the separate attacks made on this memorable day; yet, at the present moment, it is too difficult a task to be complete, without again reviewing and closely examining the terrain on which the battle was fought; the author is, therefore, constrained to confine himself to the general character and most striking features of the whole.

General von Kleist being left in and near Leipsic, with 5,000 men, and General Miloradowitsch, at Zeitz, with 12,000; the Allied Army, 70,000 strong, after passing the Elster, crossed the Flossgraben in small compact columns, in close succession, to form in line of battle, wheeling, as they deployed, rather to the right; so that the right wing leaned on the Flossgraben, and halted behind the heights about a mile and a half from Gross-Görschen. It was now noon; and the troops were absolutely in want of some repose, the Prussians having marched without intermission during the last six-and-thirty hours.

From these heights the gleams of hostile bayonets were seen at a great distance, and the enemy's cavalry in full march by the way of Lützen to Leipsic; at least so it was judged by the clouds of dust that occasionally hid them from the view of the Allied Army; but it was more reasonable to suppose that the enemy were hastily retracing their steps, on finding their original plan disconcerted by such a decisive and vigorous movement on the part of the Allies. The enemy, it was perceived, occupied the villages of Gross-Görschen, Klein-Görschen, Rahno, and Kaja, which, lying near each other, form of themselves a kind of irregular square: this occupation was thought to consist of some weak outposts, and it was therefore hoped no great resistance would be made.

The plan of the attack was, to take and occupy these villages with an advanced guard; to proceed with the front against the enemy, whose position seemed to run parallel with the high road to Weissenfels, in such a manner as to bring the principal weight of the attack against his right wing, but to undertake nothing against his left. With this concentration of force, it was the intention to throw back, if possible, his right wing, to drive Napoleon from the direct road to the Saale, and then, with the mass of the numerous cavalry of the Allied Army, to turn the enemy's right wing, and, by a furious charge on its flank and rear, to bear down all obstacles, and thus decide the fortune of the day.

The order of battle was as follows: the army of General von Blücher formed the first line; that formerly belonging to Count Wittgenstein, the second; and the corps of General Winzingerode, together with the Russian guards and grenadiers, the reserve. The Russian and Prussian reserves of cavalry were to be united. (See Map of the Battle of Lützen.) After an hour's rest, the army, so formed, marched onwards at about half past one o'clock, p.m. Colonel Klux's brigade was ordered to attack the first village; namely, Gross-Görschen.

From three to four batteries were erected within 800 yards, and the village heavily cannonaded; the enemy's battalions, of which three or more were drawn up before the village, supported the fire with wonderful firmness for a considerable time; the brigade then advanced, with steadiness and discipline, to close action, and, although more troops were encountered in the village than had been expected, yet the attack was made with such an irresistible impetuosity, that the French were in a few minutes driven out of it with great loss.

They soon rallied, and, being reinforced, returned to the attack with redoubled fury, and the action continued with violence without the Allied troops being compelled to relinquish a foot of ground, As the enemy continued bringing up fresh troops every moment, General Ziethen's brigade was ordered to advance to the right of the village, and the Prussians soon acquired a visible ascendancy; the enemy's infantry fought bravely, but the two brigades still pressed forward, and carried, after an obstinate resistance, the two villages of Rahno and Klein-Görschen, that lie about the distance of a cannon-shot to the right and left of Gross-Görschen. For several hours the conflict was dubious; but the discharges of musketry raged with such indescribable destruction, and the troops on both sides were so near to each other, that the number of killed and wounded was incredible.

The artillery was then gradually brought forward, and small detachments of cavalry, of one and two squadrons, that formed the second line of the Prussian brigades, endeavoured to find favourable opportunities to charge: the enemy was not remiss in bringing up his artillery and squadrons of cavalry; and on a terrain of about one thousand to one thousand five hundred square yards, intersected by villages, hamlets, meadows, and ditches, the most severe and galling attacks of all arms took place in close contact with each other, and on which, it may be said, fell Slaughter, in all his horrid terrors, crowned with desolation, and, prodigal of death, reigned triumphant.

The number of Prussians engaged amounted to about fourteen or fifteen thousand men. The enemy, who, for the moment, acted on the offensive in striving to regain possession of the villages, brought up continually numerous bodies of fresh troops into action, and at last attained a superiority of numbers that obliged the weakened and thinned battalions of the Allies to evacuate Klein-Görschen; but, again led on and inspired by their generals, and profiting of some fortunate charges of the cavalry, Napoleon was soon deprived of his precarious advantage; and here it was demonstrably evident, that the enemy's infantry was not, in any respect, equal to the Allied in moral value, though superior in numbers; they displayed neither firmness nor discipline; and the unremitting, steady fire of the Prussians in platoons, soon forced their dismayed battalions to desert the field of battle in disordered crowds.

When it was observed on the side of the Prussians, that an important crisis presented itself to carry Kaja, but that the troops on the spot were too weak in numbers to maintain themselves in it, the reserve brigades, consisting of the guards and grenadiers, were brought into action; and these gallant files arrived on the ground at a most critical juncture. Napoleon incessantly pushed on into fire, fresh battalions from all points. The two brigades were already so thinned in their ranks, that they could only keep up a partial and irregular fire, like the open lines of a rifle-corps. The guards, however, pressed forward with incomparable bravery and order; they took Klein-Görschen, and the village of Hahalati to the right of it, by storm, driving the French before them to the other side of Kaja: in vain did the enemy endeavour to stop their progress with the bayonet; their resolution was not to be daunted: the ground over which they marched was strewed with the dead and wounded, "and blood and carnage paved the way to glory." Kaja was in flames, and it was not occupied from either side.

This was the most brilliant period of the battle. It might be about six o'clock in the evening; and the Allies had gained a mile and a half in advance upon the foe, amidst a continual and murderous fire, the violence and fury of which baffle all attempts at description. This dear-bought bloody conquest must have proved the first step towards a most splendid victory, if, under the existing circumstances, it were to be gained in any way. But the arranged plan for this battle, of which we have just depicted the most important features, now met with considerable difficulties in its execution and continuance.

The unexpected and obstinate resistance of the enemy in the first villages, and the number of troops he brought into the line of battle, soon convinced the Allies that no very inconsiderable part of Napoleon's army was engaged with them; it was, however, impossible, instantly, on this being ascertained, to break off and decline the combat

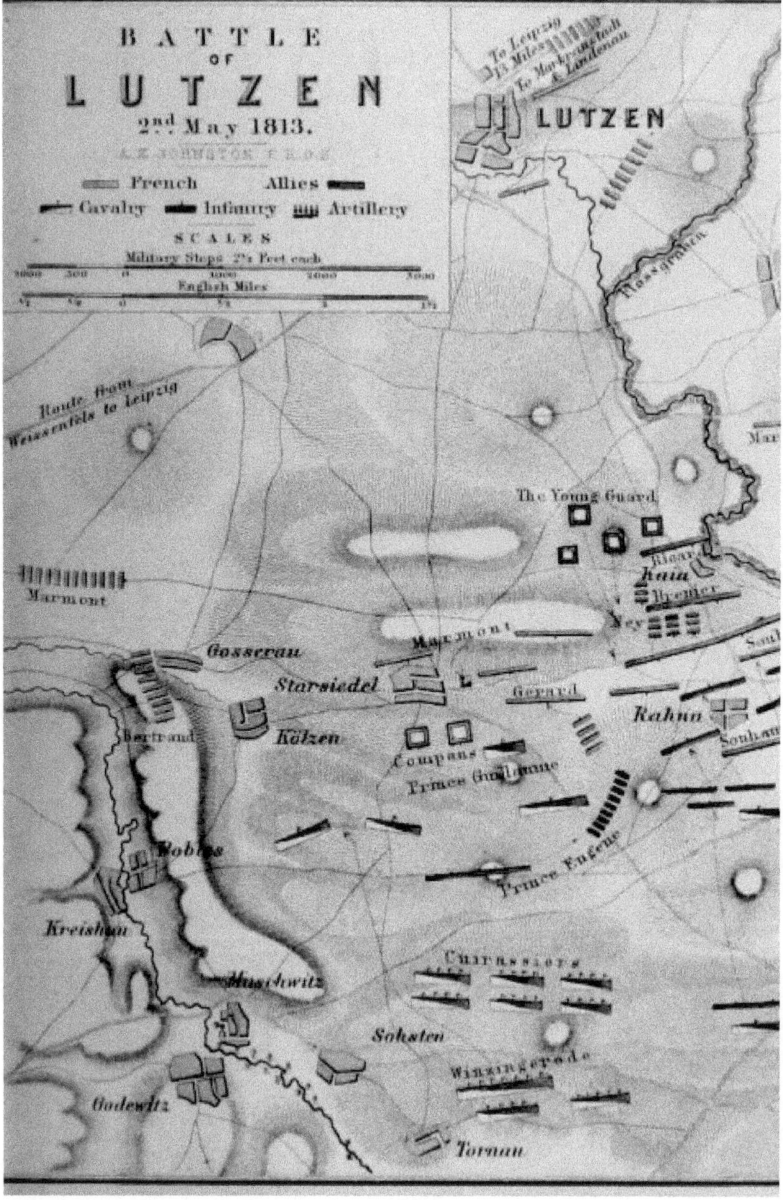

BATTLE
OF
LUTZEN
2nd May 1813.
French
Allies
Cavalry
Infantry
Artillery
SCALES
Military Steps 2½ Feet each
English Miles
To Leipzig 13 Miles
To Markranstadt & Lindenau
LUTZEN
Flossgraben
Route from Weissenfels to Leipzig
Marmont
The Young Guard
Ricard
Kaia
Bremer
Ney
Marmont
Gosserau
Starsiedel
Gerard
Rahna
Bertrand
Kölzen
Compans
Prince Guillaume
Prince Eugene
Kreishau
Cuirassiers
Muschwitz
Sohsten
Winzingerode
Godewitz
Tornau

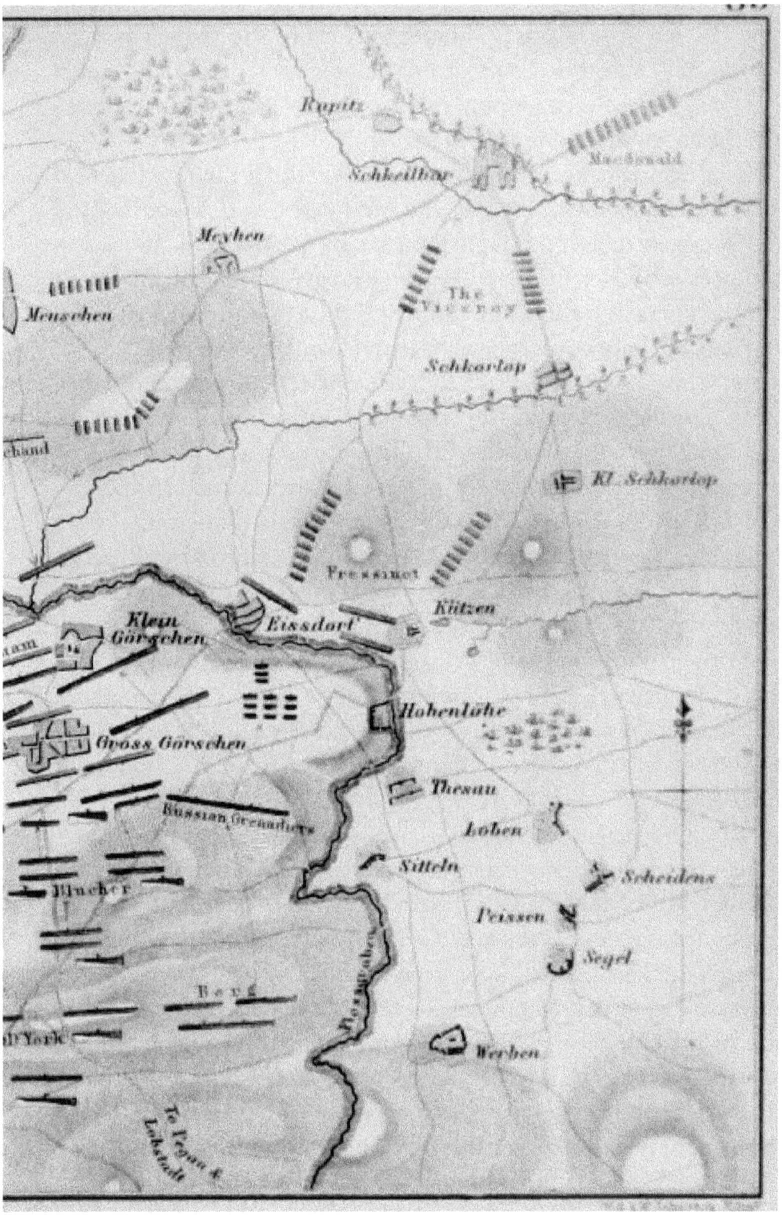

Rapitz
Schkeitbar
Meyhen
Menschen
The Viceroy
Schkorlop
Kl. Schkorlop
Kitzen
Eissdorf
Klein Görschen
Gross Görschen
Hohenlöhe
Thesau
Löben
Sitteln
Scheidens
Peissen
Segel
Werben
Russian Grenadiers
Blucher
Berg

by leaving the affair undecided, as their adversary would have soon acted on the offensive, had they given him time, by slackening their fire, or revived his hopes by a retrograde movement in the heat of action. No other option was left the Allies, therefore, but to carry their point at all hazards, It was a momentous crisis; the fate of nations seemed to depend on the issue of this sanguinary struggle, and much was to be left to the goodness of Providence, whose omniscience mocks the short-sighted policy of men.

General von Blücher's army, that is, the whole of the first line, had been hotly engaged with the foe, and even defeated that body of the enemy opposed to him, though superior in numbers; yet there was no prospect whatever of directing the principal weight of the attack against the enemy's right wing; and it was therefore resolved to order up the second line, consisting of General von York's corps of 8,000 men, and General von Berg's of 5,000, to support General von Blücher.

With the view of attracting the attention of the enemy's right wing, and by this feint to profit of the first opening in which, perhaps, a movement of the front line of the enemy, that leaned on the village of Staarsiedel to the right, might afford their numerous cavalry a favourable opportunity to charge the hostile infantry; the Prussian cavalry in reserve, and a considerable part of the Russian heavy cavalry, were so drawn up on the plain as to support General von Blücher's left with their right wing, and to stand opposite with their left to the village of Staarsiedel. A brisk cannonade now ensued on the whole of this line. The reserves of infantry, both Russian and Prussian, were posted on the high commanding grounds in the neighbourhood, out of the range of the enemy's artillery.

At the time that the Prussian guards penetrated to Kaja, the enemy's first line being threatened on their left wing, and much annoyed by the hot fire of the artillery of the Allies, drew back from five to six hundred yards, and evacuated the village of Staarsiedel, which the want of infantry prevented them from occupying.

It was apparent that Napoleon considered the occupation and possession of the five villages already mentioned, as decisive of the fate of the battle; for he did not hesitate to bring into action more than a fourth, if not the half of his infantry, in order to retake and maintain them (namely, from forty to fifty thousand men); and thus continued an obstinate engagement for hours, in which both the Allies and the French were victorious and vanquished by turns.

The corps of General von Blücher may be rated at 20,000 men,

GENERAL YORCK ENTERS KÖNIGSBERG

without the cavalry in reserve: the enemy once more became his superior in numbers, and it required the most heroic exertions to preserve those points from whence he had dislodged the foe, until General von York's, and a great part of General von Berg's corps could advance to support him. Napoleon, in bringing up his forces, spread them far to the left of the villages, thus obliging the Allied troops of the second line to deploy more to the right, and, consequently, the assistance intended in aid of the first line was much weakened. A considerable number of the first line had fallen, and many of the battalions belonging to it, reduced to inconsiderable bodies, had retired behind the villages to rally and collect themselves.

For the purpose of giving some decisive turn to this most obstinate and sanguinary contest, the General-in-Chief, Count Wittgenstein, gave orders that the infantry, under the command of Prince Eugene of Würtemberg, should fall upon the left flank of the enemy, to ensure the advantages already gained near the villages. They were put in execution; but the Viceroy of Italy, who had just arrived on the field with his corps from Leipsic, advanced with confidence on the prince at this juncture; and, instead of having it in his power to outflank the enemy, he was himself outflanked, an event which called forth all the gallantry and firmness of this young hero, and the intrepid valour of his distinguished division, to keep, their position in this unequal trial.

In the meantime, the Allied cavalry kept up a brisk cannonade with their horse-artillery on the right wing of the enemy, which cost the life of many a brave soldier, without any important consequences ensuing. The brilliant charges which the Prussian cavalry repeatedly made to penetrate the French ranks, were often crowned with success; but the principal line of the Gallic infantry ever standing firm and unbroken, no object of importance could be attained by the charges of cavalry alone.

The enemy was foiled in all his repeated attempts, to regain possession of those obstinately contested points of his position which the Allies had acquired during a severe action of eight hours, although the battle raged till night.

To maintain the conquered ground during the night, however, would require the advance of more reserves of infantry. On the side of the Allies about 38,000 infantry had been engaged; and as the whole force of their foot did not exceed, 53,000 men, of course, only 15,000 fresh troops of this description were in reserve. Supposing the enemy had brought from sixty to seventy thousand men into the field, which might be presumed after the arrival of the Viceroy, he had at least from forty to fifty thousand men remaining untouched. This being maturely weighed, it naturally followed that the Allies had it not in their power to keep pace with the physical strength of the enemy, on which account, it was determined to attempt, in the obscurity of the night, to surprise him by an unexpected charge of cavalry, which, if successful, might lead to very important events.

With nine squadrons of the Prussian reserve cavalry that were on the spot favourable for the operation, but reduced in their efficient numbers by the murderous cannonade of eight hours' duration, the advanced troops of the enemy were undauntedly charged, broken, and hotly pursued to some distance, where, falling in with enormous masses of infantry in the rear, and owing to the darkness of the night, and a hollow way which the cavalry was obliged to pass to make another charge, they had eventually dispersed in all directions, depriving the Allies of any immediate advantages to be derived from this dashing attempt.

If the Allies would not set everything at stake in continuing to oppose a superiority of infantry in the enemy, that nearly trebled theirs, it was incumbent on them to make good their retreat on the following day, that so they might be nearer their reinforcements, and, with as little sacrifice of position as possible, await Austria's declaration of war, and the call on Germany, to rouse her dormant spirit, to assert her liberties, and to avenge her wrongs.

The Allies had suffered no other loss in this battle, but of killed and wounded.

******

The humane inhabitants of Leipsic and Altenburg, although Saxons, with a noble emulation, endeavoured to outvie each other in bringing prompt assistance to the wounded Prussians and Russians lying on the field of battle; the country-people voluntarily lent their aid to carry them on biers, from off the ground, to the temporary hospitals, particularly to that in Altenburg, where the poor-house was hastily converted into an hospital, exclusively for the brave Allies, and in which they were nursed and attended with the tenderness of relations.

The wards in the poor-house more resembled ballrooms than the chambers of the sick; both married and single ladies of rank and fortune, held it an honour to bring refreshments, bandages, and; medicines of every description, and in many cases to distribute them themselves. Wreaths of laurel, garlands of flowers, festoons of oak, were hung round the walls, and replaced fresh and blooming every three or four days. The French were taken care of in the town-house, but not a man of them dared to put his foot within the hallowed edifice solely devoted for the relief of the gallant and adored guardians and defenders of Teutonic liberty and independence.

★★★★★★

The enemy could scarcely have made a few hundred prisoners; and they had not to boast of having captured a single piece of artillery: the Allies, on the other hand, had established themselves on the principal points of his position, and a few cannon and tumbrils, with six to eight hundred prisoners, constituted the trophies of the day.

All this was effected in a conflict with an enemy very superior in numbers; and if we place this battle in a point of view similar to an affair of honour, it might be looked upon as a victory that only increased the splendour of the Allied arms, and served to convince the neutral German princes of the zeal and unanimity that governed the councils of the Confederates.

★★★★★★

The Emperor of Russia transmitted to our veteran general the order of St. George, accompanied by the following gracious letter in his own handwriting:

Dresden, May the 5th, 1813.

General of the Cavalry, von Blücher,

The bravery which you have evinced in the battle of the 2nd of May, the services you have done on this memorable day, your devotion, your zeal, your eagerness to be found on the post of danger, and your firmness in not deserting the field of honour, although wounded; in a word, the whole tenor of your conduct during the battle has filled my heart with gratitude and admiration. Inspired with the desire of giving you proofs of my sincere sentiments in this respect, I send you the insignia of the second class of the order of St. George. It will remind you of a battle that must interest you in so lively a manner by the conduct of the gallant troops you commanded, that have so highly distinguished themselves; and may it likewise serve as a mark of my personal attachment. As for the rest, I pray to the Almighty that he may ever take you under his holy protection.

Alexander.

★★★★★★

The retreat of the Allied Army from the plains of Lützen, could not be considered as proceeding from the consequences of the battle; it originated solely in the evident superiority of the foe; and if the battle had not been fought at all, would have become so much the more necessary.

★★★★★★

According to an official statement of the French Army, under Napoleon, prior to the Battle of Lützen, the corps of which it was composed, and their numbers, were as follow:

6 old and 16 young battalions guards Marshal Mortier
16,000
3rd corps, under Marshal Ney, consisting of 5 divisions
45,000
6th corps, under Marshal Marmont, consisting of 3 divisions
25,000
4th corps, under Count Bertrand, consisting of 3 divisions
25,000
12th corps, under Marshal Oudinot, consisting of 3 three divisions
5,000
5th corps, under Count Lauriston, consisting of 2 divisions
15,000
11th corps, under Marshal Macdonald, consisting of 2 divisions
15,000
Cavalry of the guards under Bessières
4,000

170,000

★★★★★★

That these observations do not spring from an empty vaunting, or any inclination to deceive ourselves, is sufficiently proved by the conduct of Napoleon after the battle: according to his own account, he had withdrawn his corps to some distance in his rear, during the night, and did not occupy the villages which the Allies had left, till the noon of the following day, and then only with weak detachments; he remained inactive during the whole of the third, and, on the fourth, put his army in motion in pursuit of the Allied Armies, and to follow out his plan.

On the second, the Allies marched to Borne and Altenburg; on the fourth, to Röchlitz and Kolditz; on the fifth, to Döbeln and Nossen; on the sixth, to Meissen and Wilsdruf; on the seventh they crossed the Elbe, and took the road to Bautzen on the eighth, where they hoped to be enabled to offer a second general battle to the enemy.

******

General von Blücher received on this day the following letter from the Emperor Alexander:

Dresden, May 6, 1813.

The Prussian troops, on the 2nd of May, have, by their resolution, their firmness, and their zeal, not forgetting their distinguished bravery and discipline, excited my most unfeigned admiration, and that of the whole Russian Army. I entreat you, noble General, to be the interpreter of these my sentiments towards them, which impose upon me the agreeable duty of publicly giving proofs of my esteem and gratitude to those brave men who have covered themselves with glory, on that splendid day. Therefore, General, you will have the goodness to make known to me those generals and officers who have had opportunities of doing signal services, that I may, accordingly, fix the kind of distinctions which I wish to confer upon them. In the meantime I place at your disposal three hundred crosses of the order of St. George, fifth class, to be distributed to those subalterns and privates who have the most highly distinguished themselves by brilliant deeds of arms. A chief, who, possesses your esteem and confidence, wilt deliver to you these distinctions, and, at the same time, prove to you how much I do justice to your conduct. Your, fellow-soldiers in arms will hereby be convinced that they share with yourself an honorary badge, on which you place a great value, and which only the regard and devotion that prevails between you, in so high a degree, can preserve and confirm. Please to accept, noble General, the assurance of my most sincere esteem.

Alexander.

******

During the battle, General von Kleist, who, on the approach of the enemy's Grand Army, had retired from Leipsic, again occupied that city. He left it on the 3rd, and passed the Elbe at Mühlburg.

******

1. The French General of Division Lauri had, on the 3rd of May 1813, forced the Prussian General Kleist to evacuate Leipsic. A

few Cossacks had, however, loitered behind, and a patrol of eight French *chasseurs à cheval* rode down the Peter's Street, to clear this quarter of stragglers, and then stopped a few minutes at the Peter's Gate: at this instant, a single Cossack, on a gentle trot, passed within a few yards of them, with as unconcerned an air, holding his pike balancing in his hand, as if they had been his own comrades: the writer of this, an eye-witness, was astonished at the calm manner in which he eyed the French; who, seized by an unaccountable surprise, or rather a kind of irresolute torpor, actually permitted the Cossack to advance more than fifty paces through the gate, before they bethought themselves of taking him prisoner. On galloping off after him, they fired their pistols, but the intrepid Cossack had already got clear of the gateway, and with wonderful presence of mind turned the first corner at full speed, and escaped.

2. On the same day, the French piquets being pushed forward towards Wurzen, and their patrols having scoured the roads on all sides, their light cavalry seemed to think all danger far distant, and began to disperse themselves in different parts of the city. Two of them rode their horses to a farrier's, in the suburb of Halle, to have them shoed; they dismounted, and hanging their bridles on the hook in front of the smith's shop, stepped in, stating their wants, and, as usual, demanding a bottle of wine, "*pour passer le tems:*" scarcely were they seated with their wine, on a bench before the door, when a prowling Cossack, who had been on the watch, rode up at full speed, with his pike couched towards them; the dragoons, taken by surprise, hastily retreated into the smith's workshop, and the Cossack, little heeding them, with an agility bordering on enchantment, unhooked the bridles, and galloped off unmolested with his booty; leaving the Frenchmen to enjoy their wine at leisure, but with what relish may be easily conceived.

******

General von Bülow had, on the second of May, taken Halle by storm, capturing six pieces of artillery. This glorious exploit proclaimed, like many others, the fine spirit that animated the troops, but their results were for the moment absorbed in the unavoidable vortex of general events.

The advanced guard of the French came up with the Prussian rear-guard, on the fifth, at Kolditz, and a severe action took place, without accelerating or retarding the march of the Allied columns. No further attempt was made by the enemy on this rear-guard. Against General Miloradowitsch, who commanded the rear-guard of the Russian columns, the adversary made some attacks that led to no advantage to himself, but for which he was several times severely punished, by the success of the Russians.

******

The severest conflicts took place on the 12th, by Kapellenberg, near Bishoffswerda. General Miloradowitsch defended every foot of ground with incomparable bravery, and the enemy, foiled in his obstinate and repeated attempts to penetrate the lines of the rear-guard, and full of rancorous revenge at his heavy loss, plundered without mercy the pleasant country-town of Bishoffswerda to the bare walls, then set it on fire, and did not leave three houses standing.

******

In casting a retrospective glance over this first opening of the campaign, it may be remarked, that the issue was a very natural effect of the general state of affairs in Germany. Only one of the Germanic states, and but a small part of a growing power, assisted by a moderate army of his faithful ally, fought and attempted to make head against the concentrated forces of colossal France. It was to be lamented, that, even at this eventful epoch, many German princes added their files to the host of the oppressor, that the rest of Germany was calm and torpid, and (except the bright examples of the Duke of Mecklenburg-Schwerin, (see note 1 following), and the ancient city of Hamburgh; see note 2 following) awaited with solicitude the hour of deliverance, but wanted the courage to hasten its approach!

******

1. Mecklenburg-Schwerin was the first state that threw off the trammels imposed on it by fear and coercion, through the hated confederacy of the Rhine, No sooner had the French deserted the right bank of the Elbe, than the people, in zealous haste, anticipated the call of their prince, and flew to arms.

History will not forget the burst of patriotism, which, on the approach of the Russians, in February, converted the faithful subjects of the duke into a band of heroes. The well-appointed corps of volunteer yeomanry cavalry, headed by the duke's third son, Prince Gustavus, gallantly charged the Danes, on the 10th of December 1813, at the affair on the Eider, between

Eckernförde and Flendsburg; but being unsupported by infantry, through the tardy and vacillating measures of the Crown Prince of Sweden, their retreat was obliged to be made through a defile defended by some battalions of the enemy. This brave young prince, at the head of his squadron, attempted to cut his way through; but his horse being shot under him, and himself wounded, he was taken prisoner.

On being conducted to Prince Frederick of Hesse, who commanded the Danes, he was released on his parole of not serving against Denmark during the war. The Crown Prince of Sweden was very lavish of expressions, in extolling the intrepid conduct of the worthy descendant of the great Coburg, and appointed the prince a commander of the Swedish order of the Sword. A conduct to be compared to a man's standing by, very unconcernedly, whilst his friend is well drubbed by others, and afterwards consoling him with proffers of friendship. (Related to the editor by Baron von K—n.)

2. A weak garrison of about 2,000 men, of all arms, being left in Hamburgh, under the command of General Carra St. Cyr, and those troops fit to take the field having been marched to the vicinity of Magdeburg, to join the Viceroy of Italy, but little penetration was wanting to foresee, that the spirit of Liberty, so long enchained, would seize the first favourable moment to burst her galling fetters. On the 24th of February 1813, when the French authorities, both civil and military, made evident preparations to evacuate the place, and leave it to its fate, the populace were not backward in expressing loudly. The arms of Napoleon were torn down, and treated with every mark of contempt, the custom-house offices sacked and demolished, and several other acts of popular fury were committed.

Six persons were, in consequence, arrested by order of General Carra St. Cyr, and dragged before a military-tribunal; their trial was of the most summary kind, no witnesses were confronted, no counsel allowed, and, after a short hour of examination, they were sentenced to be shot as traitors, in having aided an insurrection; and without being permitted any communication whatever with their relatives or friends, and even denied the solace of spiritual comfort in their last moments, they were inhumanly hurried to the place of execution, and into eternity, unable to make their peace either with God or man. Never were liberty, justice, and the natural rights of mankind more flagrantly violated, than in this instance.

It is a lamentable fact, that one of the unhappy sufferers was with his uncle in the country during the whole of the day on which the pretended rebellion had taken place. Such are some of the infamous deeds of a few of those flagitious miscreants and followers of Napoleon, who have wantonly stained with innocent blood every city, and every river, from the Scheldt to the Elbe, and from the Rhine to the Danube; evincing in all their actions a marked disdain and mockery of religion, and an avowed opposition to everything sacred in the laws, customs, and governments of other countries.

It would not, however, be doing justice to the French nation, to blend them indiscriminately in such remarks: contrast is the soul of description, and it is our duty not only to present a faithful and animated picture of the actions of Napoleon's satellites, but to enrich our pages with a narration of authentic occurrences, that may afford a fair opportunity of giving praise, and bestowing censure, wherever their sentiments of freedom and detestation of their tyrants, both vehemently and they may be due. These considerations demand of us a case in point.

When the Crown Prince of Sweden entered Hamburgh, as Prince de Ponte-Corvo, and as commander in chief of a French-Spanish corps, the French *gens d'armes*, and other officers of the police, first began to exercise their functions; and it was soon discovered, that a Monsieur D——, living in Hamburgh, and author of a French and German Grammar, that had already run through five editions, had inadvertently inserted in one of the exercises the following phrase; "General Bernadotte is a good captain of *banditti*, but unworthy to be a marshal of France."

The *gens d'armes* dragged him to prison, as a libellous emigrant; and, in a few days, he was brought into the presence of the prince, who mildly asked him, "If he were the author of the Grammar, and if he knew, from his own personal experience, the truth of the assertion he had made in it?" Upon the prince being answered in the negative, the latter replied; "In your next edition, I trust, the offensive sentence will be expunged; and my now dismissing you, without punishment, will prove to you that I know how to value men of letters, when they set bounds to their opinions, taking it for granted that you have only been in an error." The author retired overwhelmed at his clemency; and if he had formerly felt indignant at the name of a republican, he had now learnt to confess, that the truly great can ever discriminate between error and premeditated; malice. Would d'Avoust, Vandamme, and St, Cyr, have acted thus?—Alas, No!

★★★★★★

Austria had not yet completed her armaments; and only a brave and resolute resistance against the overbearing power of the conqueror, who seemed again to lift his fallen crest, could arrest his further progress, destroy his martial strength, force him to respect the Allies, inspire the rest of Europe with confidence in their arms; and, above all, diffuse and keep up that reliance on themselves with which their corps were already animated.

Should it be ever questioned whether this resistance was made, no Prussian need to shrink from the answer. Prussians, you may review with complacency your past deeds in arms. You have done your duty, what your country expected of you, and what God demands from the champions of a righteous and sacred cause. The nation with gratitude acknowledges your exertions, sacrifices, and privations; and the warlike spirit aroused in it, is still heightened and elevated by the innate and noble pride with which it views your glorious struggle in relieving your native land from a state of bondage, that openly violated every principle of justice, humanity, and religion.

The Battle of Lützen has restored the ancient splendour of the Prussian name, and quieted the perturbed shade of Frederick the Great; their cotemporaries in the field have borne witness, that, on this memorable day the military glory of the Prussian monarchy burst forth from behind the clouds that had hid its lustre, evermore to beam in the eyes of all Europe with undiminished fervency.

The combined army went into camp on the 14th of May, in a well-chosen position, about three miles from Bautzen. The town and its environs were occupied by General Miloradowitsch, commanding the advanced guard of the army. The camp itself stretched its left wing behind Klein-Jenkowitz, the centre was behind Gross-Jenkowitz and Baschütz, and the right wing towards Kreckwitz. The line of heights, situated between the water of Klein-Bautzen and the army, and those from Kreckwitz to Nieder-Gurke, were left unoccupied, that the position might not become too extended.

But when General Barclay de Tolly, after the reduction of Thorn,

A SAXON CUIRASSIER

joined the army with 14,000 men, on the 17th, by the way of Sprottau, he posted himself on the heights of Kreckwitz to Nieder-Gurke, forming the right wing of the army. In the rear of Gross and Klein Jenkowitz and Baschütz, entrenchments and breastworks were thrown up for the artillery, that it might have the advantage of cannonading the enemy under cover, as a long and violent cannonade was to be foreseen. Here the army enjoyed a repose of eight days, of which, after so many actions and marches, and their attendant fatigues, it stood much in need. On the 15th, the enemy showed himself to the piquets, but advanced no farther than to drive them in; he pitched the camp of his advanced guard on the opposite commanding grounds, the videttes and outposts of the Allies still remaining on the other edge of the valley between them.

After the Battle of Lützen the army had been reinforced with 5,000 men, under General Kleist, 14,000 under General Barclay de Tolly, 3,000 of the Prussian reserve, and some thousands of Russians. These reinforcements amounted to about 25,000 men; and if we estimate the losses of the Allied Army at the Battle of Lützen, and subsequent affairs, at 16,000 men, its force might be fixed at 80,000 men, on the day of the Battle of Bautzen. Nothing certain can be staled of the strength of Napoleon's army: his activity to recruit it was, no doubt, stretched to the utmost, during the eight days he passed before Bautzen and the intrenched camp.

According to later accounts, fresh troops, in considerable numbers, had marched through Dresden, and a part of d'Avoust's corps had arrived from the Lower Elbe. The Saxon garrison of Torgau, and the King of Saxony's heavy cavalry out of Bohemia, together with Würtemberg's contingent, had likewise joined; so that the losses of the enemy at Lützen, and in other engagements, might be considered as sufficiently replenished, and his army reinstated to its original number of 120,000 men.

Under the pressure of such a situation, in having to engage with as great a superiority of numbers as at Lützen, it would not have been advisable to give battle, if it had not formed a part of the system of the Allies to dispute every inch of ground with their opponent, to convince Europe that they had suffered no defeat in the first battle, and were neither morally nor physically incapable of making head against him, and moreover to convince the Austrians that they were resolutely determined not to spare their powers, nor in fearful expectation leave the deliverance of Germany entirely at the discretion of Austria.

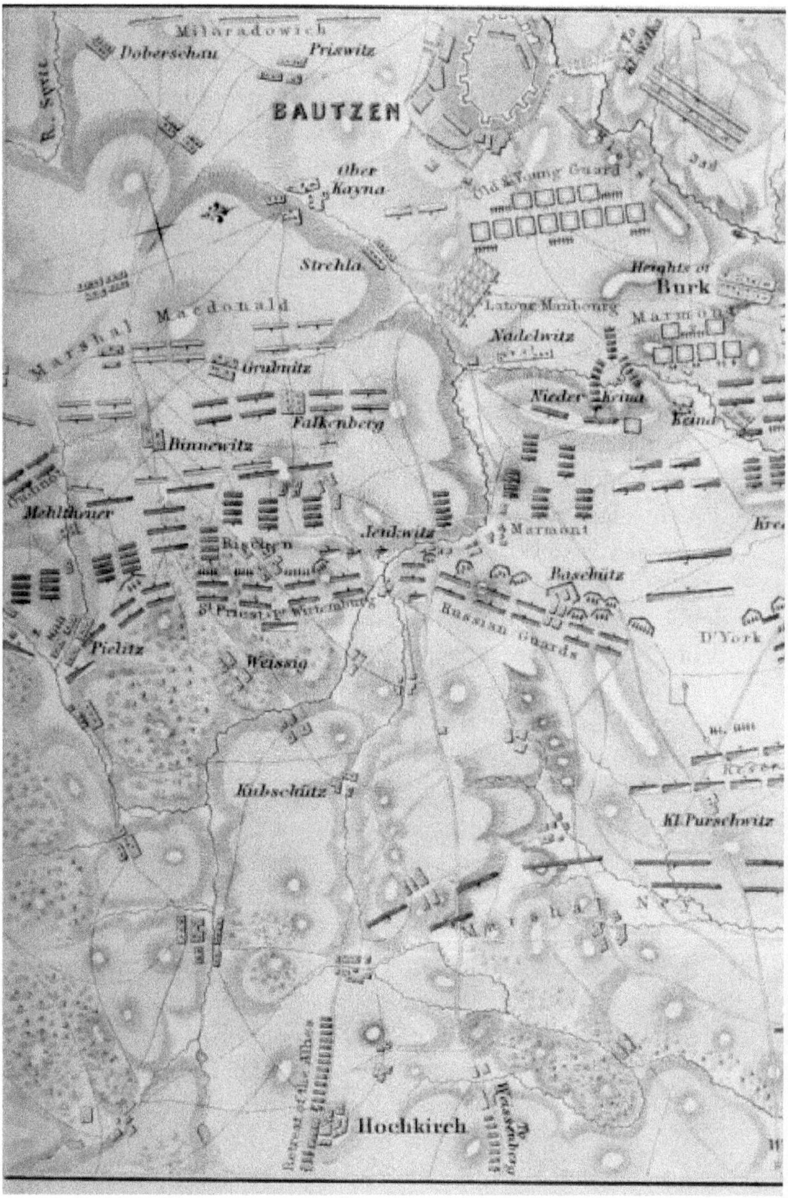

Milaradowich
Doberschau
Priswitz
BAUTZEN
R. Spree
Ober Kayna
Old & Young Guard
Strehla
Heights of Burk
Marshal Macdonald
Marmont
Nadelwitz
Grubnitz
Nieder Keina
Falkenberg
Keina
Binnewitz
Mehltheuer
Jenkwitz
Marmont
Baschütz
St Priest
Wurtemburg
Russian Guards
D'York
Pielitz
Weissig
Kubschütz
Kl. Purschwitz
Marshal Ney
Hochkirch
Retreat of the Allies

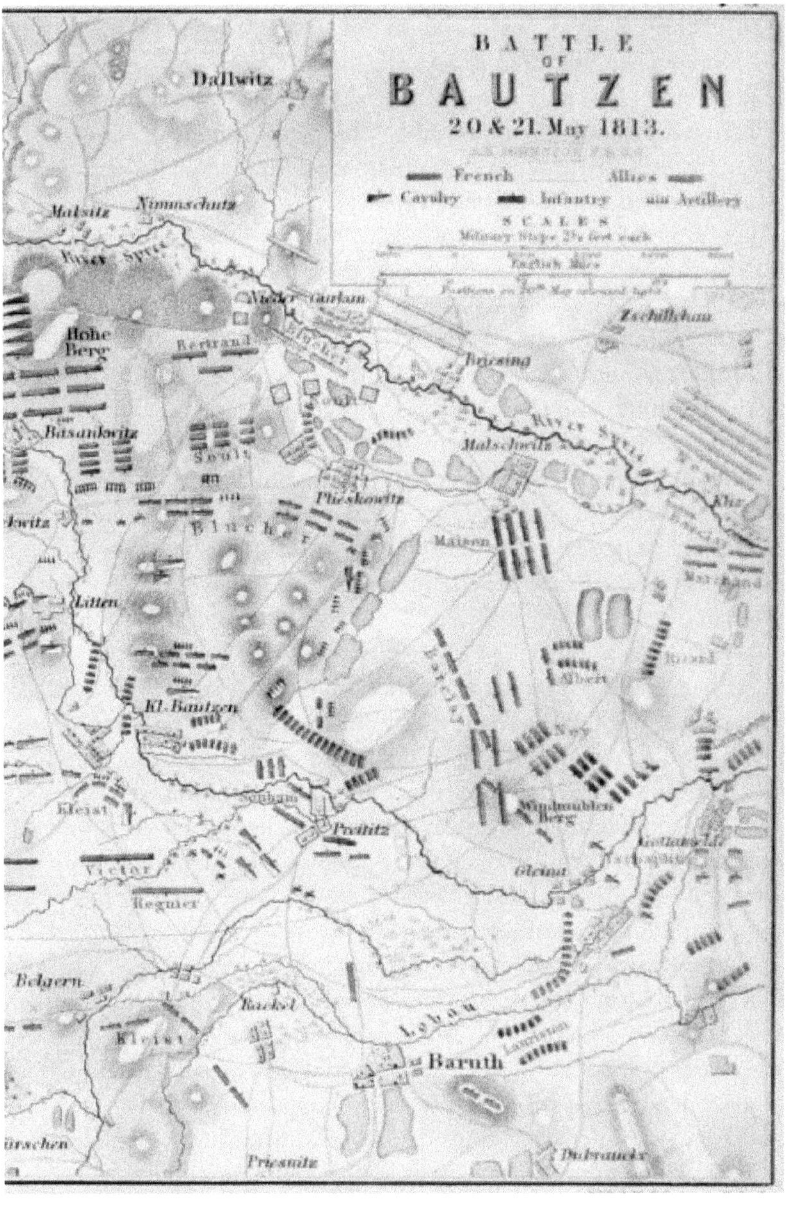

BATTLE OF BAUTZEN
20 & 21. May 1813.
French
Allies
Infantry
SCALES
Dallwitz
Malsitz
Nimmschutz
River Spree
Hohe Berg
Bertrand
Basankwitz
Soult
Pliskowitz
Blucher
Malschwitz
Zschillchau
Maisen
Litten
Kl. Bautzen
Kleist
Preititz
Victor
Regnier
Windmuhlen Berg
Gleina
Ney
Belgern
Rackel
Kleist
Baruth
Priesnitz

******

Count de Bubna, formerly Ambassador from the Imperial Austrian Court to that of France, was intrusted by his emperor to deliver private proposals, and to make overtures to Napoleon concerning a general peace; and on the 16th of May 1813, was, in consequence, admitted to an audience at Dresden.

The count delivered his dispatches in person to Napoleon, who, after reading them, abruptly observed: "Too late;" and then turning his back to the ambassador, pretended to look with attention out of the window,

After a short pause, the count asked: "Sire, is that the whole of the answer I am to bring my emperor?—If that is the case, permit me to demand leave of absence."

"Stop a moment," replied Napoleon, and went into another apartment. After a few minutes had elapsed, he returned, and addressed himself to the count in the following terms;

"Monsieur Bubna, if your emperor had made these proposals to me four weeks ago, I might have listened to them; but now, after the Battle of Lützen, I am become *master of Europe*; and when I have settled affairs with the Emperor of Russia and the King of Prussia, I may have leisure to attend, to those of your monarch; *adieu*."

******

The army, strongly feeling their moral pre-eminence, entertained no other wish but to close with their implacable foe. The attempt of retreating farther would only have tended to dispirit the troops, and shake their unbounded confidence in their popular commanders. The face of the country about Bautzen was favourable to their arms, and it was therefore determined once more to court the smiles of fortune, and try their strength, valour, and discipline, with the superior forces of the common enemy of mankind.

On the 18th, the Allies received the intelligence, that General Lauriston, with a strong corps, probably under the supposition that the Allied Army was capable of no further resistance, had been detached to the Mark, and was in full march, by the way of Hoyerswerda; upon which, General Barclay de Tolly, with his corps, and that of General von York, were detached towards Hoyerswerda. They began their march in two columns on the night of the 18th: the column of the left wing, under the command of General Barclay de Tolly, fell in with General Lauriston near Königswartha, and repulsed him after a severe contest, taking from him 2,000 prisoners, and 14 pieces of cannon.

The column of the right wing under General von York, about 5,000 strong, encountered Marshal Ney's corps at Weissig, who intended to effect a junction and co-operate with General Lauriston; the repeated attacks made by General von York on his much more numerous enemy, prevented Marshal Ney from sending any support to General Lauriston; and these exertions, which were continued till late in the evening, contributed not a little to the glorious termination of the engagement between the latter and General Barclay de Tolly. During the night of the 19th, the several columns returned into camp.

GENERAL YORCK AND HIS SNUFF-BOX

Chapter 6

Blücher's Ambuscade at Haynau

The direction which the corps of Marshal Ney and General Lauriston seemed to take towards the right flank of the Allied position at Bautzen, plainly evinced the intention of attempting to turn that position from the side of Glein and Preititz, the former village lying behind the posts of the right wing by Krekwitz. There was consequently, on the part of the Confederates, a necessity of changing their lines, and taking up another position, which on the 20th was as follows:

The left wing now stood on a rising ground, behind Klein-Jenkowitz. The lines in front stretched across the villages of Gross-Jenkowitz and Baschütz, towards Krekwitz, and from thence in the direction of Nieder-Gurke on the Spree, on which spot the right flank formed a curve, and keeping the Spree in front, passed on to the windmill of Glein, where it terminated.

Klein-Jenkowitz lies near a brook flowing from the high ridges on which Hochkirch stands, and these were in a parallel line with the left flank of the position. The brook running from Klein-Jenkowitz to the villages of Nadelwitz, Nieder, Kayen, and Pasankwitz, to Krekwitz, and, turning more to the right by Klein-Bautzen, Preititz, and Glein, made a bend before the front, and, receding from the centre about fifteen hundred yards, formed of itself a complete segment of a circle. But at Krekwitz, the brook crossed the position, the right wing there taking in the ground between the brook and the Spree, that river running parallel with the brook about a mile and a half.

At Glein the brook touched the extreme right flank of the position, from the rear, because this flank extended itself from Nieder-Gurke diagonally between the Spree and the brook, as far as Glein. In the same manner as the brook covered the front line to Krekwitz, the Spree covered the flank line from Nieder-Gurke to Glein. The space between Krekwitz and Nieder-Gurke is about fifteen hundred yards broad, and quite open, the heights forming the edge of the Spree valley, at the village of Burg, lying before it. The whole of the ground from Klein-Jenkowitz, as far as Krekwitz, might be considered as one large plain, although the left wing stood rather higher.

In the rear of the position, the ground gradually rises towards Hochkirch. General von Blücher was posted with his whole corps on the commanding grounds from Krekwitz to Nieder-Gurke; the villages in front of his position, close to the Spree, were occupied by light troops. The extreme right wing, under General Barclay de Tolly, stood near Glein, and on the advantageous Windmill-Hill in its vicinity, having before them the defile of Klix, over the Spree, within reach of their artillery. It being necessary to establish their defence on the Spree, behind the villages of Nieder-Gurke, Doberschütz, Pliskowitz, and Malschütz, the Windmill-Hill afforded a strong point of defence in disputing the passage of this river below Malschütz.

On this day the troops of the whole army were posted in the following manner:

Lieutenant-General von Berg's corps, about 4,000 men strong, stood on the left wing behind Jenkowitz: on his right, Lieutenant-general von York's corps, not exceeding 5,000 men, extending behind Baschütz. There was an open space of two thousand yards, forming a plain from Baschütz to Krekwitz, on which no troops were placed in the first line, being covered by the reserves of *cuirassiers* drawn up behind it.

The front of Blücher's corps, which might be rated at 18,000 strong, besides the reserves of *cuirassiers*, extended from Krekwitz to Nieder-Gurke, and from thence by Doberschütz to Pliskowitz.

General Barclay de Tolly was posted at Glein, with 14,000 men. Marshy grounds, full of pools, connected with each other, and having but few passages between them, formed a line of defence from Pliskowitz, on the Spree, to Preititz, on the rivulet in front, between this corps and that of General von Blücher. General Miloradowitsch stood before this front, in and by Bautzen, with a force of 10,000 men; and on the heights by Burg, General von Kleist with 5,000. The Russian Imperial Guards, and the rest of the Russian infantry, near 16,000 in the whole, stood as reserves in the rear of the left wing and centre.

Partly behind these, and partly to their right, the Russian reserves of cavalry, consisting of 8,000 *cuirassiers*, were drawn up. The front line from Klein-Jenkowitz to Krekwitz, and by Nieder-Gurke to Glein, was more than six miles in extent.—(See Map of the Battle of Bautzen.)

The nature of the ground unavoidably forced the Allies to occupy too large a terrain, not very compatible with precautionary suggestions; and the obvious necessity of taking possession of the high ridges that ran parallel to the left wing towards Hochkirch, whenever the enemy advanced his columns, did not contribute to contract it. A part of the reserves, consisting of the Prince of Würtemberg's division, and a detachment from Miloradowitsch's corps, were afterwards ordered to occupy them; by which movement the lines in front were lengthened more than three miles. The defence of the left wing in the mountains had of course many advantages.

No apprehensions could be entertained, that the enemy would penetrate over the plain from Klein-Jenkowitz to Krekwitz, as the crossing of the marshy banks of the rivulet must be attempted under the fire of a numerous and well-served artillery, protected by intrenchments and breast-works, and, therefore, not easily to be first silenced. The villages of Gross-Jenkowitz and Baschütz were prepared for defence, strong detachments of cavalry were at hand, and that part of the plain from Baschütz to Krekwitz was so strongly flanked by the height of Krekwitz being rather in advance of the position, and upon which stood Blücher's left wing, that the enemy could not here advance a step, without being previously in possession of Krekwitz.

General von Blücher's position was on the advantageous heights near Krekwitz and Nieder-Gurke, having the valley of the Spree, full of meadows, intersected with ditches, before him; his front was, without doubt, difficult of access, but the extension of his line to three miles from Krekwitz by Nieder-Gurke to Malschütz, might be considered as much too great for a body of only 18,000 men; and being a mile and a half from the Grand Army, if he met with a repulse, he would be obliged to retreat through two defiles over the boggy sides of the rivulet, to reach the main body; he could not, therefore, spare any considerable reserve, nor, in arranging his dispositions, post less than 12,000 men in his front.

General Barclay de Tolly had to defend a point of the general position, that afforded in itself some good natural bulwarks of defence; but he was surrounded by woods, and at a greater distance from the centre than General von Blücher.

Thus situated, towards noon of the 20th of May, the enemy assaulted General von Kleist, on the heights near Burg, and at the same time, General Miloradowitsch, near Bautzen; and a furious fight for some hours was maintained with the greatest bravery, by General von Kleist and his intrepid corps. It seemed as if the enemy held the possession of these heights as a necessary prelude to the battle, by his bringing up fresh columns of troops into fire, and repeating his attacks; but five battalions from General von Blücher's corps were ordered up in support of General von Kleist, to keep his physical strength in equiponderance with that of the enemy, who, about three o'clock in the afternoon, after suffering murderous repulses, endeavoured to turn General von Kleist's left flank, by penetrating to Nieder-Gurke; he was, however, baffled in the attempt, on finding some battalions of von Ziethen's brigade and artillery posted on the heights close behind the defile, and only a brisk fire of sharpshooters was now kept up in the valley at this point.

These stubborn efforts of Napoleon, so wasteful of human blood, were frustrated by the good countenance and undaunted valour of General von Kleist's corps, to whose glory and renown, fresh and ever-blooming laurels were added on this day. It is to the incessant assaults made by the enemy, that followed each other like the waves of a tempestuous sea, from twelve o'clock at noon till eight in the evening, with the view of overwhelming the gallant Prussians, and driving them from their impregnable position, by the mere force of numbers, that we are to ascribe the enormous loss which he suffered in the Battle of Bautzen, and of which, some calculation may be formed, by the authentic and official fact of 18,000 of his wounded having been transported to Dresden.

A sharp action took place with General Miloradowitsch, on the side of Bautzen, and, in the meantime, the enemy had forced back General Emanuel, with his corps of Russians, towards the mountains to the left of Bautzen, and pushed forward considerable masses of infantry; but the Russians being timely reinforced, the adversary did not succeed in breaking through any of the lines of the Allied corps in advance, or in taking post on the left flank of the army, as was his evident intention. On the extreme right wing, under General Barclay de Tolly, no movements were made on either side, which might be explained, by the corps of General Lauriston and Marshal Ney not being yet in the field.

The firing began to cease at nightfall, and thus ended the action of the 20th, of which it was difficult to decide, whether it were a battle, or only the first opening of the operations; for although, on the part of the Allies, those points only were defended and maintained, that served to obstruct the advance of the enemy, and his pressing on the position itself; yet, in considering the heroic resistance and invincible courage and intrepidity Of their troops, and the conduct, example, and bravery of their generals, added to the advantages of the ground, and the severe losses already felt by the disturber of the peace of Europe, great hopes might be entertained, that, on a renewal of his attacks, discomfiture and disgrace might become his bitter portion, and the Allies, satiated with victory, might tranquilly repose on their arms, to enjoy the heart-thrilling satisfaction of having done their duty.

But, it not being the intention of the Allies to make those disputed points the field of battle, in case of the enemy's acting on the offensive the next morning, while more advantages were to be drawn from the position itself; and as the expected attack on General Barclay de Tolly would cause these advanced points of the position not to be exactly adapted to the whole, the corps of General Miloradowitsch and von Kleist were withdrawn in the night, into the position: the former joined General von Berg, and the latter General von York. The Allied troops passed the night under arms on the field of battle, cheering each other with gratulations of having made a gallant defence; and if there be anything that could ensure or prognosticate the happy success of a future day, it was the peaceful order that everywhere prevailed amongst the troops, so seldom found after such inveterate and sanguinary conflicts.

Soon after daybreak, on the 21st, the first shots were heard along the line. The enemy, in renewing his attacks, directed them against two principal points of the Allied position, namely, General von Blücher's and General Barclay de Tolly's; and after these attacks had been opened by the sharp-shooters and artillery, he gradually displayed his whole force down the full extent of the Allied line.

From the eminences of the Allied centre they had a full view of the enemy's columns, marching over the heights to the right and left from Bautzen, and drawing up in heavy compact masses, directly opposite to their position, but out of the reach of the artillery. These masses of troops might be estimated at from 30,000 to 40,000 men, and they were scarcely drawn up in order of battle, when pillars of smoke were seen rising from the high grounds near Burg: this was the signal of attack for Marshal Ney and General Lauriston, who instantly pressed forward, with about 30,000 men, and threw themselves with great impetuosity on General Barclay de Tolly, at Glein. A very hot engagement ensued, which lasted till near ten o'clock a.m.

The superiority of the enemy in numbers obliged the general to lose ground, to relinquish the strong post of the Windmill-Hill, and, step by step, to retreat over the rivulet in his rear, and across the Löbau water, to the commanding heights of Barutis. This side being a very vulnerable part of the position, General von Kleist was immediately ordered to his support; his corps had, however, in the bloody affair of the day before, been reduced to near 3,000 effective men, and, instead of being able to drive back the enemy, in co-operating with de Tolly, they could only succeed in silencing his fire in part, and keeping him in check.

In the meantime, the conflict in the mountains had commenced with redoubled animosity, but the inflexible spirit and steady fire of the Allied battalions prevented the enemy from making any progress in this quarter during the whole day. The Prince of Würtemberg and General Miloradowitsch supported this point with their infantry, and the favourable terrain cost their obstinate foe an inconceivable number of men.

The cannonade in the centre now began, as the enemy seemed to menace an advance. General yon Blücher having before him the wood on the side of the Spree, could form no judgment of the strength of his adversary, and only some trifling affairs between the rifle-corps and light troops occurred in the valley. This was the state of the battle about noon, as Marshal Ney and General Lauriston pushed on columns to their right, and occupied the village of Preititz: this village lay between General von Blücher and General Barclay de Tolly, on the brook so often mentioned, close to Klein-Bautzen, consequently behind the right wing of General von Blücher.

Nothing could be of more importance to this general, than the occupation of this village: if the enemy proceeded from thence to the unoccupied villages of Klein-Bautzen and Puschwitz, the general had no other line of communication with the Grand Army than through Krekwitz; but Krekwitz lay in front of the position, within the range of the enemy's artillery, and could, besides, only be occupied by a single battalion; the enemy were already standing in the village of Pasankwitz, close to it, and it was a matter of uncertainty whether the village of Krekwitz could finally be maintained or not.

Under such dubious circumstances, General von Blücher resolved to part with the only reserve he had at his command, and therefore ordered his reserve brigade to march to the support of General Barclay de Tolly, for the sole purpose of retaking the village. He was in hopes, that, not being himself seriously engaged, this brigade would be able to give another turn to the affairs of the right wing, by falling upon the right flanks of Marshal Ney and General Lauriston.

A detachment of the Prussian reserve cavalry was, at the same time, sent towards the Spree, that now separated General von Blücher from Marshal Ney, to observe the passages, to threaten the enemy still more in his right flank, and to cannonade him with their horse-artillery. These dispositions were hardly made, and the troops marched off, when the enemy attacked General von Blücher himself in his whole position, first at Pliskowitz, then at Nieder-Gurke, and at last throughout the whole line of the Spree: a most heavy and destructive fire of musketry was kept up without intermission, which having lasted about an, hour, and his second line of infantry coming into action, General von Blücher began to discover, with that quickness of foresight so peculiar to this military hero, how unsafe it was to maintain his extended lines, and issued prompt orders for the reserve brigade to return, and post themselves ready for an emergency, at Baschütz.

But this brigade had already marched to Preititz, and, in combination with the corps of General von Kleist, entered at once with great vigour and resolution into the village, and gallantly carried it at the point of the bayonet, although with a very heavy loss. They kept the village occupied, and the rest of the brigade returned according to orders. Such was at this period the situation of General von Blücher's corps, that it was obliged to present a front on three sides; namely, between Krekwitz and Nieder-Gurke, against the enemy advancing from the heights of Burg; from Nieder-Gurke to Pliskowitz, to defend the low grounds of the Spree, and from Pliskowitz to Preititz, at the back of the pools, against the advance of Marshal Ney.

The whole of the reserve had been detached to retake the village of Preititz, in the rear, and thus to keep open the threatened fourth side of the position, the only one by which reinforcements could be received, or a retreat, if necessary, be made. The action in his front had about this time taken a very unfavourable turn; two Russian batteries, the one by Krekwitz, the other by Nieder-Gurke, that formed the principal defence of these points, had expended all their ammunition, the enemy, an over-match in numbers, had made himself master of the heights behind Nieder-Gurke, from which alone this point could be defended, and he now marched forwards over the low grounds between the rivulet and the Spree; and although the brigade of Colonel von Klux had twice repulsed him with severe loss, by bravely charging him with the bayonet; yet, it was evident, the heights were not to be retaken.

General von Blücher demanded reinforcements, and General von York was ordered up to secure the execution of his dispositions, who immediately marched to the village of Krekwitz, to fall on the right flank of the advancing enemy; but the expected succour came too late; the two brigades of General von Blücher's front had gradually withdrawn themselves out of their convex position to the high grounds about Krekwitz; but here not a spot was found adapted for further defence, and, in consequence, only one measure to keep himself master of the terrain, remained at his option, and that was to unite the weak battalions of the brigades with the rest of the reserve, and, waving all other considerations, to act, with impetuous firmness, on the offensive.

No doubts can be entertained, that, by this very rapid movement, he would again have penetrated to the valley of the Spree; but the brigade reserves were at the instant not yet returned, and, besides, very important consequences were here previously to be regarded. If Blücher had reconquered this ground, still the battle was not gained; the less so, as the terrain already lost, on the extreme right wing, was so decisive an event, that, from the moment the impossibility of moving onwards, on this point, was perceived, the commander-in-chief did not expect any favourable issue to the contest in general. General von Blücher, in hazarding everything to recover his former position, and even if crowned with success, had unavoidably dislocated his whole corps; he was unacquainted with the advance of General von York; the battle raged with Generals Barclay de Tolly and von Kleist, and the maintaining of their occupied lines was a matter of uncertainty.

He therefore resolved to undertake no operation until he had received fresh orders, and wishing to wait the return of his reserves to Purschwitz, he directed the two other brigades engaged, to maintain themselves to the last extremity in their positions, before they retreated to Purschwitz. The reserve cavalry, being of little service on this close ground, were ordered to draw back across the defile, that the retrograde movement, if obliged to be made through it, might not meet with any impediment.

At this period the centre was yet untouched, the enemy only making demonstrations, showing and deploying his columns, and keeping up a brisk cannonade.

******

The Emperor of Russia and the King of Prussia were standing together, in the rear of one of their batteries, from which a heavy fire was kept up on the enemy with great effect, who answered with a shower of shells, when one of the shells fell within ten yards of the spot where the Allied monarchs were conversing. A Prussian veteran, of the artillery, no sooner saw the shell take ground, but running up with an intrepid presence of mind, was fortunate enough to extinguish the *fusee* before it burst. The King of Prussia, who saw the action, called out to him, asking his name, and how long he had served.

"Thou shalt be rewarded, my brave fellow," said the king; "I here on the spot promote you to the rank of an officer."— "I humbly thank Your Majesty for this gracious mark of your favour," replied the man; "but I cannot accept it: I might have been a corporal years ago, if—— (he could not write.) Your Majesty, however, will not, I hope, be displeased, if I mention that *the pay* of an officer would make my family and myself happy for life." The king understood him: his boon was granted, to which were added, the order of the Iron Cross from his sovereign, and the order of St. George from the Emperor of Russia.

★★★★★★

It was clear that their opponent feared the strength of the Allied position at this point; and he, perhaps, expected that the centre of the Confederate Army, in sending support to the hard-pressed right wing, would be so weakened, as gradually to prepare for the favourable crisis of its attack by close action, on the event of which might depend his gaining a complete and decisive victory over the Allies.

Since the opening of the campaign, it had always been kept in view by the Allies, for very sage and political reasons, rather to break off before a battle was ended, if its tendency was doubtful or uncertain, than to expose themselves to the chance of a total defeat; and as the whole contest had actually taken an unfavourable turn, this step was here the more necessary, inasmuch as their undisputed superiority in cavalry enabled them to throw this choice into the balancing scales of their operations, whenever it was held judicious.

The same causes which rendered it dubious, whether the last exertions of General von Blücher, to recover the lost ground, would prove beneficial for the whole, or not, but might place Blücher's corps in a very dangerous situation, determined the commander-in-chief, between three and four o'clock p.m. to decline the contest on this position, and to order a retreat.

The retreat was made in the most perfect order and regularity in two columns. The Russian troops of the centre and left wing took the direction of Hochkirch to Löbau; the Prussians, that of Würschen to Weissenberg. General Barclay de Tolly and General Kleist, with the reserves of Prussian cavalry, drew up again in line of battle, on the advantageous heights of Gröditz, to keep Marshal Ney and General Lauriston in check, which was done the whole evening with such good success, that Generals von Blücher and von York had time to pass Weissenberg with the extremities of their columns: this measure was very requisite, the enemy being much nearer Weissenberg from Barutis, than the former were from the points of Krekwitz and Baschütz. When the centre of the Allies broke up, the enemy did not attempt to follow.

This stupendous battle afforded the enemy but few prisoners, and not a single piece of artillery fell into his hands: it must be allowed, however, that he succeeded in forcing the Allies, after a hard struggle, to relinquish a part of their strong position; but it was accomplished by such an enormous and inhuman sacrifice of men, that Napoleon's loss may be moderately estimated at double that of the Allies, they having had from 14,000 to 15,000 men killed, and wounded, and, as already related, the enemy sent 18,000 of his wounded back to Dresden; and it has since been indubitably ascertained, that the small town of Bautzen and its vicinity alone had to provide hospitals for 7,000 of his severely wounded men after the battle.

On this vast theatre of carnage, where, but a few hours before, the most luxuriant crops, peaceful villages, and hamlets, decked the fertile fields, smiling in all the native graces of a fruitful spring, everything perished and was blasted by the untimely blight of wasteful war, and the dire ravages of the ruthless sons of spoil, insatiate in destroying whatever could refine and embellish nature. The horrid transactions of these French military-barbarians are written in blood, and bear that hideous character by which the voice of God and nature has designated the most flagrant of human offences. They can never be forgotten: the affrighted inhabitants fled into the woods, and the face of the country was suddenly transformed into a savage, wild, and desolate wilderness.

Napoleon, in the midst of his mathematical calculations and theorems, might feel the instability of human events, and find an error in the definition of such kind of victories as the present one. It had been his custom totally to defeat his adversary with a very disproportionate and trifling loss on his side, and then to extort a rash and precipitate peace. The attributes of his station as conqueror demanded this. And here, after having experienced in Russia a reverse of fortune, unparalleled in history, that involved him in difficulties scarcely surmountable, he could have nothing more at heart than to destroy in their bud the dawning hopes of Europe, to crush the rising spirit of liberty, now spreading far and near, and to appal his enemies arming on all sides by rapid, splendid, and decisive victories.

It is notorious that this was not done. Partial advantages formed the utmost confines of his boastings, presenting, of themselves, but a weak and tottering dam against the irresistible rolling tide of self-confidence that was now set in against him. Fresh calamities awaited him in his rear, and were ready to burst over his power and his plans. The victorious hero of Spain, Lord Wellington, now stood on the frontiers of France to chastise, on his own threshold, their haughty and abhorred enemy.

There was, therefore, no well-founded cause for the Allies to complain of their situation, and they might be convinced that order, perseverance, and intrepidity would inevitably bring them to the desired goal, in defiance of those ostentatious accounts of victories so industriously published to Europe by their wily antagonist.

The Allied Army continued on the 22nd, its retrograde movement from Löbau and Weissenberg to Görlitz. At Reichenbach the rear-guard had a lively affair with their pursuers, that cost the French Army a marshal and two generals, and Napoleon his most intimate friend. Buonaparte being dissatisfied that his generals of the advanced-guard sent in no prisoners from a supposed defeated army, undertook, in a sudden burst of indignation, the command of it himself for one day, to teach them, as he said, a more vigorous execution of his infallible orders. The rear-guard of the Allies was posted at Reichenbach, having a very numerous cavalry and artillery, the former burning with impatience to try a charge upon equal terms with the French.

A sharp cannonade was kept up, some regiments of French dragoons actually showed themselves, and the Allied horse had an opportunity of wreaking their vengeance, by repulsing them with heavy loss. It happened that, during the cannonade, a fatal ball struck General Kirschner dead, close to Napoleon, tore open the bowels of Marshal Duroc, and mortally wounded General Labruyère.

★★★★★★

Marshal Duroc, Duke of Frioul, lived on a very intimate footing with Napoleon. He was born in 1772, at Ponte-Mousson, and was the son of a house-painter of that place. By the help of a relation he was educated at the military school, made a lieutenant in 1792, and rose to the rank of captain in the artillery in 1796; at which period Napoleon became acquainted with him, and found in him a fit person to execute, with implicit devotion, some of his barbarous mandates. It is well known that he assisted in poisoning the wounded French in Syria in 1799. Since which he had been sent on several diplomatic missions to St. Petersburg and Berlin, and was afterwards, as Marshal of the Imperial Palace, much about the person of Buonaparte,

★★★★★★

Napoleon, shuddering at this sudden stroke of fate, levelled so near his sacred person, turned round the head of his horse, and, without a word or exclamation. escaping his lips, or altering a muscle of his countenance, rode off in agitated haste from the spot.

The pursuit was afterwards followed up in the usual manner; and the excellent and matchless cavalry of the Allies gathered fresh laurels at every rencounter.

From Görlitz the march of the Allied Armies was continued in two columns, by the way of Naumburg to Queisz, Bunzlau, Haynau, and through Lauban, Löwenberg, Goldberg, Striegau, to the camp of Pültzen, near Schweidnitz, where it arrived on the 1st of June.

The Prussian Army marched, with the corps of General Barclay de Tolly, in the column of the right wing that proceeded through Haynau.

It being the object of the commander-in-chief to continue the retreat as slowly and leisurely as possible, without entangling himself in any general or serious affair; and the enemy having begun to press and harass the rear-guard very closely, a plan which General von Blücher had conceived with that boldness of genius which displayed itself on all momentous occasions, was now arranged and put in execution. An ambush was to be placed for the enemy's van-guard, to chastise them severely for their rashness, and to distress their further operations: the terrain behind Haynau seemed well fitted for this purpose.

About a mile and a half on the other side of Haynau, is situated the village of Michelsdorf, and from this spot to Doberschau, about the distance of three miles, it is quite an open and champaign country, except the villages of Pantenau and Steudnitz, which, lying in a kind of valley, form a defile. To the right of this flat open country, is a defile, formed by low grounds and copses, which, beginning at the village of Ueberschaar, continue, without any break, as far as Baudmansdorf, lying about three miles on the same level to the right of Doberschau.—

(See the Map of the Ambuscade near Haynau.)

On the 26th the Prussian Army left Haynau on the high road to Liegnitz. The rear-guard followed, at a distance of twelve miles, and passed Haynau the same day.

It was General von Blücher's well-concerted plan to let the actual rear-guard, which consisted of three battalions of infantry and three regiments of light-horse, under the command of Colonel von Mutius, retreat over the plain to Steudnitz, after halting before Haynau till the enemy came out to attack; and they should then endeavour to draw and allure the enemy after them. In the meantime, the whole of the reserve cavalry, consisting of twenty squadrons, with two batteries of horse-artillery, were placed in ambush at Schellendorf, under the command of Colonel von Dolfs. They were to advance through the defiles with all the rapidity and secrecy in their power, so as to push forward over the plain through Ueberschaar, and to fall unexpectedly on the right flank of the enemy's advanced guard, at the moment when they were occupied in attacking Colonel von Mutius.

A windmill between Baudmansdorf and Pohlsdorf, which could be distinctly seen by both parties, was to be set on fire, as a signal for the reserve cavalry in ambush to advance. General von Ziethen's brigade was drawn up as reserve behind Pantenau and Pohlsdorf, and the conduct of the whole intrusted to this general. Our veteran General von Blücher, anxious for the accomplishment of his premeditated surprise, remained in the neighbourhood. The enemy pursued Colonel von Mutius, in appearance with much precaution, and did not show himself out of Haynau till past three o'clock, p.m. marching slowly and warily as if in doubt. Colonel von Mutius, according to orders, retreated in seeming haste.

The division of General Maison composed this advanced-guard; and Marshal Ney, to whose corps it belonged, left it just before the attack. General Maison, as if warned by a presentiment of his danger, expressed his fears concerning the safety of his advancing into the plain, to the marshal himself, who ridiculed them. The marshal proceeded to another point, and General Maison marched with a heavy heart into the plain. He however neglected sending detachments into the defiles on his right, as the only way to secure that flank in a proper manner, and prevent any surprise.

The enemy having passed Michelsdorf about fifteen hundred yards in advance, the reserve cavalry put itself in motion, having about a mile and a half to march before they could be as near to the enemy as Colonel Mutius. They left the ground at full trot, and General von Ziethen fired the mill as a signal for the attack. General Maison, on seeing this, suspected some ambush, and immediately ordered his troops to form in squares; but little time was left them to perform the evolution, for Colonel von Dolfs, leaving two regiments as reserve, and without stopping to make use of his artillery, seized the favourable moment, and precipitated himself on the enemy with the swiftness of the winds.

The French cavalry betook themselves to flight, leaving the disorderly masses of infantry in the act of forming, to their fate. They were furiously charged, and rode down in the space of a few minutes. Those that were not cut in pieces or taken prisoners fled through the village of Michelsdorf, towards Haynau. The whole affair lasted but twenty minutes; and by the quick dispersion of the enemy, Colonel von Mutius was almost deprived of a share in the brilliant action.

The trophies that fell into the hands of the Allies, consisted of 18 pieces of cannon, their whole artillery, and the usual spoils of baggage, tumbrils, horses, and stores; but a scarcity of harnessed horses prevented their bringing away more than 11 pieces of artillery, and from three to four hundred prisoners were taken. The Allied cavalry, covered with glory, then retired to Lobentau: the rear-guard took a position there, and kept up videttes and outposts on the plain close to Haynau. During the whole of the following day the enemy kept himself close in Haynau; and it was not till the 28th, that the rear-guard retired to Kloster-Wahlstatt.

The cavalry obtained in this splendid engagement that renown so difficult to be acquired in modern times, owing to the superior tactics of the infantry; it is, however, here incontestably proved that there are opportunities in which this superiority is of no avail, and cavalry can perform wonders, and cut their way through every obstacle that may oppose their progress, when disciplined valour, and the enterprise and foresight of experienced officers, are happily blended together.

The brave Colonel von Dolfs fell in gallantly leading his squadrons to the charge.

Napoleon no sooner arrived at Liegnitz with his army, and perceived that the Allies retreated towards Schweidnitz, and not to Breslau, than he immediately detached a corps of 30,000 men to the Neumark, which entered Breslau on the following day.

Prior to the Battle of Bautzen, Buonaparte had himself offered an armistice, and to enter into negotiations.

******

It was on this day that Napoleon sent a letter, written with his own hand, by a flag of truce, to the Emperor of all the Russias, in which he made, it was supposed, very flattering overtures for a cessation of arms.

His Imperial Majesty, having received it, and being pre-informed of its probable contents, demanded of the bearer, "Whether he had likewise brought a similar epistle for the King of Prussia?" On being answered in the negative, Alexander observed: "Then I cannot open this: I can listen to no communications from the Emperor of France but in conjunction with the King of Prussia."

The flag of truce was obliged to return without fulfilling his mission, and Napoleon saw himself under the necessity of offering proposals for a cessation of arms conjointly to the two Allied, potentates, and which was accordingly done.

******

These offers were now renewed, and on the part of the Allies accepted. (The plenipotentiaries from both sides had a long conference on the 30th, which lasted eighteen hours, at Kloster-Wahlstatt, near Liegnitz.) A preliminary armistice of thirty-six hours was first regulated, and soon after prolonged to three days.

As the Allied Armies were on their march to Silesia, General von Bülow, with an army of 20,000 men, had advanced from the Mark into Lower-Lusatia. A corps under General Oudinot was detached by Napoleon to check the progress of this general, whom he found posted at Luckau, and a smart action ensued on the 4th of June, which principally turned on the possession of Luckau; the French, however, were unable to drive the Prussians out of the place, although in flames; and the enemy being at last attacked in their rear by General von Bülow's cavalry, under General Oppen, they were forced to relinquish the field of battle, with a loss of from 400 to 500 prisoners, and one gun.

The enemy's lines of communication with the Elbe were threatened to be intercepted, and a vexatious war of posts and skirmishes was now carried on with constant success against him. On both banks of the Elbe, and even to the borders of Franconia, Prussian and Russian detachments scoured the country in every direction; a considerable number of prisoners were brought in, and several of the expeditions were particularly fortunate: Captain von Colomb, our hero's brother-in-law, having passed the Elbe with a squadron of volunteer light horse, at the time the two conflicting armies were standing on its banks, had penetrated as far as the borders of Franconia, where he surprised a transport of 18 pieces of artillery, 6 howitzers, and 40 tumbrils, proceeding to the French Army under the escort of Bavarian troops.

He spiked the guns, blew up the tumbrils, and made from 200 to 300 prisoners. The Russian General Czernischeff crossed the Elbe with a body of 1,800 men, light troops, and near Halberstadt unexpectedly fell in with the Westphalian division of General von Ochs, with about 2,500 men, 14 pieces of cannon, and a number of ammunition-waggons, of which the latter formed in haste a circular bulwark, on a rising ground near the road; but General Czernischeff did not hesitate cannonading him with his light artillery; and several of the ammunition-waggons having blown up, he rapidly charged the enemy with a rare intrepidity: the Cossacks succeeded in breaking through the fortified circle, and General von Ochs, with all his infantry, about 1,000 men, were taken prisoners; 14 pieces of cannon, 60 tumbrils, and 800 artillery horses, and large quantities of. military stores fell into the hands of the Cossacks, and were conveyed in safety over the Elbe.

A detachment from General Woronzoff's corps, under the command of Colonel Borizoff, had likewise passed the Elbe; and on the 23rd of May, encountered near Cönnern, between Halle and Bernburg, a body of French *cuirassiers*, 400 men strong, under General Pinsot; after an obstinate conflict of two hours, the whole were either killed, wounded, or taken prisoners by the Cossacks; and a train of 19 waggons, with stores, baggage, &c. became their booty on the road to Merseberg. The Russian General Emanuel surprised a transport of artillery, between Reichenbach and Görlitz, took 2 pieces of cannon, spiked 6, and blew up 15 tumbrils. General Lasalle, another French general, and 300 men, were killed, and 600 taken prisoners. General Woronzoff having afterwards formed a junction with General Czernischeff, they both put themselves in march towards Leipsic, the Duke of Padua being employed there in remounting depots of French cavalry: they would have had the most brilliant success, if at this moment, intelligence of the armistice had not reached them.

★★★★★★

As this duke (Arrighi), during the armistice, was carrying on his acts of oppression at Leipsic, a Russian officer arrived with a flag of truce, to treat concerning the exchange of the remains of Lützow's corps that had been so basely surprised.

From the midst of the crowd that accompanied the Russian

officer to the hotel of the duke, very lively acclamations and cheering huzzas, in compliment to the brave Russian, were distinctly heard, even under the windows of the duke's apartments. He appeared much incensed at these marks of disrespect, and strict orders were issued to punish those culprits who could dare to be so insolent towards one of Napoleon's marshals.

Rewards were even offered to apprehend the delinquents, and to those who could discover any individual guilty of so great a crime; but the duke's proclamations, and his threats, were equally useless; for, lo! they were his own soldiers that had alarmed the fancied dignity of this ape of a tyrant's despotism: some hundreds of honest Westphalians, whose breasts glowing with a true patriotic flame, could not forget the name of Herrmann, and that Teutonic blood still flowed in their veins!

******

Negotiations respecting the armistice had been, in the meantime, carrying on, and, on the 1st of June, it was concluded at Plaszwitz, for a period of seven weeks; namely, to the 20th of July, allowing a notice of six days. On the 26th of July it was prolonged at Neumark in Silesia, to the 10th of August. This armistice was, in every point of view, of a very different complexion from those which in former times had been forced upon, or offered by Napoleon to his adversaries. Here no sacrifice of territory was made; no fortresses were delivered up, nor were even those besieged, to be uninvested.

******

It must not be forgotten that the greatest sacrifice made by the Confederates, was their granting the *uti possidetis* in the 32nd French military division; a measure, the policy of which still continues enveloped in a degree of mystery, and by which Hamburgh remained in the hands of a vengeance-breathing despot, forcing upon him, as if in his own despite, the means of punishing those brave spirits who had first dared to manifest a patriotic zeal, by flying to arms and unfurling the banners of unanimity for the deliverance of Germany, and their own independence.

Enormous were the exactions which Napoleon imposed and levied; cruel and relentless the robberies and spoliations that were committed and justified by his Satraps, so as utterly to destroy and undermine for a series of years, the opulence and prosperity of this venerable head of the Hanse league.

It is surely difficult to conceive any character more odious and despicable than that of a ferocious hireling, who, trembling at a tyrant's frown, issues the mandate that is to devote virtuous citizens to starvation, to desolate happy and peaceful hamlets, to wring agonizing tears from the widow and the fatherless!—Such is d'Avoust. An official and moderate estimate states the total amount of the losses caused to this city and its environs by d'Avoust, at thirteen millions sterling.

The population was reduced from 120,000 to 40,000 souls; more than 1,500 houses were either burnt or demolished; and by d'Avoust's unnatural, stubborn, and vindictive cruelty, more than 1,600 families were stripped of their bedding, furniture, and cattle, turned out to live under the canopy of heaven, in the midst of a severe winter, and, in short, became beggars on the high roads. And yet, this honourable officer—this moralising marshal, has the effrontery to justify his callous deeds, by asserting, they were needful for the defence of Hamburgh: now this is an abominable falsehood; for, after the conflagrations of the distant villages, instead of attempting to defend the burning ruins,; they were abandoned at the first onset of the bold and hardy Russians.

✶✶✶✶✶✶

The French troops were to occupy, according to the fourth article of the armistice, a line of demarcation in Silesia (see the Map), which extended from the borders of Bohemia, near Schreibershau, on nearly a straight line by the way of Parchwitz, Liegnitz, Lähn, and Goldberg, along the banks of the River Katzbach, till it falls into the Oder. The lines of the Confederate Army in Silesia, under Blücher, commenced at Dittersbach near the frontiers of Bohemia, passed through Pfaffendorf and Landshut, following the course of the Bober to Rudelstadt, and from thence to Kanth, Bettlern, and Althof, to the left bank of the Oder: the whole of the territory between these lines of demarcation being declared neutral. The 12th of June was the time fixed, on which all the troops and detached corps were to be in the rear of their lines of demarcation.

A body of 10,000 Danish troops had arrived in the vicinity of Hamburgh, with the supposed intention of making a common cause with the troops of the Allies; but owing to the political discussions of the Danish cabinet, with England and Sweden, this design had at this period undergone a change. The Danes suddenly declared themselves for France, entered into the views of Vandamme and d'Avoust, and thereby forced General von Tettenborn to evacuate Hamburgh.

******

It was under the immediate command of Vandamme, that Hamburgh was bombarded. A few authentic anecdotes of the early part of this man's life may serve to amuse the reader.

Vandamme is the son of a citizen in humble life, of Cassel in Flanders. After receiving a common day-school education, he was clerk in an office for some time, but being intrusted with a sum of money, he decamped with it, and commenced the life, of a swindler and vagabond; detection soon following, he was publicly whipped, and set in the pillory at Bergen in Flanders. Indeed, he had received sentence of death; but through the intercession of Mr. Schubitz, a respectable merchant of, Dunkirk, his life was saved.

Soon afterwards he was sent to the galleys at Marseilles, where he remained till he was liberated by the Jacobins in 1793. He distinguished himself by his abominable cruelties towards the Royalists in Paris, and on this account was made a general by the National Convention, and sent to command a body of troops in Flanders, He began his new career in a manner most fitting his character and Jacobin principles: upon entering Dunkirk, he ordered his former patron and deliverer, Mr. Schubitz, to be arrested, and sent him to Paris, denounced as a furious aristocrat and dangerous royalist. He ended his life, of course, under the guillotine. Such a signal instance of base ingratitude and atrocious perfidy can scarcely be equalled in history. But are not the satellites and adherent of Napoleon, wretches of one common stamp, a brotherhood of butchers

******

Thus fell for a second time, into the hands of the French, one of the most ancient free imperial cities of Germany, whose exertions in the cause of liberty made her so worthy of the freedom she aspired to, and whose loss may be esteemed one of the severest and most painful which the Allies had as yet suffered.

Two very cogent reasons may be here adduced, why it was the interest of the Allies that an armistice of seven weeks should be concluded with the enemy: the one, to restore the exhausted strength of the army by every possible reinforcement, and to prepare for a vigorous renewal of the war; and the other, because Austria had secretly given Russia and Prussia to understand, that such a period of time was necessary to complete her armaments.

In this war undertaken against France, there were some events on which the Allies ought to have solely depended, and by which alone they could be placed in a situation to stand on an equal footing with the preponderating power of Napoleon. The Allies were either to rely on a general insurrection in Germany, the disallegiance of the Confederation of the Rhine, on partial revolts in the north of Germany, Tyrol, and Italy; or they must look to the coalition of Austria as admitting no doubt. By a continuation of the war, one of these favourable events, if occurring to its full extent, would yield such an accession of strength, that the possibility of success might be confidently cherished.

Hopes were, at that time, not entirely given up, that the northern powers, Sweden and Denmark, might enter the league; and, indeed, Sweden had already expressed herself in very unequivocal terms.

Certainty being unknown in the political world, the Allies were constrained to tranquillize themselves with a greater or less degree of probability, that such events could be brought about. But the sequel has proved that their calculations were free from error. Austria did declare against France; and the conqueror, in the zenith of his power, soon found himself deceived in the unfailing effects of his imaginary and vain-glorious omnipotence.

What man amongst the Allies could have hoped, in December 1812, that, in June 1813, Russia, Prussia, and Austria, would stand on the banks of the Oder and the Elbe, with a power both formidable and superior; forcing Buonaparte to subscribe to other laws than those of his over-ruling will and imperious commands? Who had not thought, on being told that Napoleon, in six months, would again have an army of several hundred thousand men in Germany, have fought the Allies with an overmatch in numbers, in two pitched battles, that the consequences must inevitably have been, a general despondency prevailing amongst the Allies, a retreat far into Poland, ending in their total destruction, and Austria silenced for ever?

It is with unceasing gratitude towards Divine Providence, the Allies have to acknowledge that their hopes were more than realised. With what a sense of immeasurable benefits conferred, ought they not to be grateful, that the Emperor Alexander, trusting to Prussia and Austria, boldly pursued the enemy to the Oder; and towards the Monarch of our illustrious hero, who, unshaken by misfortune, and unbiassed by the voices of desponding cavillers, flew to arms, threw off the disgraceful yoke, to protect the honour and independence of the Prussian nation: towards the Emperor of Austria, who, disregarding the extorted tie of affinity, fearlessly declared himself as champion for the emancipation of Germany, and the liberties of Prussia!

During the period of the armistice, the efforts of the Confederates were particularly. directed to the following objects:

> 1. The necessary reserves and reinforcements, for the Russian Army were accelerated on their march to join; and an army of reserve was organised in Poland of at least 100,000 men.
>
> 2. The regiments in the Prussian Army were completed, and measures adopted for supplying the depots promptly with recruits,
>
> 3. The procuring of arms and ammunition from England and Austria.
>
> 4. The preparation of all kinds of accoutrements.
>
> 5. To arm, form, and discipline the militia.
>
> 6. To provision, arm, and repair the fortresses, particularly Schweidnitz.
>
> 7. To throw up the necessary *têtes de pont* on the Oder.
>
> 8. The procuring and collecting of provisions for the army during the next campaign.

On the other hand, Napoleon did not relax in increasing his means of resistance in the same proportion. All the troops he could possibly form during the period of the armistice, were put in march. To fix the exact number of combatants, with which he took the field, is rather difficult. What we know as certain is, that he drew no army from Spain, but only drafted veterans and subalterns to organise the new battalions of conscripts in France.

The troops that arrived from France and Italy in Germany, in the month of April, were calculated at 100,000 men, and in the month of March, at 60,000; and if we, upon an average, suppose that Napoleon formed, in the last three months, the same number of troops as in the four' months previously to the armistice, namely, 160,000 men; by adding the army of 60,000 men still on the Elbe, the whole amount would then be 380,000 men; from which we are to deduct, at least, 50,000 men for his losses in the Battles of Lützen and Bautzen, and all the other bloody encounters, and by sickness and desertion. To this, also, must be superadded the Danish and Confederate troops 70,000 men, and the aggregate number will be 400,000.

The writer is, however, convinced that this is over-rated by about

50,000 men; for, according to all subsequent accounts which have been collected, the sum total of 350,000 men seems the nearest to truth, and to exclude the reproach of any palpable exaggeration. Here we have to observe, that these 350,000 men found a considerable counterpoise in the combined powers of the Allied Army: and when we reflect that an army of only 80,000 Allies bravely stood their ground against 120,000 French, in two battles, without suffering a defeat, obliged the enemy to continue his operations with unusual precaution, and at last made him eager to conclude an armistice, no doubt could be entertained of a favourable issue to the approaching campaign.

If the Allies had in part failed, the failure might be attributed to the want of a sufficient physical force; but, on a renewal of warfare, they had now to contend with an army formed of heterogeneous troops—their opponent, with an armed nation: there could be no reason to doubt whether any force might ensure success, as the condition of the Allies could not be accounted desperate; Germania's sons had neither lost their courage nor their hopes, and could look forward with confidence to still more glorious and greater exertions than those already made.

If, with all the difficulties and disadvantages under which Russia and Prussia laboured at the onset and commencement of the former campaign, they achieved a certain degree of success in repelling the enemy, might they not entertain much better hopes from the issue of a second, with a whole nation in a state of military organisation? In war, no one can ensure success and victory; but here, with the preconcerted resistance of a brave, powerful, enthusiastic, and well-disciplined army, the highest probability was certainly on their side.

Of all the Allied powers, Prussia appears to have made the greatest exertions, in proportion to her extent of territory and comparative population. The active army was completed during the armistice to its full numbers, and the most provident and wise measures were adopted to fill up its losses in the expected campaign with promptitude. It was divided into four principal corps; and our hero, the veteran general of the cavalry, was appointed commander-in-chief.

The first corps was commanded by Lieutenant-General von York; it consisted of four brigades of infantry, one brigade of cavalry, and a due proportion of artillery: its force may be computed at 38,000 men. The second corps was headed by Lieutenant-General von Kleist, of nearly the same strength. The third corps was under the command of Lieutenant-General von Bülow; and the fourth, of Lieutenant-General Count Tauenzien. The efficient strength of the whole Prussian forces in the field, at this period, a few days previous to the 10th of August 1813, may be calculated at nearly 150,000 regular troops. The militia counted 170,000 men in its ranks; and the levy *en masse* presented a very formidable body for defensive operations. General von Blücher now took the immediate command of the Prussian Army in Upper Silesia, posted on the lines of demarcation as already mentioned.

Soon after the conclusion of the armistice, the French Army went into more extended cantonments. A part of the Young Guards, and the 2nd, 3rd, 5th, 6th, and 11th *corps d'armée*, remained in Silesia, in the neighbourhood of Liegnitz, Goldberg, Bunzlau, Löwenberg, Glogau, and Grünberg.

The following dispositions were made with the Allied Army of Russians and Prussians in Upper Silesia. The Prussians were composed of the first corps, under the command of General von York, and the Russians, of two strong corps, under the command of General Count von Langeron, and General Baron von Sacken. General von Gneisenau was appointed quartermaster-general of the staff to this army, which now consisted of about 70,000 men.

GENERAL GNEISENAU, BLÜCHER'S CHIEF OF STAFF

CHAPTER 7

Blücher's Victory on the Katzbach

The armistice was denounced on the 10th of August. According to the convention of the 4th of June, hostilities were to commence on the 17th of August: but, as the enemy had repeatedly violated the neutral territory by imposing and enforcing requisitions of every kind, and had so basely surprised the corps of Lützow at the commencement of the armistice.

★★★★★★

Major von Lützow's free corps, known by the name of the Sable Knights, or Corps of Vengeance (their uniform being black), was composed of some of the most exalted characters in Germany. Young men of the first-rate talents, of the most noble families, whose grand views of national liberty, of the privileges of citizens, and the birthrights of men, had absorbed all minor considerations, served as volunteers in its ranks. His Majesty the King of Prussia gave permission for its formation in the month of February 1813.

Theodore Körner, by birth a Saxon, a promising young poet, whose works are read with delight; Mr. Göschen, son of the most famous typographer in Germany; Mr. Jahn; Mr. Humboldt; the Prince of Karolath, and a long list of gallant youths, eminently distinguished themselves. Their rapid marches in the rear of the French Grand Army, and the war of posts and skirmishes which they carried on so successfully, prior to the armistice, made them the terror of all French stragglers and detachments.

But, above all, their heroic example fanned and lighted up a flame of chivalrous enthusiasm, caused an extraordinary fermentation to be excited throughout Germania's plains, and thus materially aided the good cause. Their ultimate fate casts

LÜTZOW'S WILD HUNTSMEN

an odium on the honour and character of the Duke of Padua, which may place him on a footing with d'Avoust and Vandamme, if not with the perpetrator of the massacre at Jaffa.

The intelligence of the armistice reached the corps on the 9th of June, near Hoff; and the official annunciation on the 14th, at Plauen, where they had halted, was delivered to Major Lützow by Captain Monbe, a Saxon officer, who, at the same time, presented Captain von Jensewitz as the Saxon officer appointed by the commanding officer of the district to conduct the corps to the frontiers.

The French general commanding at Gera invited Major von Lützow, and several other officers of the corps, to dinner, and received them in the most hospitable and friendly manner. On the following morning the corps continued its march to Zeitz; and, having reached the village of Kitzen, between Pegau and Lützen, a body of the enemy's troops was observed on the advance towards them; and soon after Major von Becker, with a flag of truce, appeared, and announced to the corps that it was the Duke of Padua's express order (who then commanded in Leipsic), that the corps should not proceed on its march until French officers had arrived to accompany it farther.

The major instantly consented; and soon after another flag of truce appeared, and desired the major to proceed with him to General Fournier, commanding the column in advance. The major complied, and immediately put the question to the general, If it were his intention to act on the offensive? which was answered in the negative; adding, As long as the corps proceeded quietly on its march to the frontiers.

Major von Lützow then issued an express order, "That the corps was to refrain from every hostile act towards the enemy's squadrons, on pain of death." The enemy's horse now drew up close in their rear, forming two sides of a square, and in this state the march began. It was near nine in the evening; numbers were singing popular choruses, and each pursuing his way unsuspicious of treachery, and without a presentiment of danger, when, suddenly, they were furiously charged by the French in their rear, and all those, the fleetness of whose horses did not favour their escape, were murdered in cold blood, or taken prisoners. A few files that had time to form, and scorning to surrender, sold their lives dearly; but the whole corps was dispersed on all

PRUSSIAN VOLUNTEERS ATTACK NAPOLEON'S PICKET TROOPS

sides, and only Major von Lützow, with some brave companions, happily cut their way through the treacherous French, and reached the Elbe. The Duke of Padua sends an officer to do away all suspicion, to lull them into security; commands them to halt until an officer of safe conduct has arrived: the officer does arrive, and they fall as victims of the foulest treachery, the most diabolical perfidy to be met with in military annals.

This is an instance, amongst innumerable others that could be adduced, that some of the *Satraps* of Napoleon trampled on the most sacred pledges, without blushing and without remorse, whenever a favourite object of their revengeful, bloodthirsty *sultan* was to be attained.

★★★★★★

General von Blücher, by way of reprisal, advanced with his army into the neutral ground on the 14th, reached Breslaw the same day, and marched towards the Katzbach on the 15th and 16th, fixed his headquarters at Jauer on the 17th, and employed that day in reconnoitring the enemy's position on the Katzbach, with the view of attacking him on the 18th; for which every preparation was made by the commander-in-chief; but the enemy left the heights, on which they were strongly posted, during the night, and evacuated Liegnitz and Goldberg, which were immediately occupied by General Baron von Sacken, after a trifling affair, not far from the latter place, whereby the enemy lost 6 officers and 200 prisoners.

The rest of the army pursued General Lauriston on the road to Goldberg, towards Löwenberg and Bunzlau; and General von Blücher established his headquarters at Goldberg. General Kaisaroff had pushed on his corps at the same time to Lahn, where he was warmly attacked by a French brigade under General Zucchi, from the corps of Marshal Macdonald; but he vigorously repulsed the enemy, and took from him 160 prisoners.

At this period the positions of the several combined and Confederate armies were as follows:

The united army of Russians and Prussians, under the command of General Barclay de Tolly, consisting of General Wittgenstein's corps of Russians, General von Kleist's corps of Prussians, together with the Prussian and Russian reserves under the Grand Prince Constantin and Count Miloradowitsch, about 80,000 men strong, passed the Bohemian frontiers on the 12th of August (on which day Austria declared war against France), formed a junction with the Imperialists on the 17th;

LÜTZOW CAPTURES TWO HUNDRED RECRUITS FOR THE FRENCH ARMY AT RODA

and Field-Marshal Prince Schwartzenberg then took the command in chief, General Count Radetzky being appointed quartermaster-general.

This Grand Army, whose efficient numbers in the field may be calculated at 180,000 men, took up a position on the Saxon border, the headquarters being at Prague, at which place the Emperor of Russia and the King of Prussia had arrived on the 18th, and were there met by General Moreau, who was immediately appointed General Adjutant to the Emperor of Russia.

The Swedish Army of the Crown Prince of Sweden, strengthened by the Russian corps of Generals Winzingerode, von Woronzow, and von Czernischeff, an English Hanoverian corps under General Walmoden, and a Prussian corps under General von Bülow, were posted in the Mark, the prince having his headquarters at Charlottenburg, and from which he addressed a proclamation to his troops, full of fire and energy.

The Prussian Army under General von Tauenzien, was posted so as to act in conjunction with General von Blücher, or the Crown Prince of Sweden, as circumstances might render necessary, the headquarters being at Münchenburg.

Napoleon occupied offensive positions at all points against these *corps d'armée*: he threatened Berlin, Breslaw, and Prague, and moved from Dresden, as from the centre of a circle, on all sides of him. His Grand Army of 150,000 men, under Marshals Ney and Macdonald, and Generals Sebastiani and Lauriston, made front towards Silesia. Marshal Oudinot menaced the Mark with 90,000 men; a reserve of 60,000 men was in cantonments between Bautzen and Löwenberg; several corps of observation were stationed towards Bohemia; and his right wing was formed by d'Avoust, with 30,000 men.

It was the judiciously concerted plan of the Allies, that, if the Silesian Army was attacked by a superior, overwhelming force, it should retreat, fighting, from one strong position to another; and in this manner, by drawing the principal force of the French after it, unavoidably lengthen, and at the same time weaken, Napoleon's line of operations; and thus enable the grand Bohemian Army to reap important and incalculable advantages, when attempting to advance rapidly out of Bohemia upon Dresden.

On the 19th the Silesian Army continued its offensive movements. The corps of General Langeron crossed the Bober at the village of Zobten, and took the village of Siebeneichen, where a division of

Macdonald's corps attempted to defend the passage. The advanced-guard of the Russians, under General Rudczewitz, encountered a column of the enemy on their retreat from Lahn, took a battery, a number of prisoners, the whole of Marshal Macdonald's field-equipage, and the military chest of the paymaster-general. This daring enterprise was hardly executed, when the enemy fell upon the general with great force; but having formed his advanced-guard into a square *phalanx*, and placed his rich booty in the midst, he forced his way at the point of the bayonet, through the opposing files of the enemy, and reached his corps in safety.

General von York, at the head of his corps, had taken the direction. of Löwenberg, where he found the heights in front of the town already occupied by the advanced-guard of Lauriston's corps; General von York ordered his up to the attack, and drove the enemy's over the Bober with inconsiderable loss. During this affair, it was reported to General von Blücher, who was present, that Marshal Ney, with the cavalry of General Sebastiani, was on the march from Haynau to Löwenberg, menacing the flank and rear of the Prussian Army. Upon this, General von Blücher dispatched Prince Charles of Mecklenburg, with a brigade, to stop the progress of the enemy; but finding himself too weak to withstand his repeated attacks, he demanded support, which General von York complied with, and the prince succeeded in keeping Marshal Ney in check, so as to enable our veteran general to follow up his advantages at Löwenberg.

Marshal Ney halted at Gröditz-Berg, in a woody, intersected terrain; and General von York drew up his forces opposite to him, at the distance of a cannon-shot, while the general-in-chief directed the march of the other columns thither, with the intention of attacking the enemy the next morning. General von Sacken had marched, on the same day, towards Bunzlau, in pursuit of the enemy, who had evacuated, in great haste, both Liegnitz and Haynau. It was the 6th corps, under Marshal Marmont; but the advanced-guard of General von Sacken's corps succeeded in bringing him to action at the village of Kreibau, behind Haynau. He then took up a position on the hills of Kaiserswalde, to the left of the high road towards Bautzen.

After an obstinate engagement, which cost the enemy a great number of men, he was obliged to relinquish his strong position, and retreat on the road to Bunzlau. On his march, General Nevarofsky fell on his right flank, kept up a heavy cannonade and galling fire of musketry, and pursuing with the cavalry to the village of Ober-

Thomaswaldau, night alone put an end to the sanguinary combat. The corps of General von Sacken bivouacked between Wolfshain and Thomaswaldau.

After reconnoitring the position of Marshal Marmont, General von Sacken caused him to be attacked on the morning of the 20th, and forced him to abandon Thomaswaldau, and to pursue his march to Bunzlau, under a continual succession of severe engagements and charges. The enemy being driven out of the intrenchments they had thrown up near this place by assault, and having blown up his magazines and broken down the bridges, the town was occupied by the troops under General Count Lieven. Marshal Ney's corps, and the cavalry under General Sebastiani, had made good their retreat through Bunzlau in the night between the 19th and 20th; General von Blücher was, therefore, spared the necessity of attacking him, as the French had entirely abandoned the right bank of the Bober on the 20th August.

But, on this day, Napoleon, by forced marches, had reached Lauban with his guards and the corps of cavalry under General Latour-Maubourg, and hastened to make the necessary dispositions that his retreating army might act again on the offensive. He arrived at Löwenberg by break of day on the 21st, at the critical moment when the Silesian Army was on the point of crossing the Bober.

Napoleon lost no time in throwing bridges over that river; and General Lauriston repassed it at noon at the head of the 5th corps, the rest of his army following. This sudden return of the enemy's columns, and the great force they displayed, did not escape the penetration and foresight of our veteran general, who rightly judged that the enemy, being reinforced, was determined on giving battle; but to avoid doing so was absolutely necessary from various circumstances; and he therefore concentrated his gallant army on the Gröditz-Berg, during which his advanced-guard seized every advantage which the nature of the ground permitted, to obstruct the progress of the enemy, and keep him in check.

At noon, on the 22nd, the Silesian Army was drawn up in order of battle between Abelsdorf and Pilgramsdorf. The French threw themselves on its left wing, which General von Blücher drew back behind Goldberg, placing his army in position, with the Katzbach in front, and his left wing extending to Liegnitz. On the 23rd the French attacked Goldberg with the 5th and 11th corps: the advanced-guards of General Count Langeron and von York defended the town and the heights with the greatest bravery. General Lauriston, who had the command of the French troops, took Wolfsberg, defended only by small detachments, and debouched with columns of infantry, but was repulsed with heavy loss, three several times, during which the Prussian cavalry made many brilliant charges with great success.

The Prince of Mecklenburg, who fought the enemy on the left bank of the Katzbach, had to sustain the most violent and impetuous attacks; the great superiority of the French artillery had dismounted a part of his guns and thinned the ranks of his columns, while twenty-four squadrons of French horse, profiting by the favourable moment, made a grand charge, took a battery, and surrounded two battalions. Some squadrons of Prussian cavalry, and the regiment of Mecklenburg Hussars, threw themselves, at this moment, with indescribable fury, on the enemy's cavalry, broke their first line, forced the second upon the third, retook the guns, and released the battalions which had been taken prisoners. On this memorable occasion, the gallant Prince of Mecklenburg seized a Prussian standard, rallied some battalions that were giving way, put himself at their head, and led them on again into action.

This was one of the hottest affairs of the whole campaign. Some of the battalions of the Silesian militia highly distinguished themselves, and excited the admiration of the veterans of the army. General von Blücher learnt, from the prisoners that were made, that Napoleon was in the field with the flower of the French Army; and at the same time General von Sacken, who commanded the right wing at Liegnitz, reported, that the French, in considerable force (the third and sixth corps), were on the advance against him.

The Bohemian Army would, in all probability, advance on this day, two days' march into Saxony; it was possible also, that the Crown Prince of Sweden, with the Northern Army, would be in Lower Lusatia; General von Blücher therefore held it more advisable to draw off the French Army farther from the Elbe, so as to prevent Napoleon from finding time to unite his scattered forces to a converging point. He accordingly issued orders to break off the combat, judging the contest no longer equal, and to retreat towards Jauer. The loss of the Silesian Army, during the whole of the engagements, from the 21st to the 23rd, amounted to 3,000 men; but that of the French must have been far more considerable, as the vantage-ground was favourable for the Allied arms.

Napoleon, on the first intelligence of the progress of the Bohemian Army towards Saxony, soon perceived how necessary his presence must be on the Elbe; and scarcely had his guards arrived in Silesia, on

FRENCH TROOPS ENTER A GERMAN VILLAGE

the 22nd, before they were ordered to trace their steps back again to Dresden. He followed them on the 23rd, accompanied by Marshal Ney, leaving Marshal Macdonald commander-in-chief of the third, fifth, and eleventh corps. Marshal Marmont's corps, and the cavalry under General Latour-Maubourg, likewise began their retrograde march to Dresden. On the 23rd, General Souham took the command of the third corps, during Marshal Ney's absence.

Nothing of importance occurred to Blücher's army on the 24th; the French were posted on the Katzbach, and the Allies at Jauer. On the 25th, the advanced-guard of the latter made a movement forwards, and the light cavalry of Sacken's corps pursued the third corps to the environs of Haynau, when the latter faced about, and again moved towards the Katzbach. Upon this, General von Blücher marched the corps of General von Sacken to Malitsch, that of von York to Jauer, and directed the corps of Langeron to take up their ground on the fine position of Hennersdorf. The fifth French corps stood in the position of Goldberg, having its advanced-guard at Prausnitz; the eleventh corps behind Goldberg; and the third corps near Rothkirch, with a division posted at Liegnitz.

These corps were, however, separated in part by the Katzbach and Neisse, which, owing to the heavy rains, had overflowed their banks, and become raging torrents. The Prussians having concentrated themselves near Jauer, could either advance on the enemy, or take up an impregnable position on the mountains, in the rear; but General von Blücher, with his usual penetration, quickly perceiving that the main spring of action, Napoleon himself, was not in the field, and satisfied that the counter-march of such numerous bodies could not but be known to him, with a promptness of decision so marked in all his resolves, determined to improve the opportunity, and made dispositions for a general attack on the enemy, at two o'clock p. m. on the 26th August.

The three *corps d'armée* were to pass the Katzbach, between Goldberg and Liegnitz; those of von York and von Sacken to attack the third French corps with the utmost rapidity; during which the corps of Langeron was to cover the rear of both, towards Goldberg. The corps of General von York, having reached the heights of Brechtelshof, reported to the commander-in-chief, that the enemy was already on the advance, and had driven in the outposts; and particularly, that General Langeron was briskly attacked.

Upon this, General von Blücher halted his columns, and drew them up again in ambuscade.

A MECKLENBURG HUSSAR'S CAPTURE

A most tremendous and continual rain, and lowering sky, had so darkened the atmosphere, that every movement was rendered very difficult, and any kind of reconnoitring almost impossible.

******

As this memorable battle has been the peculiar boast of the Prussians, the greatest security to the province of Silesia, and the first check the ambitious power of Napoleon experienced on the plains of Germany, a detailed account of the occurrences that marked and preceded the glory of the day may not be unacceptable to the reader.

For several days previous to the battle, the Confederate Army had to struggle with uncommon difficulties. An incessant rain had inundated, in a great measure, the face of the country. Their marches were nothing but a continual wading, up to their knees, through innumerable rivulets, that, swollen by the rains, polled like torrents from the mountains. Each bivouac, at night, was taken up on ground ankle-deep in mud and mire, the rain falling without any intermission. Their supplies of provisions could not be brought up, and the army suffered privations with an heroic fortitude, and calm determined resignation, that form the brightest gems in their crown of victory.

******

To the left of the village of Eich-holz, some commanding ground became the key of the whole position (see Map of the Battle on the Katzbach), and General von Sacken was ordered to line it with his artillery, which was done with his usual promptitude and celerity; a Prussian battery, of twelve-pounders, strengthened his left, and their brisk and well-directed fire forced the enemy, in despite of himself, to deploy his columns slowly and disadvantageously, between Weinberg and Eich-holz. This was the moment intended by our bold veteran for the general attack.

******

The eyes of all Europe were, at this time, on the conduct of Blücher, and his able defence of Silesia has justly exalted him to a most elevated place in the military annals of the present day. Collected within himself, he in no instance hazarded the event of a battle by premature experiments on the enemy, but deliberately observed their approaches, and seized the important moment to make his attacks: his cool and temperate demeanour maintained that confidence with which he had inspired his troops, and his unaffected eloquence, when addressing them, did but increase their veneration. The cannonade had begun, the infantry were in column, when our veteran general rode down the lines, and stopping at intervals, harangued the troops in nearly the following words:

"My brave lads; this day decides! Prove to your king and to your country, that your courage is equal to your fidelity. Prove it, I say, at the point of your bayonets look yonder, there's the enemy. March, show yourselves as gallant Prussians." Reiterated huzzas, and cries of "The King for ever!" resounded from all sides, with bursts of enthusiasm,

******

The advanced-guard, and von Horn's brigade, fell on the right wing of the French, at Weinberg; the Prince of Mecklenburg's brigade followed in support, that of von Hünerbein covered the left flank against Lauriston, and the brigade of Steinmetz, together with the cavalry, formed the reserve. General von Sacken caused his advanced-guard to take post to the left of the village of Eich-holz, and two regiments of Russian riflemen occupied the village, supported by two others. Lieutenant-General Nevarofsky formed the first line, and General Count Lieven the second line of the advanced-guard.

There being an evident possibility of turning the left flank of the enemy, General von Sacken ordered Major-General von Lanskoy with the cavalry, General Karpoff with the Cossacks, and General Wassiltschikoff with the Achkirsch hussars, to leave Eich-holz to their left, and to attempt to fall on the enemy's left flank. In this position the attack began.

General Lanskoy took the French in flank, and General Wassiltschikoff, supported by the Prussian cavalry, attacked them in front; Lieutenant-General Nevarofsky supported these fierce charges with the whole of his infantry, followed by General Lieven, who advanced into the first line. With an impetuosity and a defiance of danger that baffles all description, as if animated by one soul, and impelled by one spring of action, the whole line of battle now precipitated itself on the enemy.

******

It was the second battalion of the Brandenburg regiment of infantry, that formed the head of the column which made the first onset. Cool, steady, and compact, the battalion advanced to storm three batteries, protected by two squares of infantry of the enemy's centre. The cannon-balls plunged into the ranks, mowing down whole files. The Prussian column, silent as death, moved on unshaken. A galling fire of grapeshot now thinned their ranks. No one looked either to the right or left, and shouts of "Forwards! forwards!" stifled the cries of the wounded and the dying. Whole sections fell, and the dauntless survivors did but press on the more vehemently to use the bayonet.

Closing with the enemy, a dreadful pause of irresolute suspense seemed to intervene, when, as the officers shouted, "Down upon them! down upon them!" a furious murderous charge with the bayonet ensued. In the heat of the attack no quarter was given, and scarcely ten minutes elapsed before the enemy's *phalanx* was transformed into a pyramid of ghastly corpses. The other square, shuddering at the fate of their advance, broke, and took to their heels. The tumult and confusion in the French centre were so great, that two regiments of French horse, which advanced at full gallop to cover the fugitives, passed the Prussian column at this moment, mistaking them for their comrades.

★★★★★★

The incessant rain, pouring down in torrents the whole day, had rendered fire-arms useless; not a musket would go off, when, with loud shouts and reiterated huzzas, a conflict with the bayonet took place, the most sanguinary, desperate, and destructive that is to be met with in the history of battles. Whole columns of Frenchmen were in a few minutes overpowered by the physical enthusiastic strength of the Allies, and suddenly transformed into frightful heaps of wounded, dead, and dying; not a soul escaped; no one thought of taking prisoners; "Forwards! forwards! Go on! go on!" were the watchwords, and Death stalked in hideous majesty before the impenetrable files of the Prussians and Russians; from the gleams of whose bayonets their appalled enemies shrunk aghast with horror and confusion. The Prussian cavalry charged at intervals, in single squadrons, and took several pieces of artillery.

On the left wing, General Langeron had to sustain the most furious attacks; twice did General Lauriston succeed in carrying the heights of the Russian position, and twice was he driven from them, at the point of the bayonet French impetuosity here found its overmatch in the adamantine steadiness of Russian bravery and devotion. Marshal Macdonald's efforts were at last in vain; the French could no longer withstand the determined resolution of the Allies; he attempted, as a forlorn hope, a grand charge of cavalry, but this was repulsed with severe loss, and he was obliged to relinquish the field of battle, leaving a great part of his artillery behind him, and seek his safety, and that of his routed army, across the foaming torrents of the Katzbach and the Neisse, which, swollen as they were by unceasing rains, could not be done but with great danger and difficulty, They were here pressed hard by the Allies, and driven down the steep precipices of their banks into the raging floods beneath.

★★★★★★

Who shall venture to describe the ecstatic feelings arising from the consciousness of having gained a signal victory over an implacable foe? Veterans, soldiers by profession, gratify their passion for honour on such an occasion. It is honour they seek, it is honour they gain: but the heart of the patriot, when taking the field to save that country so dear to him, to preserve the glory of that king so beloved and adored, overflows with an excess of rapturous delight, an indescribable charm, that beggars all description: such, however, was the feeling that pervaded the Prussian Army on the eve of this day.

Each column, each company, was eager (like children with their playthings) to show their comrades the prisoners they had taken, the trophies they could boast of. Blücher listened to the tales each had to relate with the indulgence of paternal partiality: "Well, my lads," he would say, "the French will think of us; they'll remember our bayonets, I warrant them."—"Hear me, father Blücher," the soldiers would answer; "This day is a day of days; if we go on so, who's afraid?"

★★★★★★

This decisive battle, by which the gigantic plans of Napoleon received a fresh check, and the foundation was laid for the emancipation of Germany, and the peace of Europe, commenced about three o'clock p.m. lasted till night was far advanced, and ended on the Katzbach. In the night, when all firing and pursuit had ceased, an enemy's reserve, with sixteen pieces of cannon, advanced on the road from Liegnitz, with the intention of harassing the right wing, to draw off its attention, and thus enable the discomfited army to retreat unmolested; but it was warmly received by the Generals von Lieven and Nevarofsky, and quickly repulsed with heavy loss; after which attack this hard-fought contest ceased entirely.

Sixteen pieces of artillery were captured, sword in hand, by the conquerors; but there was no possibility, on this day, to ascertain the exact number of guns and prisoners taken; among the latter was, how-

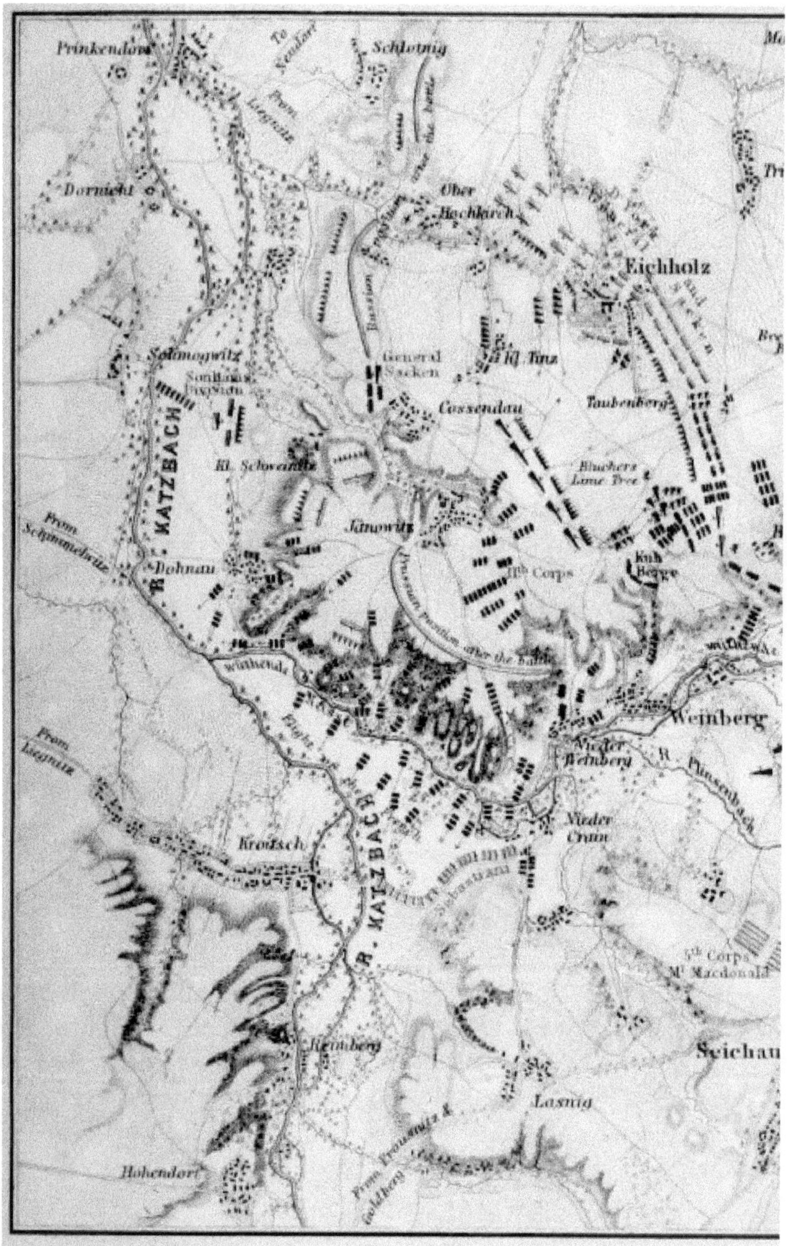

Prinkendorf
Schlotnig
Dornicht
Ober Bachkirch
Eichholz
Schmogwitz
General Sacken
Kl. Tinz
Cossendau
Taubenberg
Kl. Schweinitz
KATZBACH
Bluchers Lime Tree
Janowitz
From Schmochwitz
Dohnau
Kuh Berge
Weinberg
Nieder Weinberg
R. Plinsenbach
From Liegnitz
Nieder Crain
Kroitsch
R. KATZBACH
5th Corps Ml Macdonald
Seichau
Lasnig
Hohendorf
From Goldberg

BATTLE
OF THE
KATZBACH
26th August 1813.

French — Russians & Prussians
Cavalry — Infantry — Artillery

SCALES

Positions before & after the battle. Light colours.

ever, the French General van der Suden.

The loss of the combined army was by no means considerable. On the 27th, the advanced-guard of General Count von Langeron attacked the corps of Lauriston, retreating towards Goldberg. General Kapezewitz caused the Generals Partschoulidseff and Denischeff to attack an enemy's square mass of infantry, of three battalions, and flanked by four guns; the intrepid Russians did not let a man escape, they were all either killed, wounded, or taken prisoners; and this severe loss so discouraged the rest of Lauriston's corps, that, being briskly pursued, and losing eighteen guns, they evacuated Goldberg, and General Langeron occupied it the same day.

Blücher paused not a moment: on the 28th, the victorious Silesian Army crossed the Katzbach at Liegnitz and Goldberg, during which the several advanced-guards continued without intermission to follow up the enemy towards Löwenberg and Bunzlau, hourly capturing prisoners in every direction. The rain, falling in torrents, had swollen every rivulet to an outrageous stream, which had broken down every bridge, so that the whole country was in a state of inundation; there was in consequence no way of passing the Bober, but at Bunzlau, and to this point all the French columns were obliged to direct their march.

General Puthod had been detached, on the 26th of August, to manoeuvre in the rear of the Allied Army, by the way of Schönau and Jauer. The intelligence of the battle being lost had reached him; it was not however in his power, on account of the waters being out, to repass the Bober; he made the attempt at Hirschberg, but not succeeding, he marched down the right bank of the Bober, towards Löwenberg, and passed the night of the 28th at Zobten. On the 29th, he directed his steps to Löwenberg, where he made several unavailing attempts to replace the bridge over the Bober.

This delay gave General von Langeron time to gain a march upon him, having received advice of his movements; and as General Puthod saw the danger he was in of being attacked at a disadvantage, he endeavoured to regain the high road to Bunzlau; but General Rudzewicz, commanding the advanced-guard of Langeron's corps, having cut off his retreat on this road, he bent his march towards Zobten once again, which being reported to General von Korff and Prince Czerbatow, who had followed the advanced-guard with cavalry, as support, they threw themselves on this route by a forced march, and General Puthod, finding himself hemmed in on, all sides, drew up his corps on the heights near Plagwitz, by Löwenberg, and prepared for a desperate

THE PATRIOT FICHTE

A VOLUNTEER OF 1813

defence. General Czerbatow, in consequence, directed the march of his division to this point, and General von Korff followed along the banks of the Bober, with his cavalry.

The prince arriving on the commanding ground opposite the enemy's position, established a battery of light artillery, that began to play briskly on the French columns, and detached four regiments of riflemen to attack and gall the enemy on his right flank. The French were not slow in making the most vigorous resistance, and their batteries did great execution; but at this moment, their left flank being hard pressed by General Rudzewicz, Prince Czerbatow commanded an assault to be made with the bayonet on their right flank; it was carried, and the French driven pell-mell from the heights into the roaring Bober, and all were made prisoners that did not precipitate themselves into the river. The trophies of this signal victory over Puthod's corps were glorious to the Allied arms.

General Puthod, more than 100 officers, and 8,000 men, were taken prisoners; 16 pieces of cannon, 2 eagles of the 146th and 148th French regiments of the line, and the whole of the artillery park, fell into the hands of the gallant Confederates. The Brigade General Siblet, a colonel, many officers and privates, were drowned in the rapid stream of the Bober. The whole loss of Langeron's corps did not exceed 200 men.

★★★★★★

A praiseworthy emulation spurred on the troops, and, under the blessing of an all-ruling Providence, the success of this great day may be justly attributed to the invincible courage and intrepidity of the Confederate Silesian Army: General von Blücher never lost sight of the enemy, and attacked him almost daily. In the course of eight days he had fought him in eight bloody encounters, not to mention trifling affairs; beat him completely in a pitched battle, and directly afterwards made three serious attacks upon him. We may venture to affirm, that, in modern military annals, no example of such a succession of bloody and eventful days is to be found as those between the 18th and 29th August 1813.

★★★★★★

On the 30th of August, General von Blücher transferred his headquarters to Holstein, near Löwenberg, and continued to pursue the enemy in the most active manner. General von Bennigsen entered Breslaw on the 30th of August, with his Polish Army of reserve, and proceeded from thence to Liegnitz, marching on the same line with Blücher. In bivouac, at the village of Kielingswalde, between Naumburg and Görlitz, General von Blücher addressed a proclamation to his army:

> Silesia is cleared of the enemy. Brave soldiers, of the Russian and Prussian Army under my command, it is to your vigorous exertions and resolution, to your patience in supporting fatigues and privations, that I owe the good fortune of having wrested this fine province out of the hands of a greedy and rapacious enemy. The implacable foe, with haughty defiance, met you on the Katzbach. You issued with the rapidity of lightning, from behind the heights. You disdained to attack him with the distant fire of musketry, but advanced upon him without pausing.
>
> Your bayonets, and the nervous strength of your arm, drove him down the steeps of the raging Neisse and the Katzbach. You have since waded through torrents and rivers; you have passed the nights in storms, without shelter, short of provisions, and struggling with every want; but you murmured not, you pursued with promptitude and energy the flying enemy. I return you thanks for your exalted, praiseworthy conducts He alone is a true soldier that possesses such qualities.
>
> One hundred and three pieces of cannon, 250 tumbrils, the camp-hospital of the enemy, his provisions, a general of division, 2 generals of brigade, a great number of colonels, staff and other officers, 18,000 prisoners, 2 eagles, and other trophies, have fallen into your hands. The remainder of those who opposed you on the Katzbach, terrified at the sight of your bayonets, have taken to flight.
>
> The roads and the fields between the Katzbach and the Bober bear the unequivocal marks of the confusion and dismay of the enemy. Let us sing praises to the Lord of Hosts, by whose help you have overthrown your enemies, and return him thanks, in the hour of prayer, for the victory he has given into our hands. Three volleys shall be fired in honour of the day, and terminate your devotions. And then, once more, seek the enemy in the field,
>
> Von Blücher.

The insignia of the Grand Order of St. Andrew, which the Emperor of Russia transmitted to General von Blücher, after the battle

Trachau
Pieschen
Scheunen
Neudorf
Kaditz
Uebigau
RIVER
Ostra Gehege
DRESDEN
Friedrich Stadt
Cotta
Löbda
Bürgstädel
Ockerwitz
Wölfnitz
Gorbitz
Comptitz
Rossthal
Altfranken
General Gyulay
Pesterwitz
Plauen
Gittersee
Potschappel
Zauckerode
Döhlen
Burg

BATTLE OF DRESDEN
26th & 27th August 1815.

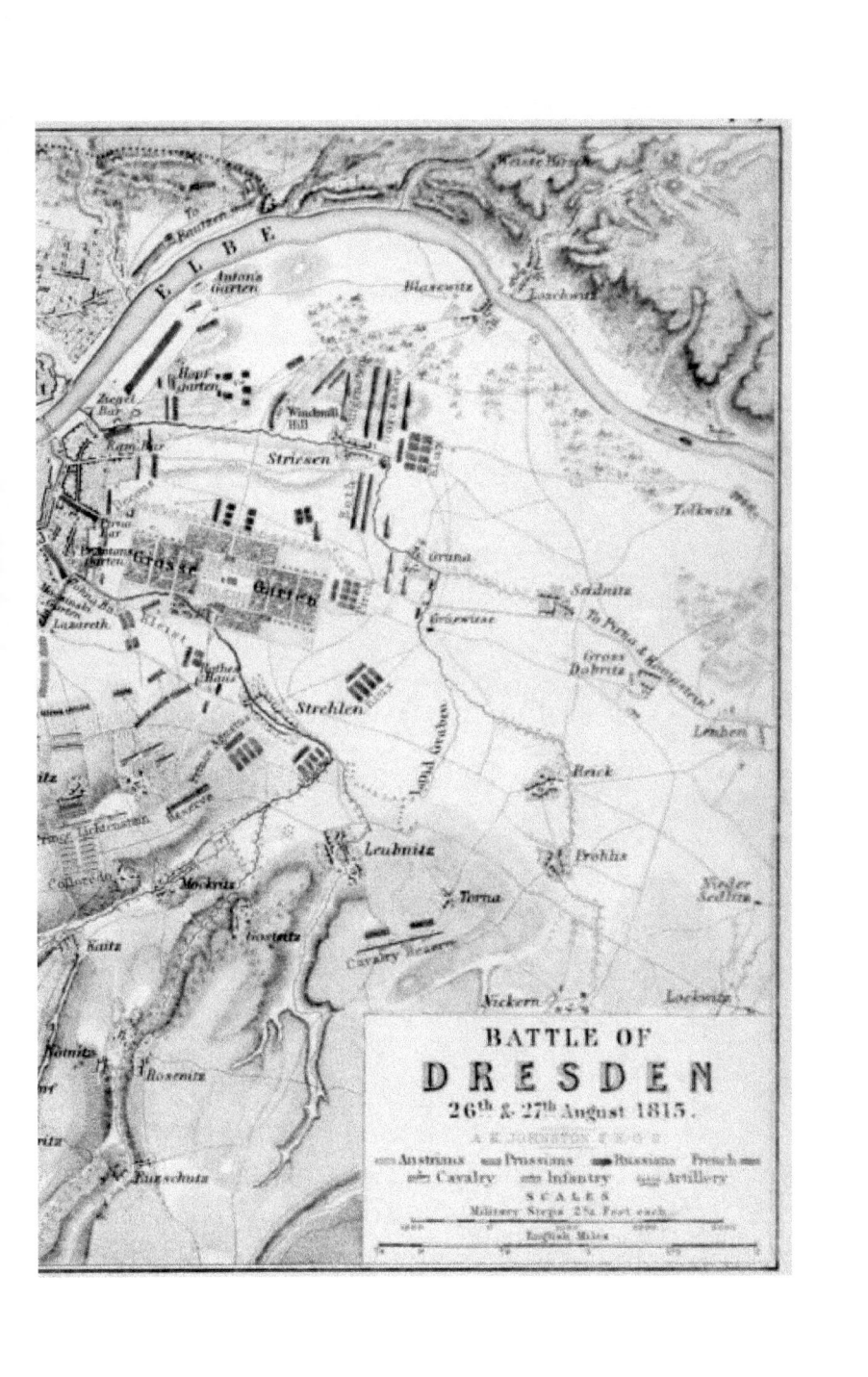

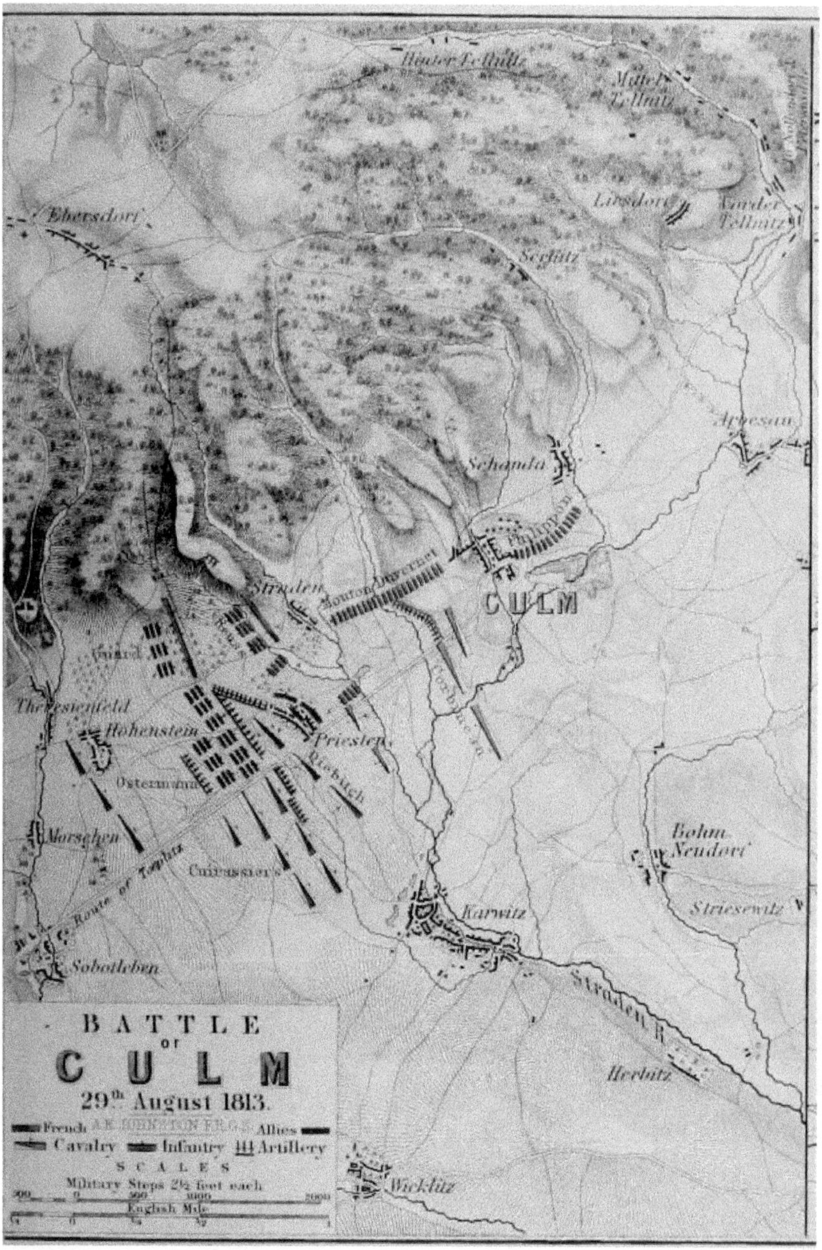
BATTLE
OF
CULM
29th August 1813.
French
Allies
Cavalry
Infantry
Artillery
SCALES
Military Steps 2½ feet each
English Mile
CULM
Karwitz
Schanda
Straden
Priesten
Hohenstein
Osterman
Morschen
Sobotleben
Cuirassiers
Route of Teplitz
Guard
Ebersdorf
Seeblitz
Linsdorf
Arbesau
Böhm. Neudorf
Striesewitz
Herbitz
Wicklitz
Diebitsch
Vorder Tellnitz
Mittel Tellnitz
Hinter Tellnitz
Strader R.

on the Katzbach, was accompanied by the following note, in the emperor's own handwriting:

General,

Amongst the most agreeable moments of the campaign, I reckon those, in which I can give you proofs of the peculiar satisfaction I feel, in doing justice to your brilliant courage, the activity of your operations, and the effect of your unparalleled movements.

In the hour in which we, on our side, have gained a signal victory, (of Culm), I send you the insignia of the order of St. Andrew, which I have myself worn. I do not suppose that this circumstance will enhance the value of this mark of my pleasure, but it will at least prove to you, that I have lost not a moment in assuring you, and those brave men under your command, of the singular gratification your fortunate progress has afforded me.

The glory of a commander is reflected upon his soldiers, as that of the soldiers upon their commander. Tell them how highly I rate their deeds, and accept the assurances of my best wishes.

Alexander.

Töplitz,
the 30th of August 1813.

General von Blücher received, from his grateful sovereign, the grand cross of the order of the Iron Cross.

After a warm affair between the brigade of von Horn and the rear-guard of the enemy, at Bunzlau, very honourable to the former, although attended with considerable loss, the French evacuated Silesia entirely. They left the banks of the Bober on the 31st of August, and, on the 1st of September, the country was cleared of them, and the wrecks of Macdonald's army fled through Lusatia.

General von Blücher's advanced-guard crossed the Queisse the same day, which was distinguished by a brilliant operation: Major von Falkenhausen, and Captain von Swanenfeld, surprised with two squadrons of hussars, between Görlitz and Bautzen, four companies of French artillery, a squadron of *chasseurs*, and a company of infantry, entirely dispersed them, and took from them the last cannon saved from the wreck of the battle on the Katzbach.

OLD MARSHAL VORWÄRTS ATTACKS THE FRENCH ON THE KATZBACH

CHAPTER 8

Blücher Crosses the Elbe

The remains of Marshal Macdonald's corps now sheltered themselves behind the Queisse, and endeavoured to recover from the universal panic that had seized them. On the 2nd of September the advanced-guard of the Silesian Army passed the Neisse, and the main body followed. The retreating and beaten French stood, on the 3rd of September, near the Löbau pools, and on the 4th pursued their retrograde march to Bautzen: they had already abandoned Hochkirch, when suddenly their columns halted and bivouacked on the nearest heights. Napoleon having, no doubt, received intelligence of the defeat of Macdonald, had, it seems, hastened, by forced marches, with a part of his guards from Dresden to his support; and the corps of Poniatowsky, from 12,000 to 15,000 strong, at the same time advanced from Zittau.

The retrograde march of the Grand Allied Army into Bohemia, having given Napoleon the power of enlarging his circle of action, he left Dresden on the 3rd of September, accompanied by Marshal Murat, passed the night at Harthau, arrived in the vicinity of Hochkirch on the 4th, and immediately issued orders for the retreating army to halt. It was soon reported to General von Blücher, that Napoleon, with his guards, the sixth corps, and the cavalry under General Latour-Maubourg, were now in the field against him; upon which he withdrew his advanced-guard under General Wassiltschikoff, behind the Löbauwater, and concentrated his army in the rear of Landskrone. In this position he remained to ascertain whether Napoleon would be contented with merely gathering up the shattered remains of Macdonald's army, or offer battle.

On the 5th, Napoleon deployed a numerous force in front of Reichenbach, and vigorously attacked Blücher's army. The general-in-chief, true to his system, did not hold it advisable to accept battle at this critical moment, but passed the Neisse and Queisse with his army in the most complete order, leaving a rear-guard on the right bank of the Neisse, to watch the enemy's movements and demonstrations of advancing into Silesia. Nothing could be more evident than that the farther the enemy could be drawn from Dresden, the more decisive the operations of the Allied Army in Bohemia must eventually prove. But Blücher's patience was in vain tried on the 6th and 7th; the foe made no attempt to advance.

Napoleon felt the whole danger of his situation; and the Bohemian Army having again threatened Dresden, he saw himself kept in constant check, and obliged once more to trace his steps back to Dresden with the reinforcements he had brought with him, where he arrived on the 6th, in the evening. In the course of these operations detachments of cavalry from Blücher's army harassed the rear of the French Army, and caused it a considerable loss. The Russian General, Prince Madatoff, surprised, on the 2nd of September, a corps of French at Wurschen, consisting of 1 colonel, 5 captains, 18 lieutenants, 2 adjutants, and 677 privates, and made the whole of them prisoners.

On the 4th, the same prince attacked the escort of a large transport of ammunition, took them prisoners, and blew up more than 100 tumbrils. Our veteran hero, on finding the enemy less impetuous, put his army again in motion on the 8th. The corps of General St. Priest crossed the Neisse at Ostritz; that of Count Langeron followed. According to Blücher's plan of operations, General St. Priest was suddenly to attack Löbau; during which, General von York was to fall on the rear and flank of the enemy's corps at Görlitz, in the direction of Landskrone, so as to cut it off, if possible, from Reichenbach.

General St. Priest was prompt and vigorous in his attack on the 8th Polish corps, concentrated at Löbau, and drove it out of Mittel-Hartwigsdorf, Ebersdorf, and Löbau; but it was not possible to execute the attack on Görlitz, as the enemy, well aware of the peril that menaced him, had made such a precipitate retreat from the place, that the Cossacks, sent in pursuit, were not even able to overtake him.

General von Blücher learnt from an adjutant, taken prisoner, bearing dispatches to the Prince of Neufchatel (Berthier), from Prince Poniatowsky, that his corps had lost 23 officers and 500 men in the affair of Löbau. Macdonald's army continued its retreat to Bautzen. On the 10th, the advanced-guard of Blücher's army occupied Hochkirch, the Cossacks surrounded Bautzen, and General Blücher fixed his headquarters at Herrnhut. A division of the Austrian Army, 8,000 strong, under General Count Bubna, formed a junction with the Silesian Army on this day, having, till then, been posted in the vicinity of Gabel, on the frontiers of Bohemia, to observe the corps of Poniatowsky.

The decided superiority of force, which our hero now possessed, urged him to move onwards; and, on the 11th, Generals St. Priest and Kapczewicz forced the passage of the Spree, and General Count Bubna advanced towards Neustädt. The French troops evacuated, by break of day, on the 12th, both Bautzen and Neustädt, and retired behind Bishopswerda and Stolpe: here they were only a day's march from Dresden, and, by the way of Pirna, in direct communication with the right wing of the grand French Army. On the 14th, General St. Priest marched in advance, and charged a column of infantry with his cavalry, near Bishopswerda, taking about 100 men prisoners.

The following days were employed in narrowing the positions of the French near Dresden, and cutting off their supplies. According to the accounts of deserters, forage and provisions of all kinds were beginning to fall short in the place. General von Blücher having received intelligence that Marshal Marmont intended to make a diversion on the side of Grossenhain with the 6th corps under his command, ordered General von Sacken to advance to Camenz; and his advanced-guard, under General Fiegner, after skirmishing with the enemy the whole of the 15th, obliged him to retrace his steps to Dresden on the 16th.

In the position of Bishopswerda the Silesian Army remained in a state of comparative inaction till the 22nd: there seemed to be a cessation of offensive operations on the part of the army; but the great plan of the Allies was only ripening, and the main object, of acting on the flanks of Napoleon's army, was never lost sight of. Our veteran general, whether on the offensive or defensive, seemed equally successful; and no commander had, as yet, distinguished himself in a more eminent or even equal degree. His talent of daring enterprise, and his consummate prudence, carried him through triumphantly, in situations the most difficult to be conceived; and his conduct at the approaching crisis established him for ever, in the opinion of Europe, as one of the first of commanders.

Napoleon having returned to Dresden on the 21st of September from his unfortunate expedition into Bohemia, and finding himself hemmed in and compressed within narrow limits by Blücher, who stood in position almost within sight of the walls of Dresden, thought it expedient to attempt disengaging himself from so troublesome a neighbour. For this purpose, he proceeded to Harthau on the 22nd, causing the 11th, 3rd, and 5th corps of his Grand Army to march in the direction of Bishopswerda, occupied by Blücher's advanced-guard under General Rudzewicz and Colonel von Katzler. Although attacked by superior numbers, the gallant Confederates maintained the unequal contest nearly the whole of the day in this position, before they yielded a foot of ground.

On the 23rd, Napoleon renewed his attack, and the advanced-guard abandoned the woods and heights near Bishopswerda; but no sooner did the French debouch out of the wood, into a favourable terrain for cavalry, than the Allies faced about, and the Russian cavalry under Generals Count Witt and Emanuel, and the Prussian, under Colonel von Katzler, charged them with intrepidity, and drove them, with heavy loss, back into the wood; on which occasion 10 officers and 300 privates of the guards were taken prisoners. Napoleon, nevertheless, by dint of numerical superiority, succeeded in penetrating to Gödau, where the face of the country gradually opens, and is less intersected by woods; while, towards Bautzen, an extensive plain presents itself, of singular advantage for the operations of cavalry.

Our veteran general here endeavoured, with his wonted decision and alacrity, to entrap Napoleon in an ambuscade. General von Sacken was ordered to lie in ambush, with his whole corps, in such a position, that, when the enemy renewed his attacks on the 24th, he could fall unperceived upon his flank and rear; but the French remained perfectly quiet the whole of the 24th; upon which, General von Blücher directed General von Sacken to act on the offensive against the left flank of the enemy. The near approach of night prevented any movement being made in his rear; and the decisive attack and execution of Blücher's daring plan was obliged to be postponed till break of day of the 25th.

Napoleon, however, as if having a presentiment of what awaited him, retired in all haste, during the night, upon Bishopswerda, In this manner was he constrained to renounce, for the third time, acting upon the offensive against the intrepid, calculating Blücher and his Silesian Army, and returned to Dresden for the tenth time since the armistice, beset on every side by his enemies: and, although his concentrated position enabled him, by shifting his troops and corps from one point to the other, to make front on all sides of him, with an imposing force; yet this severe succession of partial losses dispirited his troops, and threw whole corps into a state of absolute disorganisation.

The 8th corps, under Prince Poniatowski, passed over to the left bank of the Elbe, and marched to Penig. Marshal Victor had taken position at Freiburg, and the 1st and 14th corps were encamped at Gieshubel and Pirna. On the 27th, the French Army evacuated Grossenhain, and began to pass the Elbe at Meissen. Lieutenant-General Count Tauenzien followed sword in hand, and threw some detachments over the river to harass the enemy. This general now formed a junction with the army of General von Blücher, having his headquarters, on the 27th, at Elsterwerda; General Baron von Sacken was posted at Grossenhain, his advanced-guard before Meissen; General von York at Gröbeln; General Count Langeron likewise at Elsterwerda; General Count St. Priest in Ostrandt, and his advanced-guard towards Königsbruck; the whole of the corps forming and establishing a link, by which the various Confederate armies were at this time connected together, and surrounding and baiting the ravenous tiger in his den.

Nothing of material importance occurred to the Silesian Army during the last days of September, the fury with which Napoleon had endeavoured to break through or enlarge the narrowing boundary that formed the area of his operations, having, to appearance, nearly spent itself; and his efforts to extricate himself from his perilous situation had proved fruitless at all points. We will now present our readers with a succinct but clear detail of the operations of the grand Confederate Army since the denunciation of the armistice, and the coalition of the Austrians in the good cause; taking a view, at the same time, of the progress of the Crown Prince of Sweden, and the Prussian armies of Generals Tauenzien and Bülow.

This digression is the more necessary, from the impossibility, without it, of forming a just conception of that stupendous manoeuvre of our hero, so soon to be executed, in passing the Elbe in the face of the enemy, and throwing himself, by a series of forced marches unparalleled in the records of history, and out of the supposed sphere of man's physical powers, into the rear of Napoleon's line of operations—a manoeuvre that caused every subsequent revolution of the wheel of fortune to be favourable to the Allies, and formed a pedestal to the most imperishable monument of military fame that ever was erected to the honour of one commander.

The Emperor of Austria declared war against France on the same day that the denunciation of the armistice took place. The Austrian Army, which assembled in and near Prague, under the command of Field-Marshal Prince von Schwartzenberg, consisted of three divisions. The Russian-Prussian Army under General Barclay de Tolly, consisting of the corps of General Count Wittgenstein, General von Kleist, and the reserves under the Grand Prince Constantin and Count Miloradowitsch, marched out of Silesia on the 12th of August, and formed a junction with the Austrian troops in Bohemia on the 17th of August. This army was henceforth called the Grand Confederate Army, Field-Marshal Prince Schwartzenberg being appointed commander-in-chief, and having his headquarters at Prague.

The several armies of the Allies were posted in the following manner: the army of the Crown Prince of Sweden, called the Northern Army, formed the right wing, and took up a position between Mecklenburg and the Elbe, having his headquarters at Oranienburg, and holding communication with the army of General von Tauenzien, in position to observe the fortresses on the Elbe and Oder. General von Blücher stood in Silesia. The efficient numbers of these armies may be estimated at 350,000 men.—The Bohemian Army advanced towards the Elbe on the 18th, in four columns, and passed the defiles in the Saxon mountains on the 22nd, after some partial advantages over small detached corps of the enemy.

The severity of the weather, and the consequent bad state of the roads, prevented the Confederates from arriving before Dresden earlier than the 25th in the evening. (See Map of the Battle of Dresden.)—A general assault was made upon Dresden on the following day, a redoubt was stormed, and the French driven into the body of the place. In the interim Napoleon had arrived, by forced marches, with the flower of his army out of Silesia. He reached Dresden at nine o'clock, a.m. on the 26th. Under such circumstances the Allies deemed it prudent to relinquish the attempt of taking Dresden by assault, and, in consequence, the Confederate Army was ordered to take up a position on the heights in the vicinity of that city.

Napoleon, with his usual impetuosity, attacked the positions of the Confederate troops early on the 27th, and a bloody but indecisive conflict ensued. It having been reported to the Commander-in-chief from General von Oesterman, commanding a corps of observation near Königstein, that General Vandamme had crossed the Elbe at that place in considerable force, taking the road to Pirna, and by this movement, threatening the rear of the combined Grand Army, it was obviously necessary for the Confederates to withdraw again into Bohemia: besides, the principal object of these offensive operations was absolutely obtained, although the results, under more favourable circumstances, might have been of greater importance; for Blücher, as well as the crown prince, had thus acquired an enlarged power of acting with energy upon the flanks and the rear of Napoleon's army. The Allies, therefore, set themselves in march towards Bohemia, in the night of the 27th, and reached the frontiers on the 29th, slowly and cautiously pursued by the French.

General Vandamme had arrived at Hollendorf with his corps on the 28th, and advanced to Peterswalde on the 29th, briskly pursuing the small corps of General von Oesterman, five times his inferior in numbers, who nevertheless contested every foot of ground with determined bravery and obstinate repulses. General von Oesterman was, however, obliged to retreat to Töplitz; Vandamme followed with eager impetuosity, and came down into the valley with eight or ten battalions; he attacked him near Töplitz, but the gallantry of the Russian troops supplied the place of numbers; General Vandamme could make no impression with his ten battalions, and insensibly drew his whole corps down into the plain.

To have withstood this disproportion of numbers would have been utterly impossible for General von Oesterman, if at this critical juncture a division of Russian guards had not arrived in the field, and a brigade of Russian grenadiers dispatched as a reinforcement by General Prince von Schwartzenberg, had not come into action. General von Oesterman now attacked in his turn, and his troops fought like lions. The Russian guards showed an intrepidity on this occasion, which will long serve as an example worthy of imitation by all the defenders of the good cause. The Russian general succeeded in repulsing the enemy, and forcing him to retreat, at the close of the day, to Karwitz and Pirsten.

The happy success of this affair was of the most vital importance to the Allied arms. The grand Bohemian Army now returning from Dresden, was on the point of repairing to Töplitz, after the most fatiguing marches across the mountains, to enjoy some days of repose. If Vandamme's project had been crowned with success, the most disastrous consequences must have resulted to the combined forces. The good countenance of the Russians, and the brilliant valour of their chief, decided the combat in favour of the Allied arms, and the execution of the dispositions for the following day was thus rendered possible. Vandamme, intoxicated with the distant prospect of striking a decisive blow, with his single arm, against the operations of the Confederate Army, hurried forwards with his whole corps into the valley, and took post at Culm (see Map of the Battle of Culm), instead of keeping himself firm in position on the mountains, as was his orders, or leaving a strong detachment to occupy the passes.

On the 30th, in the morning, Prince Schwartzenberg made the following dispositions to annihilate Vandamme's corps. Besides the troops already engaged, the corps of Count Colloredo, and the divisions of Bianchi and Prince von Hessen-Homburg, were ordered into line, the latter forming the right wing in front, having Bianchi's division for support. The corps of Russians formed the left wing, and the Russian guards were posted in reserve at Sobochleben.

Count Colloredo was ordered to manoeuvre with the enemy, and, supported by General Knorring's division, to endeavour to turn their left wing. The far-famed Battle of Culm commenced by Colloredo's storming the heights occupied by the enemy's left wing, with an irresistible impetuosity, and in the most brilliant manner driving the French before him out of Neudorf. General Knorring, at the head of his cavalry, charged at the same time the enemy's battery, and took it, sword in hand; during which, the right wing and front of Vandamme's army were kept fully occupied by the Austrians and Russians. At this crisis, the corps of General von Kleist showed themselves on the heights of Nollendorf, having marched from Glashütte to gain the high road by Nollendorf. This discerning general quickly appreciated the value of his presence on the scene of action, and collecting the whole of his troops in advance, rapidly descended into the plain, and burst like a tremendous hurricane upon the rear of Vandamme's position.

This latter general attempted to make front against Kleist; yet, baited as he was on every side, the result must at all events prove disastrous, and leave him nothing but the fury of despair. Retreat was cut off, and no chance of escape at hand. In fine, Vandamme's corps suffered a complete and signal defeat, and only a few squadrons of cavalry found means of gaining the road to Eule. The field of battle was covered with the dead. Vandamme himself, and several other generals, were taken; and 8,000 prisoners, 87 pieces of cannon, and 2 eagles, constituted the immortal trophies of this glorious day. Its consequences blighted the opening blossoms of Napoleon's imaginary advantages over the Allies at Dresden.

This happy event, in combination with Blücher's victory on the Katzbach, on the 26th, and the important advantages gained by General Bülow on the 22nd, at Gross-Beeren, excited throughout the Confederate Army the most confident hopes, and elated each heart with the proud sense of victory and well-earned glory. After the battle, the Allied troops took up a position in the neighbourhood of Töplitz; their headquarters, and those of the three august Monarchs, being in

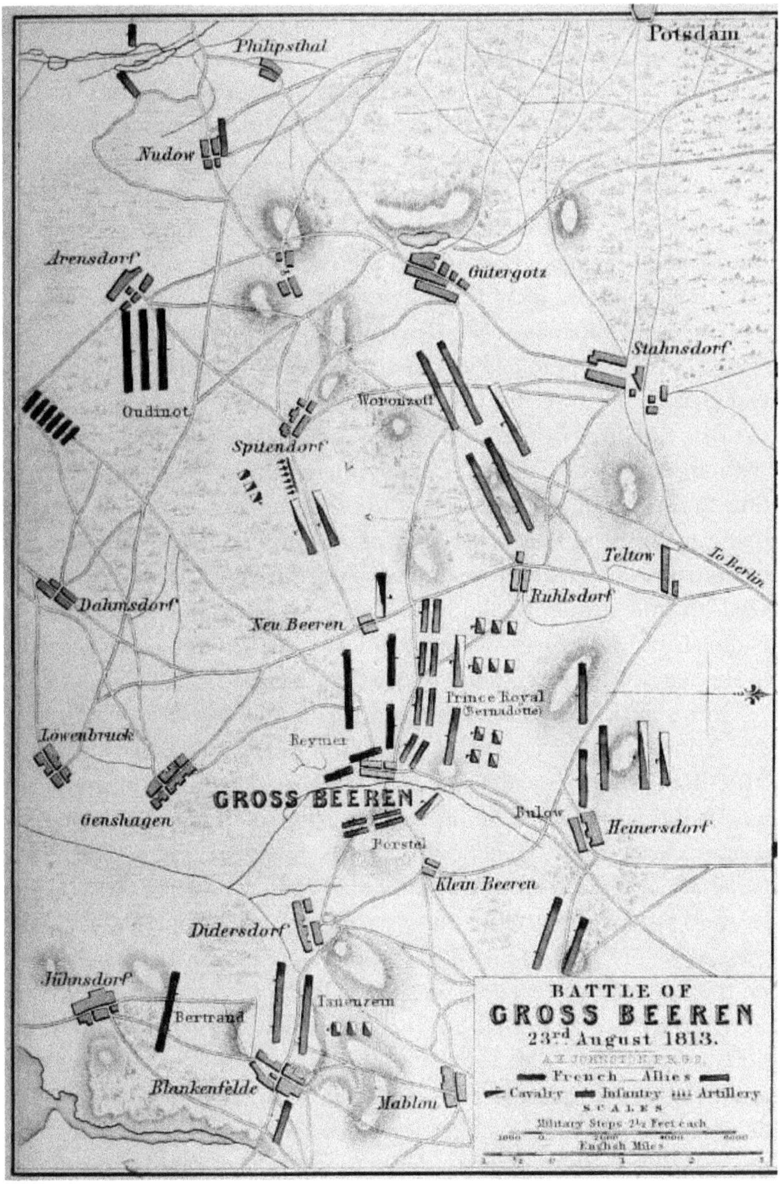
Potsdam
Philipsthal
Nudow
Arensdorf
Gütergotz
Stahnsdorf
Oudinot
Woronzoff
Spitendorf
Teltow
To Berlin
Ruhlsdorf
Dahmsdorf
Neu Beeren
Prince Royal
(Bernadotte)
Löwenbruck
Reymer
GROSS BEEREN
Genshagen
Bulow
Heinersdorf
Borstel
Klein Beeren
Didersdorf
Jühnsdorf
Bertrand
Blankenfelde
Mahlow
BATTLE OF
GROSS BEEREN
23rd August 1813.
French
Allies
Cavalry
Infantry
Artillery
SCALES
Military Steps 2½ Feet each
English Miles

the place. The French corps sent in pursuit of the Confederate Army, proceeded but slowly in advance on the 30th and 31st.

The example of Vandamme's terrible fate before their eyes, Blücher's progress, and the severe check which Oudinot had experienced, impelled Napoleon to shelter himself once more in his pestilential den at Dresden; and the Allied Bohemian Army remained in a state of repose till the 5th of September. Their ulterior movements shall be referred to in due course; and we shall now turn to those operations of the Northern Army under the command of the Crown Prince of Sweden, that led to the important victories of Gross-Beeren and Dennewitz, whose co-operating effects formed a part of those toils, now spread, and drawing closer around the implacable Tyrant, rendered so furious by repeated disappointments.

The Crown Prince of Sweden having received intelligence that the armistice was denounced, concentrated his army between Spandau and Berlin, and took up his headquarters at Charlottenburg, on the 17th of August. Napoleon, who was anxious to open the campaign with an enterprise of some *éclat*, pondered upon the project of getting Berlin into his power, and fed his ambitious hopes with thereby plunging all Europe into a stupor of astonishment at his success. For this purpose, Marshal Oudinot was charged with the command of the 4th, 7th, and 12th corps, and the body of cavalry under the Duke of Padua, forming an army of about 80,000 men, which was assembled in the environs of Baruth, on the 18th of August.

Some partial affairs occurred, and the advanced posts of the Northern Army were driven out of Jüterbock, Belzig, and Zerbst. On the 21st, the crown prince removed his headquarters to Potsdam; and as the enemy did not advance, he ordered his army to take up positions on a more extended line. General Winzingerode was posted at Saarmund; General von Bülow, between Phillipsthal and Sputendorf; General von Borstel, near Mittenwalde. The Swedish infantry occupied Potsdam, the cavalry bivouacked near Dahlen; and General von Tauenzien stood on the heights of Marienhof and Tempelhof, in front of Berlin.

On the 21st, the French advanced in two columns upon Willmersdorf, and, at five o'clock in the evening, drove in the Prussian outposts at Trebbin and Nunsdorf, taking up a position between Cliestow and Schubzendorf. By break of day on the 22nd, the crown prince drew up his army in the following order of battle (see Map of the Battle of Gross-Beeren): General von Bülow was posted near Saarmund. General von Tauenzien concentrated his corps near Blankenfelde. The

Swedish Army was posted at Ruhlsdorf. General Czernischeff occupied Belitz and Treuenbrietzen with his Cossacks.

General von Hirschfeldt, by a forced march from the environs of Magdeburg, reached Potsdam early on the 22nd. Towards noon, General von Bülow was attacked in his position, and forced back upon Heinersdorf, where he joined General von Tauenzien. The enemy having advanced to Jühnsdorf, General von Tauenzien pushed forward his corps to Blankenfelde. General von Borstel, still in position at Mittenwalde, was now ordered to form a junction with General von Bülow, in the direction of Brusendorf. Night put a stop to further operations. On the 23rd, Marshal Oudinot commanded the 4th corps, under Bertrand, to advance and attack General-von Tauenzien, who was immediately supported by the march of General von Bülow to the left towards Lichtenrade, to fall into line with General von Borstel near Mittenwalde.

The impetuous and rapid attacks of Bertrand were repulsed at all points, and the bravery of the Prussians under Tauenzien foiled all his attempts to make any impression on their line. In the meantime, the 7th French corps, under General Reynier, had succeeded in forcing General von Bülow's detachment to evacuate Gross-Beeren; but this brave and sagacious general did not hesitate resolving to attack Reynier with his whole corps, and to drive his right wing out of Gross-Beeren. It was six o'clock in the evening, and an incessant rain had fallen the whole day. He formed the battalions in square masses, and with fixed bayonets moved onwards to carry the enemy's batteries by assault, and to close with their columns.

In defiance of the showers of grape-shot, and heavy cannonade of the French, the undaunted Prussians bore down all before them: a most dreadful carnage ensued; Gross-Beeren was retaken; whole battalions of Frenchmen were bayonetted; batteries were stormed; and the cavalry, charging with equal impetuosity, effectually prevented the infantry of the enemy from rallying at any point. General von Bülow's conduct in this trying hour is above all praise; the Prussian name acquired fresh lustre under his dispositions, and the gallant band that fought with him are immortalised in the annals of Prussia.

★★★★★★

Some of the Prussian battalions of infantry suffered an enormous, and almost incredible loss, very disproportionate to that of their Allies; but they were determined to conquer or die; as for instance:

THE SMITH SPIKING THE GUNS ON THE LANGE BRÜCKE

The Colberg regiment of infantry lost 26 officers, and 763 privates.

The 9th regiment of reserve, 10 officers, and 572 privates. The 1st regiment of Neumarkt militia, 34 officers, and 551 privates.

✶✶✶✶✶✶

It was only after his arrangements were made, and the men were pressing forward into action, that he received orders from the crown prince to attack. Prompt measures are ever the forerunners of success, and, when combined with prudence and steady perseverance; never fail to plant unfading laurels on the brows of the victors. General von Borstel, having penetrated through Klein-Beeren, and cannonaded the enemy's right flank, contributed not a little to the fortunate issue of this bloody conflict. In possession of Gross-Beeren, General von Bülow ordered the reserve, under General von Thümen, to come into line, and the cavalry to turn the enemy's right wing. The Swedish and Russian corps were drawn up, at this moment, in order of battle. General Count von Winzingerode was at the head of 10,000 horse. General Count von Woronzow commanded the Russian infantry.

The village of Ruhlsdorf, but weakly occupied by the Swedes, to keep up a communication with Bülow's corps, was attacked by the enemy's sharpshooters; but the crown prince having ordered up some reinforcements, the French were soon obliged to retire. Victory was, however, decided principally by the rapid assault of the Prussians under Bülow. The corps of Reynier was broken and dispersed on all sides, and opened a chasm in the French line of attack, which all the efforts of Oudinot and Bertrand could not fill up. The retreat of the French was directed to Trebbin, and the Cossacks harassed them without intermission.

Up to the 24th at noon, the trophies of the day consisted of 26 pieces of artillery, 60 tumbrils, a large quantity of stores and baggage, 40 officers, and 1,500 prisoners. The 25th was occupied in pursuing the enemy to the Elbe; and a considerable number of prisoners fell into the hands of the light troops. General von Bülow took up his headquarters on the 26th at Trebbin. The Swedes marched to Saarmund, and the Russians to Treuenbrietzen. Pending these events, the French general Girard, with 10,000 men, of the garrison of Magdeburgh, somewhat emboldened by the absence of General Hirschfeldt, passed the Elbe, and moved towards Berlin, by the way of Ziesar. He was kept in check four days by the Prussian General von Puttlitz, with some battalions of militia; by which delay, Oudinot was already defeated before Girard could reach him.

On the 25th, General Girard made a vain attempt to dislodge the Cossacks under Czernischeff, out of Belzig, and then took position near Lübnitz. General von Hirschfeldt, after the Battle of Gross-Beeren, had marched with his corps back to Brandenburg, where he arrived on the 24th. Early in the morning of the 27th, General von Hirschfeldt reconnoitred the enemy's position at Lübnitz, and immediately determined on an attack. The heights were taken and retaken several times: the gallant Prussians maintained themselves on them at last, and Czernischeff, with his Cossacks, having come into action from Belzig, the French were completely routed.

General Girard was wounded, 8 pieces of cannon, 140 officers, 3,500 prisoners, a number of tumbrils, and all the baggage of the enemy, fell into the hands of the victors. The whole plan of Marshal Oudinot's operations was in this manner rendered abortive. His intended combinations were frustrated, and Napoleon's arrogant pride of omnipotence felt a severe abatement.

General von Bülow entered Elsholz on the 27th; General von Tauenzien was posted at Baruth, and sent General von Wobeser, with his division, to take the town of Luckau, where the French had intrenched themselves. After a brisk cannonade, the French *commandant* capitulated; and 9 pieces of artillery, and 1,000 prisoners, were the fruits of this enterprise. General von Woronzow, at the head of the advanced-guard of the Northern Army, dislodged the enemy, after an obstinate engagement, out of Jüterbock, which they had again occupied on the 27th; and the Crown Prince of Sweden thereupon removed his headquarters to Belitz. General von Bülow advanced to Treuenbrietzen, and took an advantageous position between that place and the village of Nicheln.

The headquarters of the Northern Army were, on the 30th, at Buchholz, and on the 31st at Treuenbrietzen. On the 1st of September, General von Bülow took post at Frohnsdorf, the French rear-guard retreating to Thiesen. The outposts of General von Borstel occupied the defiles of Köppenig, and the brigade of Krafft marched to the heights of Kropstädt: at the same time, General von Tauenzien made himself master of the high grounds in front of Zahne, keeping up a communication with General von Borstel. The remainder of von Bülow's corps took position at Marzahne. The Russian corps drew up near Pflighof.

The French, who, from the side of Coswig, endeavoured to pen-

THE PURSUIT AFTER GROSS BEEREN

etrate their lines, were repulsed with heavy loss by General Woronzow. On the 4th of September, the Grown Prince of Sweden fixed his headquarters at Rabenstein. His Highness now directed the whole of his attention to the necessary preparations for crossing the Elbe, by throwing over a bridge at Roslau, with the corps of Swedes and Russians under his command, and to march to Leipsic.

Napoleon, obstinately bent upon having his favourite plan against Berlin put in execution, and but little dispirited by Marshal Oudinot's miscarriage, fancied that the failure of the first attempt proceeded from the want of good dispositions. He accordingly gave Marshal Ney the command of the 4th, 7th, and 12th corps, and the cavalry under the Duke of Padua; who, since their very recent defeat, had sought protection under the walls of Wittenburg, to collect and organise their remains. Marshal Ney joined his army on the 3rd of September, and on the 4th, he began those offensive operations that served as a prelude to the signal victory of Dennewitz.

In the afternoon of this day General Dobschutz was briskly attacked, by a superior force, near Zahne; but this general defended his position with such bravery and prudence, that the French, after many fruitless attempts to force him, were repulsed, and driven back into their intrenchments near Wittenburg. The whole of the 12th French corps renewed their attack on General Dobschutz, on the 5th, in the morning, and, after a bloody combat, and acts of heroic bravery on the side of the Prussians, they got possession of the position. Upon which, General von Tauenzien was attacked at Seyda, dislodged by superior numbers, and the French occupied the post.

✶✶✶✶✶✶

A young Prussian officer being taken prisoner in the early part of the action, he was conveyed in all haste to the rear, and brought, without any preparatory intimation whatever, into the presence of Napoleon, at Dahme; who, in his usual hurrying manner, first asked him questions, concerning his name, rank in the army, and the regiment to which he belonged, and then abruptly demanded:

"Where is Bernadotte?"

"I do not know such a person," answered the officer,

"Well, well; I mean the Prince of Ponte-Corvo."

"I know just as little about him."

"Bah! where is the Crown Prince of Sweden?"

"O! I know him very well:—he is—I do not know where he is

exactly; but—he is everywhere, I believe—"

Napoleon turned his back on the officer, with a furious frown, and dismissed him.

General Tauenzien was with the Crown Prince of Sweden, on the 5th, at his headquarters at Rabenstein, to be present at a conference held concerning the measures to be adopted. In the evening, on his return to his corps at Seyda, being unacquainted with the result of this affair, he struck into the wrong road, and soon found himself surrounded by parties of the enemy. Firmness and presence of mind saved him. On being challenged by the enemy's patrols, the general and his adjutants represented themselves as Saxon officers of the regiment of Prince Anthony, and were accordingly suffered to pass on unmolested; they happily reached the general's corps, which, together with the advanced-guard, under General von Dobschutz, had in the meantime made a retrograde movement to Jüterbock.

******

The Crown Prince of Sweden occupied, on the 6th, the heights of Lobessen. General von Bülow, upon its being reported to him, that the French Army was in motion, in the direction of Zahne, with his usual promptitude and decision determined on falling upon the rear and left flank of the enemy's army; and in consequence issued orders for his troops to concentrate themselves, near Kurz-Lippsdorf and Kaltenborn. (See Map of the Battle of Dennewiiz.)—In the evening of the 5th, the French corps were drawn up in the vicinity of Naundorf, Seehausen, and Seyda. By break of day, on the 6th, Marshal Ney began his operations. The 4th corps, under Bertrand, marched by the way of Naundorf to Jüterbock; the 7th corps, under Reynier, to Rohrbeck; and the 12th, under Oudinot, towards Oehna. As a feint, the 4th corps was to turn Jüterbock, to mask the march of the two others corps.

The enemy knew nothing of General von Bülow's movement, he having ordered no watch-fires to be lighted during the night. The division Morand, forming the advanced-guard of Bertrand's corps, fell with impetuosity on General von Tauenzien's advanced-guard; but the moment the intentions of the enemy were developed by this attack, General von Bülow put himself in march with his corps, to attack the left flank of the French, reporting his intention to the crown prince, and desiring General von Borstel might be sent, to form his support.

In the meantime, General von Tauenzien bore the brunt of Bertrand's impetuous attempts to force him from his position, and gallantly stood his ground. General von Bülow brought up in haste his artillery, and briskly cannonaded the enemy, to afford General von Tauenzien some advantage from his demonstration; An obstinate conflict, attended with various success, now took place, in the course of which General von Thümen's division stormed the village of Nieder-Gersdorf, and made a great slaughter of the enemy. For four hours the battle raged with indescribable fury. The enemy, driven from Nieder-Gersdorf, still made a most lively resistance. Marshal Ney had sent the 7th corps to support the hard-pressed 4th, and with it menaced Bülow's, right flank.

The great superiority of the enemy's force, particularly of artillery, obliged the divisions of Bülow's right wing to take up a more advantageous position in the rear; and although the reserves were evidently sufficient to preserve the position taken, yet the prospect of being able to act on the offensive was, at this juncture, very doubtful. In this important moment General von Borstel arrived on the ground with his corps.

★★★★★★

That this battle terminated so gloriously for the Prussian arms, and so disastrously to the French, may be attributed in part to the prompt support afforded to General Tauenzien's right wing by the bold movement of General von Borstel. This latter general was in line with the Swedish Army till eleven o'clock a.m. on the 6th, when he received orders to march with his corps of Prussians to Eckmannsdorf; but having had the precaution to send an adjutant forward to Lieutenant-General von Bülow for intelligence, he gained, at this crisis, the important information how necessary the presence of his corps was to support the right of General Tauenzien's position.

And, giving way to the gallant feeling of succouring his brethren in arms, he changed his line of march to Gehlsdorf, sending a report of his movement to the right, to the crown prince, and, happily arriving on the ground at the most dubious period of the conflict, he drew up his troops to the right of General von Kraft's division; and, by an impetuous onset with the bayonet, took Gehlsdorf, and the heights near it, by storm, almost instantaneously ; which bold and prompt attack materially contributed to the ultimate success of this brilliant day.

★★★★★★

This excellent general, by a forced march, and overlooking trivial

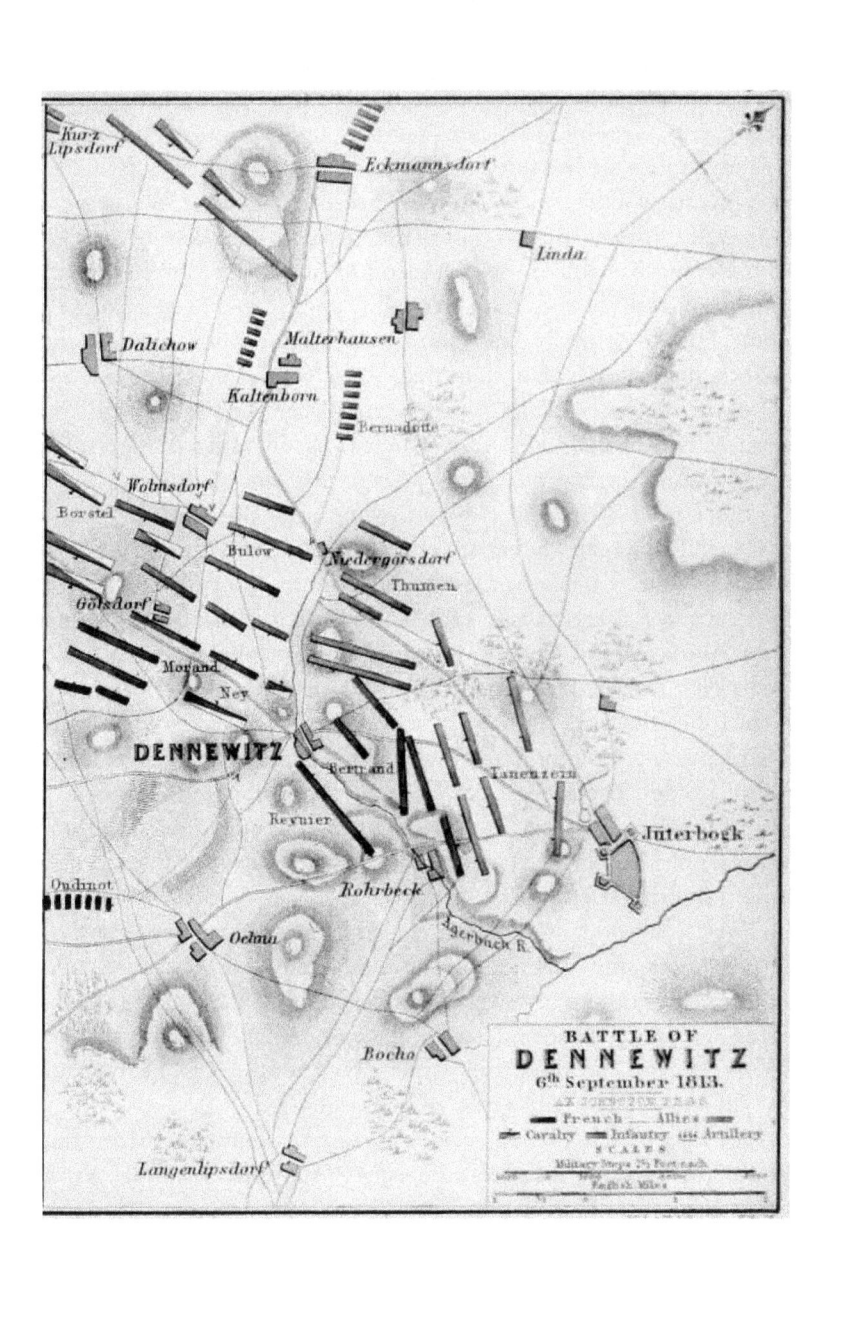

BATTLE OF
DENNEWITZ
6th September 1813.
French ——— Allies
Cavalry ▬ Infantry ⋯ Artillery
SCALES
English Miles

formalities, has, by his vigorous conduct on this occasion, established his fame, and added another name to the list of Prussian worthies. By immediately storming the high grounds to the right of Gehlsdorf, at the head of his brigade, he broke the enemy's line, and paved the way to the glorious conclusion of the Battle of Dennewitz. During these events, General Tauenzien kept firm in his position. A charge of French cavalry was repulsed with heavy loss, and driven upon their own infantry. General von Thümen's brigade forced the enemy upon Dennewitz, which, after an obstinate resistance, was taken by storm.

It was in this manner that the second Prussian corps of Bülow and Tauenzien, with the most rare intrepidity and exalted bravery, kept the whole French Army, 70,000 men strong, in check for several hours, withstood the shock of all their fierce onsets, repulsed their reiterated charges at the point of the bayonet, and placed the crown of victory on the brows of their adored Monarch so firmly, as never more to be wrested from him by any earthly power whatever.

The Crown Prince of Sweden, who, upon the first intelligence of General Tauenzien being attacked, had put himself in march from Lobessen to Eckmannsdorf, now came into action. Four thousand Swedish and Russian cavalry, with horse-artillery, attacked the French corps. At the sight of such numerous reinforcements Marshal Ney immediately beat a retreat, pursued by 70 battalions and 10,000 cavalry, of the Allies, that had not been in action. After the French were driven out of the woods near Dennewitz, their retreat was turned into a complete rout. The French 7th corps first gave way, and drew with it part of the 4th. Marshal Ney led on his reserves into fire, but a panic terror seemed to have seized the whole French Army, and this general could not bring them to stand.

The cavalry of the Confederates charged, with an impetuosity bordering on fury, the horse of the enemy, that covered their retreat, and. broke it entirely. The fugitives rode over their own infantry; the confusion became general, and each sought his individual safety in flight. The 4th corps, and the cavalry under Ney, retreated to Dahme, and the 7th and 12th took the road to Schweidnitz.

The loss of the French, in this battle, was immense. More than 10,000 prisoners, 80 pieces of cannon, 400 tumbrils, 3 pair of colours, and 1 standard, fell into the hands of the victors.

On the 7th General von Wobeser attacked Dahme, carried it, and made 2,500 prisoners. The rest of the French corps fled towards Annaberg.

That heroic example, which the Prussians gave the world on this day, will be handed down to future ages, in the remembrance of every warrior, whose breast glows with the pure flame of patriotism; and will serve to animate, in after-times, all those whose sacred duties may call them to fight for the civic freedom and independence of Germany.

Marshal Ney, with the disorganised wrecks of his army, crossed the Elbe at Torgau, and fixed his headquarters at Eilenburg, on the 9th; and his troops went into cantonments in Leipsic and its vicinity. Here he employed himself till the 25th, in recruiting and reinstating his shattered corps. The Crown Prince of Sweden, with the main body of the Northern Army, moved down the right bank of the Elbe, towards Roslau, where he commanded considerable works to be thrown up, to serve as a *tête de pont* to a bridge, which he intended to throw across the Elbe at that place.

A swarm of Cossacks was sent over the Elbe, towards Dessau and Cöthen. General von Bülow was posted before Wittenburg. The advanced-guard of General Tauenzien occupied Elsterwerda and Hoyerswerda. General Wobeser stood at Falkenburg. The Russian light troops blockaded Torgau, Detachments from the Northern Army now scoured the country in all directions in the rear of the French Grand Army, with constant success. General von Bülow bombarded Wittenburg, in the night of the 25th. Marshal Ney, having at this time recovered from his panic, and foreseeing how pernicious the threatened passage of the Northern Army over the Elbe at Roslau, might prove to the French Grand Army, if it should experience any reverses, now made demonstrations to attack the Grand Army of the Crown Prince, and to destroy the bridge at Roslau; but he was repulsed in several partial affairs, and the month of September ended very honourably to the Swedish arms.

Quitting the Northern Army for the present, we will follow the operations of the Bohemian Army.

The grand Bohemian Army, having derived every advantage from its short breathing-time, soon found itself in a renewed state of vigour, to enter the lists again with Napoleon. Having received reports that Napoleon was in motion towards Silesia, the advanced-guards passed the frontiers, and the light cavalry, on the 5th and 6th, appeared before Dresden. General Count von Wittgenstein arrived, on the 8th, at Dohna. Napoleon made a demonstration towards Bohemia, and General von Wittgenstein retired upon the Grand Army. On the 12th, Napoleon, with a considerable part of his army, was at Bärenstein. It was in vain that the Confederates waited for him with nearly 150,000 men, in the same position which had proved so fatal to Vandamme.

Napoleon appeared irresolute, and drew in his advanced posts; the Allies followed step by step; and he returned to Dresden on the 13th, his army taking the following position towards Bohemia. Count Löbau was posted with the 1st corps at Nollendorf; Marshal St, Cyr occupied the heights of Borna, and the defiles of Fürstenwalde; Marshal Victor stood in position at Altenburg, with the 2nd corps; and Marshal Mortier was in camp at Pirna, with the Young Guards.

It was deemed proper to reconnoitre the whole of the enemy's line on the 14th; and, for this purpose, several corps were pushed on in advance, who succeeded in obtaining some advantages. Napoleon, in judging that the Allies meditated a grand attack, left Dresden on the 15th, and advanced, with his whole disposable force, on the route to Bohemia. On the 17th, he reached Nollendorf; some partial affairs were favourable to the Allied arms, and he was repulsed with Joss, to the heights near that place. It not lying in the plan of operations laid down by the Confederates, to pursue Napoleon through the defiles of the Saxon mountains, he was permitted to retrace his steps to Dresden, where he arrived

Once more on the 21st of September, from his unfortunate expeditions into Bohemia. The proximity of Blücher's army urged him to leave it again on the 22nd; and his return, on the 24th, was accompanied by no laurels, no arrogant bulletin, and no one mark proclaiming the presence of the conqueror of Europe, and "the first captain of the age."

******

Early in the month of October, Napoleon held a council of war at Dresden, at which all his Marshals and Generals of Engineers in the field assisted. After some very unimportant matters had been discussed, he demanded their undisguised opinions on the state of things, the positions of the enemy, and the situation of his army.

They all unanimously gave him the advice to withdraw, with the grand body of his army, behind the barriers of the Rhine, to organise it anew, and then to face the Confederates in the field. On hearing this, Napoleon started up in a rage, vowing that, if they had lost all confidence in him, they might of themselves seek their way back to France; but he should, for his part, find means, in despite of them, to crush the enemy himself.

******

The affairs of the Confederates assumed, at this epoch, the beginning of October, the most favourable aspect at all points; and from their ulterior operations during this month, the most fortunate results might be with confidence expected. A convention was signed, on the 8th of October; between Prince Reuss and General von Wrede, by virtue of which Bavaria made a common cause with the Allied powers; and her powerful co-operation for the independence of Germany, might be daily expected. We hasten, in consequence, to give a detailed description of those military events which will ever render this month memorable in history, and endeavour to facilitate the perception of those stratocratic manoeuvres, that have immortalised the name of Blücher and the august Allies, by stating the exact position of all the Allied Armies on the 1st of October, 1813.

The Grand Bohemian Army was still in its position near Töplitz; some detachments of its light troops had penetrated through the defiles of the mountains into Saxony. General von Bennigsen had arrived with his army, and taken post on the right wing.

The Silesian Army occupied the right bank of the Elbe, from Stolpe to Elsterwerda, and had its advanced-posts close to Dresden. The headquarters were at Elsterwerda.

The Northern Army observed the right bank of the Elbe, from Hertzberg to Zerbst, kept up a direct communication with the Silesian Army, and detached light troops on the left bank of the Elbe.

The French Army was in a manner surrounded and hedged in by these three armies. Napoleon was at Dresden with his guards, and the 1st, 3rd, 5th, 11th, and the shattered remains of the 12th corps of his army. The 2nd corps stood near Freiburg; the 8th, together with the cavalry, under Lefebvre-Desnouettes, near Penig and Altenburg; the cavalry of the Duke of Padua at Leipsic; and the 6th corps was on its march thither, where it arrived on the 2nd of October. Marshal Ney was with the 4th and 7th corps, near Dessau; and Marshal Augereau, who had left Würzburg on the 26th of September, was on his march to Jena, having orders to join the Grand Army with the greatest celerity: his corps was estimated at 16,000 men.

It was easy to perceive that a simultaneous and combined operation, on the part of the Allied Armies, verging to one point, must very shortly produce a decisive blow.

At this important period, the whole of Europe felt within herself a shuddering fear, an anxious state of incertitude, that kept expectation wound up to the highest pitch, and set at nought the issues of cool

Augereau   Napoleon   Lannes   Hegel

TWO PHILOSOPHERS MEET AT JENA

reasoning and deliberate reflection. It was clear to the comprehension of every man, that a mighty conflict, at once decisive and destructive, must be approaching. The Teutonic nation, miserable and oppressed, disgraced in their honour, and humiliated in their name, longed for the hour of retribution, and consequent liberty, that they might return to the enjoyment of those happy times, when, blessed with independence, no foreign foe dared attempt to rob them of their birthrights.

The prior events of this campaign had caused a considerable agitation in the minds of the people in Germany. Patriotic zeal had bloomed afresh, and the ancient deadly hate towards the French had taken deeper root than ever: sources from whence that enthusiasm mainly sprung, which proved so disastrous, in its effects, to the fortunes of the cruel and unrelenting despot on the plains of Leipsic.

The forces of the Confederates, by the arrival of General Bennigsen with the Polish-Russian Army of 40,000 men, had been considerably augmented, and the plan of the Allies, of crossing the Elbe with their several armies in conjunction, could now be carried into execution.

Bennigsen could occupy Prince Schwartzenberg's position in Bohemia, and the latter march his army into Saxony in the direction of Leipsic, to form a junction with Blücher and the crown prince, who were to come from the right bank of the Elbe; and, by this combined manoeuvre, converge the whole mass of their effective strength in the rear of the French Army, and thus compel Napoleon to quit his strong position at Dresden, and constrain him to a general decisive battle.

A more daring promptness, vigour, and alacrity, in carrying on an operation with an army, than our bold, enterprising hero showed, when effecting his passage over the Elbe, were surely never exhibited in any former exploits of the like nature.

General von Blücher, at the head of the gallant Silesian Army, broke up from Elsterwerda and its vicinity, on the 1st of October, and was the first to Commence offensive operations, by a sudden, rapid, and unexpected march, that completely confounded the enemy. After leaving the two corps of Generals Count Bubna and Prince Czerbatow, before Dresden, he reached Herzberg on the 1st of October, and Jessen on the 2nd, with his whole army.

Though clogged with the conveyance of two bridges of pontoons, he marched with such astonishing rapidity, as to reach Elster, a village situated between Annaburgh and Wittenberg, near the confluence of the River Elster with the Elbe, on the evening of the 2nd, and succeeded in throwing two bridges of pontoons over the Elbe the same night, in the face of the enemy; and early in the morning of the 3rd, the Silesian Army began to defile over them. (See Map of the Battle of Dennewitz.)—General Count Bertrand, who had departed from Dessau in the night of the 1st of October, had already taken up an almost impregnable position, with about 20,000 men, near Wartenberg, on the left bank of the Elbe.

The corps of General von York was the first to pass the bridges, and they soon encountered the enemy, who in vain endeavoured to prevent or obstruct their deploying over. Prince Charles of Mecklenburg was detached, by General von Blücher, to turn the enemy's right flank, in the direction of Bleddin; during which operation, Blücher himself attacked the front of the enemy's position. Prince Charles had a warm affair, and the French retarded his advance nearly two hours; but the village of Bleddin was stormed, and the enemy driven from his position.

At two o'clock, p. m. the Silesian Army had gained a complete victory, although only von York's corps had come into fire, the Russian troops having followed later, and been drawn up as reserve. The enemy fled towards Kemberg and Wittenberg, and was hotly pursued, sword in hand, at all points. The trophies consisted of 11 pieces of artillery, 50 tumbrils, and above 1,000 prisoners. In consequence of this fortunate combat, General von Blücher moved his headquarters to Düben on the 5th of October.

★★★★★★

Blücher received, soon after this victory, the following autograph letter from his sovereign:

Töplitz, Oct. 8, 1813.

General von Blücher,

The manner in which you have forced the passage of the 1st *corps d'armée* over the Elbe, and the advantages you have gained over the enemy near Wartenberg, have exalted your fame still higher, and laid fresh claims to my thanks. In expressing them to you, I add the wish that you may therein find the greatest proof of my satisfaction, combined with my intention of making them publicly known to you.

Frederick William.

★★★★★★

No sooner had the news of this grand movement of Blücher's reached the headquarters of the Crown Prince of Sweden, than, with a readiness that reflects upon him great honour, and solely bent on a powerful and immediate co-operation, he marched the whole Northern Army, under his command, over the Elbe at Roslau and Acken, on the 4th and 5th of October. Several other corps passed the Elbe at this period. General Count Tauenzien marched to Halle. The crown prince took up his headquarters at Dessau, and pushing forward his advanced-posts to Raguhn and Jesnitz, opened a communication with Blücher's army; and on the 7th, the crown prince and General von Blücher formed a junction with Prince William of Prussia, at Mühlbeck, on the Mulda.

The joint forces of the two armies, amounting to 125,000 men, had taken a firm footing on the left bank of the Elbe. None but the most active measures were now adopted. In the interim, Napoleon had left Dresden, marched on the 9th to Eilenburg, and on the 10th, to Düben; he seemed to have the intention of attacking the Silesian Army, and to entertain hopes of meeting it singly in the field; but our veteran general had foreseen his movements, and, in conjunction with the crown prince, left his position on the Mulda, marched onwards, and passed the Saale. The Silesian Army marched to Halle, and the Northern Army to Rothenburg and Bernburg.

The crown prince ordered General von Tauenzien to proceed to Dessau, to observe the passage of the Mulda, to cover the bridge at Roslau, and, if necessary, to collect all the detachments on the right bank of the Elbe, and, according to circumstances, to cover the marches of Brandenburg from the enemy. This corps concentrated itself at Dessau on the 10th of October, and the general pushed his advanced-posts to Oranienbaum and Wörlitz.

This bold march of the Silesian Army astonished Napoleon; nay, it almost confounded him: he little expected such manoeuvres, so well-conceived, and a combination of movements, however complex in appearance, yet so simplified in their rapid execution. He found the two armies drawn up in battle array on the Saale, and wisely desisted from any attack.

Frustrated in his plan of fighting Blücher separately, Napoleon seems to have suddenly changed his line of operations, and to have intended making Magdeburg the centre of his ulterior enterprises. To follow out this plan, General Reynier was ordered to march to Wittenberg, and to act on the right bank of the Elbe; and Marshal Ney was to proceed to Dessau, and occupy that place. These movements were executed on the 11th of October. General Count von

Tauenzien, on the first report of these events, felt, very strongly, the possibility of his being attacked by superior numbers, and therefore determined to withdraw over the Elbe, to call in all detachments, and, in conjunction with General von Thümen before Wittenberg, take up a defensive position to cover Berlin.

After some partial affairs with the enemy, the two generals marched to Zerbst on the 12th, and from thence to Potsdam; in the meantime, General Reynier, with the 7th corps, had only made a demonstration, and had returned to Wittenberg. This operation, however, of Napoleon, at the moment, induced the Crown Prince of Sweden to suppose that he had the intention of throwing himself towards Magdeburg, in the direction of Wittenberg, down the right bank of the Elbe; and to paralyze, as much as possible, the effects of this manoeuvre, His Highness made his army repass the Saale, and march towards Cöthen.

This was a very judicious step, and proclaimed the military talents and penetration of the crown prince in a very eminent degree, forming a striking contrast to those tardy, vacillating measures that, subsequently, in so unaccountable a manner, directed the operations of the Swedish Army: for, if Napoleon really intended to reach Magdeburg by the way of Wittenberg, the crown prince could thus encounter him at Zerbst, and force him, to give up his plan, or else to fight; in which case the Silesian Army might act with success in Napoleon's rear. Early on the 14th, the 7th French corps was at Wittenberg; the 3rd, at Dessau; the 6th, at Delitsch; and the imperial guards at Düben.

In direct opposition, however, to all these seeming intentions of reaching Magdeburg, Napoleon, on this day, caused all his *corps d'armeé* to face about, and, by forced marches, to direct their route to Leipsic, where he arrived at noon the same day with his guards, taking up his quarters at Reudnitz, a short distance from that place.

******

On the 14th of October, Napoleon took up his headquarters at the country-house of a banker of Leipsic, at Reudnitz, near that place. The apartment he occupied was hung round with a few excellent English prints, representing some of the last melancholy scenes of the life of the unfortunate Lewis XVI. The prints must have arrested his attention; and what an impression must they not have made upon him! what serious reflections must they not have created in his mind! The same throne from which he had shaken half the governments of Europe to their foundations, was stained with the blood of him who here, in the last moments of his sufferings, seemed to remind him how fleeting and evanescent is human greatness. No blood, unjustly shed, filled *him* with remorse in the hour of death, who was once beloved to enthusiasm by the same people now groaning under Napoleon's iron sceptre.

To have observed the emotions of this gloomy man, when he glanced his eye over these mementoes of fallen, degraded majesty, might, to many, have been invaluable ; and it may be presumed that these faint resemblances of the departed victims of popular fury made a deeper-impression on the tyrant than the hosts of vengeance-breathing adversaries that then surrounded him,

******

The sound policy of this march is ever to be doubted, and it will always remain a problem why Napoleon did not prefer the fine position behind the Saale, so easily in his power to take, rather than, by marching to Leipsic, suffer himself to be surrounded by the Allied Armies, and no choice left him but to give battle whenever the Confederates pleased. The crown prince marched his army to Halle on the 15th, and General von Blücher advanced the same day, with the Silesian Army, to Skeuditz.

We will now turn our attention to the proceedings of the grand Bohemian Army, since the 1st of October, that our readers may be prepared to form a clear idea of that unequalled scene which was preparing to be acted on the wide field of carnage around the city of Leipsic.

The grand Bohemian Army had put itself in motion in the beginning of October, and, in the direction of Commotau, proceeded in several heavy columns to Saxony. Prince Schwartzenberg left Töplitz on the 4th of October, and arrived at Marienburg on the 5th. The Emperor of Russia, the Emperor of Austria, and the King of Prussia, likewise followed the route of the Grand Army.

On the 5th of October it occupied the following positions : the Austrian Field-Marshal Crenneville was posted, with the light troops, at Zweckau; General Meerveldt's corps at Marienburg; General Klenau's corps at Chemnitz; the Russian and Prussian corps, under General Barclay de Tolly, and the reserves under the Grand Duke Constantin, stood likewise in position near Zweckau; General von Bennigsen, and Count Colloredo, with their several corps, reoccupied the positions of the Grand Army near Töplitz. It being known that

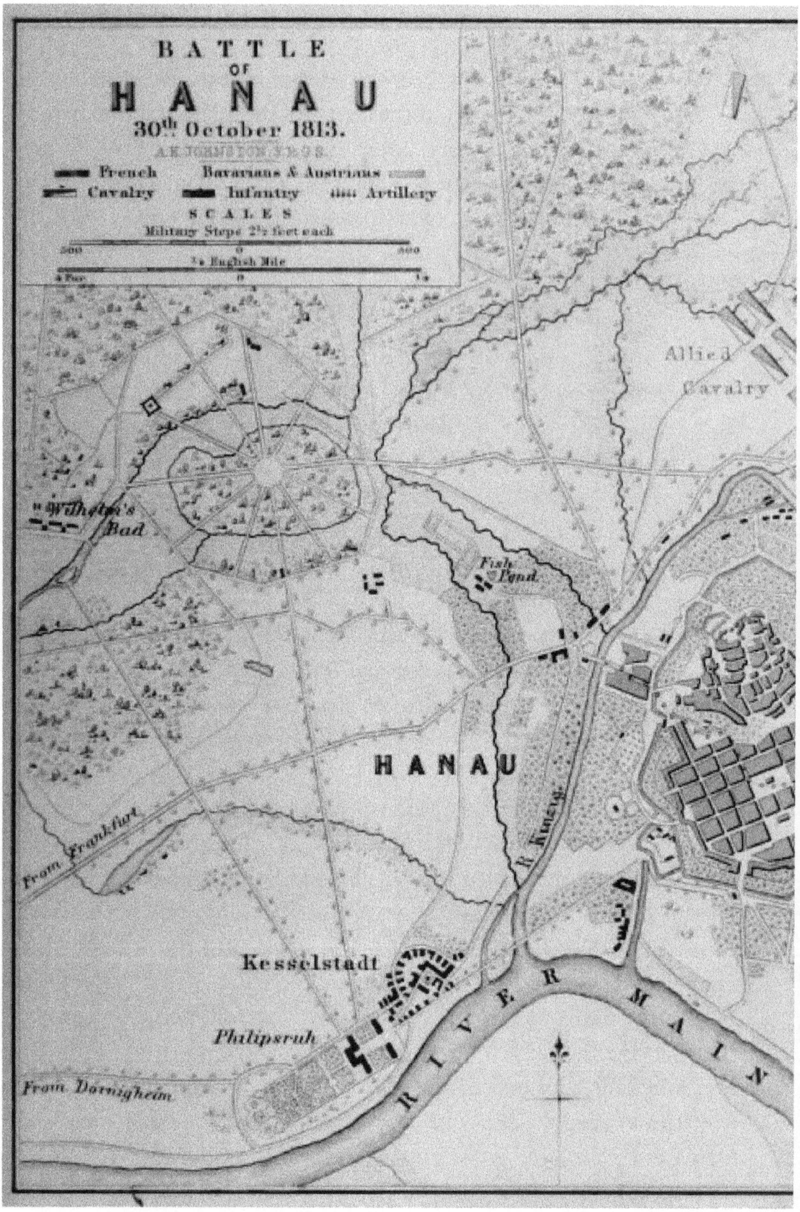

BATTLE OF HANAU
30th October 1813.
French
Bavarians & Austrians
Cavalry
Infantry
Artillery
SCALES
Allied Cavalry
Wilhelm's Bad
Fish Pond
HANAU
R. Kinzig
From Frankfurt
Kesselstadt
Philipsruh
From Dornigheim
RIVER MAIN

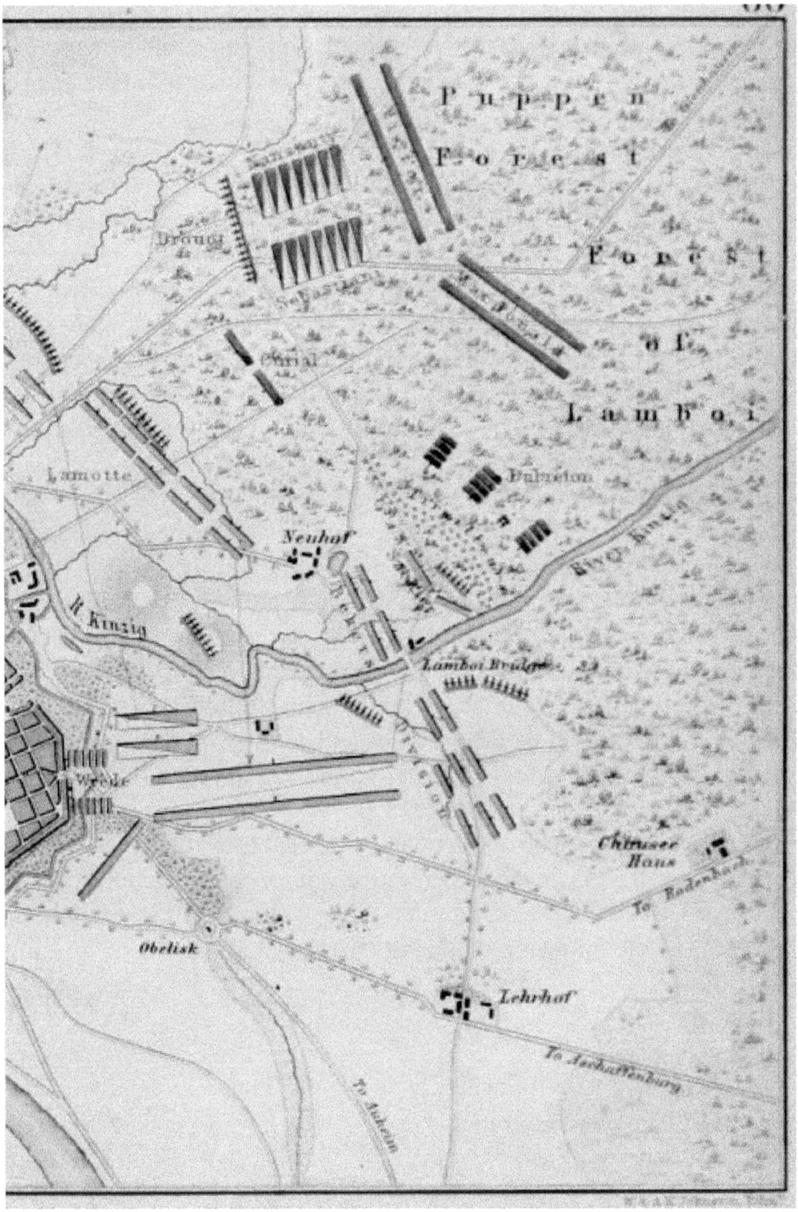

Puppen Forest
Forest of Lamboi
Lamotte
Neuhof
R. Kinzig
River Kinzig
Obelisk
Lehrhof
To Aschaffenburg

Napoleon was still in Dresden with the major part of his army, this precaution was indispensably necessary to cover Bohemia from any irruption on this side.

General Prince von Lichstenstein was ordered, with a corps of light troops, to advance, by the way of Eger, Hof, and Schleitz, and, in co-operation with General Thieleman, to retard the march of Augereau's corps upon Leipsic.

Some partial engagements took place by the advance of the several corps during the 6th. General Count Wittgenstein marched with his corps, on the 7th, to Altenburg; and General Klenau ordered General Mohr to occupy Penig, which, after a smart action with the enemy, was taken possession of. The headquarters of the commander-in-chief, Prince Schwartzenberg, were transferred to Chemnitz on the 8th. The advanced-guard of General Mohr drove the French from the heights near Penig, and forced them to fall back upon Rochlitz on the 9th. General Count Platow scoured the country in the vicinity of Leipsic, and endeavoured to open a communication with the crown prince.

The offensive movements of the Allied powers, now undertaken on a scale bold, grand, and energetic, are not, perhaps, to be equalled by any military operations recorded in modern history. The Confederates, by their execution, exposed their richest provinces to the inroads of the enemy, and, by attempting to throw themselves between Napoleon and France, left close in their rear an army of 200,000 men, headed by an enterprising military genius, and a number of strong holds well garrisoned, while they themselves had no fortified place to serve them as a rallying point, or as a position to rest upon.

******

According to dispatches, which afterwards fell into the hands of the Confederates, it appears, from the muster-master-general's return, that the French Army, prior to the Battle of Leipsic, consisted of the following corps and effective numbers:

			Men
Old guards			4,000
Young Guards			24,000
Cavalry of the guards			6,000
1st *Corps d'armée*—Mouton-Löbau			6,000
2nd	"	Victor	18,000
3rd	"	Ney	22,000
4th	"	Bertrand	14,000
5th	"	Lauriston	10,000

6th	"	Marmont	20,000
7th *Corps d'armée*—Reynier			8,000
8th	"	Poniatowsky	10,000
11th	"	Macdonald	14,000
14th	"	Gouvion St. Cyr	20,000
"	"	Augereau	10,000
1st Division of cavalry—Latour-Maubourg			6,000
2nd	"	Sebastiani	6,000
3rd	"	Padua	3,000
4th	"	Valmy	4,000
5th	"	Milhaud	3,000
			208,000

The 1st and 14th corps remained in Dresden.

The Confederate Army, at this period, has been estimated as follows:

	Men
1. Grand Army, under Schwartzenberg	140,000
2. Northern Army, under the Crown Prince	50,000
3. Silesian Army, under Blücher	50,000
4. Russian-Polish Army, under Bennigsen	40,000
	280,000

★★★★★★

But the superiority of numbers which the Allies now possessed, the glow of patriotism that pervaded the country into which they had entered, and an unbounded confidence in themselves, placed them out of all danger, as to the consequences, however exceptionable such measures might be, when judged by military rules. Napoleon, meanwhile, hastily left Dresden, with the King of Saxony, on the 7th, to prevent his being completely cut off; and arrived at Wurzen on the 8th, accompanied by the 3rd, 5th, and 11th corps, and his guards. To mask, in some measure, his march, Marshal Macdonald, with a small corps, attacked General Bubna near Stolpen, but was repulsed with loss. On the 8th, General Bubna pursued his advantages, and stormed the *tête de pont* at Pirna.

On the 9th, the advanced-guards of the grand Bohemian Army drove back the enemy at different points, near Mittweyda and Walheim, and took a number of prisoners.

General Prince, von Lichtenstein, in conjunction with General Thieleman, attacked Augereau on the 10th, near Naumburg; and, after an obstinate conflict, in which the French lost 1,500 men, the Allies were, at last, obliged to yield to the superiority of numbers, and to retreat to Zeitz.

The advanced-guard of General Count Wittgenstein, under the command of General Count Pahlen, had a warm affair on the 10th with the cavalry of Marshal Murat. The latter made a vigorous resistance, but was, at the close of the affair, taken in flank, and obliged to fall back to the advantageous position of Eylau.

The grand Bohemian Army, during these events, made progressive advances. Prince Schwartzenberg's headquarters were removed to Altenburg on the 11th; General Count Wittgenstein and Lieutenant-General von Kleist were at Borna, and Count Bubna at Pillnitz. The general of artillery, Count von Giulay, marched, on the 12th, with his corps, to Weissenfels, surprised Naumburg on the night of the 12th, made a number of prisoners, and liberated 8 officers and 150 men, which the French had taken in the affair at Wethau on the 10th.

The advanced-guards of Generals Count Wittgenstein and Klenau were engaged in several warm, attacks on the 12th and 13th, repulsed the enemy, and took from him 800 prisoners; pending which, the Grand Confederate Army advanced upon Leipsic, narrowing, at every step, its circle of operations.

It being held highly important, under the present circumstances, that the commander-in-chief, Prince Schwartzenberg, should know the exact strength of the enemy, General Count Wittgenstein was ordered, on the 14th, in combination with General Count Klenau, to reconnoitre the enemy's positions. The French had evacuated Gröbern and Gossa early in the morning, showing themselves in great force on the heights of Wachau and Liebertwolkwitz. As soon as the advanced-guard, under General Count Pahlen, supported by General Wittgenstein's cavalry, had penetrated beyond Gröbern and Gossa, the Russian horse-artillery cannonaded the enemy's masses of infantry with great effect; the Allied infantry following, drawn up in echelons.

General Count Klenau directed his march to Liebertwolkwitz; and, on finding the enemy had thrown a considerable body of infantry into the place, he stormed it at the head of the Archduke Charles's regiment.

******

It seems very probable that Napoleon, on the 14th of October, was taken by surprise through the offensive operations of the Confederates from the side of Liebertwolkwitz. He was at his bivouac, near the gallows, not far from Leipsic, when he ordered one of his adjutants to inquire of a Saxon officer, in what part of the country the terrain of the field of battle lay. The Saxon officer having given in his details, he was again asked to be very particular and exact in his description, as the emperor was anxious for information on which he could depend.

★★★★★★

The enemy, in consequence drew up their cavalry, near 8,000 strong, into a solid, compact body of great depth, supported by a numerous and heavy artillery, and were led to the charge by Marshal Murat in person.

★★★★★★

It is almost needless to observe, that much has already been before the public concerning the origin of Murat; but whether well-founded or otherwise, we will not determine; we shall content ourselves with stating that, from sources, the authenticity of which we have no reason to doubt, it has been ascertained that Murat is the son of a very rich landholder in Provence, and was sent by his father to Toulouse to study theology, being intended for the church.

Young Murat, early and deeply imbued with an attachment to military studies, devoted the occasional leisure afforded him, during his residence in Toulouse, to the cultivation of the art of war. After regularly finishing his theological studies, he, it seems, entered, without his father's consent, as a common soldier, in the Ardenne rifle-corps. In the year 1792, we find him a lieutenant in the constitutional guards of Louis XVI. which were soon after disbanded. And in 1793 he served in the Army of the West as a violent republican, against the Royalists; from which period Fortune has been unusually lavish towards him in the distribution of her fickle favours.

★★★★★★

The first lines of Count Pahlen's cavalry were obliged to give way to such superior numbers, and a furious and bloody conflict with cavalry ensued on the plains of Wachau. The Russian horse, in their usual brilliant style, charged the enemy on all sides, and repulsed him. The French cavalry rallied four times, returning each time with redoubled fury to the charge; but the Prussian *cuirassiers* and dragoons, under General Klenau, with conspicuous bravery resisted their impetuous attacks, repulsed them, and finally put them to the rout. Five hundred of the enemy lay dead on the field of battle; and several hundred prisoners fell into the hands of the victors.

General Count Wittgenstein, having now gained certain information that the 2nd, 5th, 8th, and Augereau's corps, under the immediate command of Marshal Murat, were in the field before him, ceased all further attacks, and a heavy cannonade was now kept up till night was far advanced.

Prince Schwartzenberg's headquarters were transferred to Pegau on the 15th of October, and the Austrian Army likewise advanced in the same direction.

These positions of the respective armies rendered a battle inevitable; and it was resolved upon, at the headquarters of the Confederates, that the general attack should be made on the morrow.—(See Map of the Battle of Leipsic.)

To present a faithful and striking picture of this gigantic battle of nations, fought in the environs of Leipsic, may be accounted the most difficult task that ever was imposed upon a writer. This mighty conflict seeks in vain for its equal in history; its political consequences will extend through remote ages; and all the dreadful evils that had been engendered out of the detested French revolution, and the diffusion of Jacobin principles, during a period of twenty-five years, were, at one blow, reduced to nothing.

Chapter 9

Battle of Leipsic

Our veteran general, at the head of the Silesian Army, left his position near Skeuditz, early on the 16th, to attack the enemy posted at Möckern. Marshal Marmont, with the 6th corps, occupied the position of Möckern and Eutritsch, having strong detachments at Lindenthal and Radefeld.

★★★★★★

During the first week in October, Marshal Marmont had taken up his quarters at the country-seat of ———, at Schönfeld, near Leipsic. The sergeant, who one day commanded the guard before the house, had, by his insinuating address, gained the confidence of the steward left in charge of the premises, to whom he appeared an amiable, well-informed young man. In the course of a conversation with him, he gave him to understand that his parents were people of substance in Marseilles, and he was a student at the university, when the strict enforcing of the conscription-laws had obliged him to march, although his father had already paid for a substitute.

He had devoted his time, he said, to the arts and sciences; but, like many thousands of his countrymen, had been compelled at last to make a campaign. "Ah, thus we are treated by our emperor!—thus we are driven to be slaughtered by his insatiable ambition!" he exclaimed in a tone of despair—"How often have I not sustained hunger! what privations and fatigue have I not endured!" A long string of degrading epithets against Napoleon then followed with great volubility. The apparent frankness of his heart, and his youth, excited pity; and he was kindly treated with wine and a hearty meal by the good-natured, unsuspecting steward.

BLÜCHER ON HIS WAY TO LEIPZIG

The next morning early, the marshal left the house with his suite. Soon after, the whole of the poultry was missed from the yard; not a hen was left. In the course of the day, the marshal happened to return, with his troops, to the neighbourhood, and sent one of his adjutants to bespeak a good dinner at his old quarters. The robbery was immediately pleaded as an excuse for the impossibility of serving the table with poultry to the French taste.

Marshal Marmont seemed much exasperated that such delicacies should have escaped him, and ordered the guard of the day before to be searched, when, lo! seven of the purloined cocks and hens were found, without their heads, in the possession of this young student of the arts and sciences. He received a sound flogging; and was placed at the gate, with a sentinel over him, for three hours, exposed to the taunts and bitter jokes of his comrades.

If every criminal and act of this kind in the French Army had received such a punishment, that, and the whole army of the Confederates together, had hardly furnished sentinels in sufficient number,

★★★★★★

Marshal Ney, with the 3rd corps, had stood on the right wing of the 6th corps as a support; but observing, at ten o'clock, a. m. that no enemy appeared on this side, he had marched his corps off the ground in the direction of Cönnewitz. General von York advanced on the road from Skeuditz to Leipsic, and General Langeron took the route of Landsberg to the same place; General von Sacken followed with the reserves. On General Langeron approaching Radefeld, he fell in with the enemy at Freyroda; and after a sharp engagement drove them out of both places, continuing his march to Gross-Wetteritsch, by the way of Breitenfeld. General von York pushed forwards his light troops, close to the River Elster, and dislodged the enemy, after a feeble resistance, from the villages of Stameln and Wahren; during which, General von York marched, with the main body of his corps, to Lindenthal, carried the village, and drove the enemy towards Leipsic.

Between Eutritsch and Möckern, General von York encountered Marmont's army, drawn up in order of battle. General von Blücher ordered an immediate attack, about two o'clock, p. m.; and a warm contest ensued. Marshal Marmont supported his infantry by a battery of forty pieces of artillery, and General von York's whole corps came into fire; pending which, General Langeron, upon the left wing, had taken, lost, and retaken, alternately, the villages of Gross and Klein Wetteritsch, and Marshal Ney had advanced again in support. The combat having continued for some time with dubious fortune, General von Blücher caused the reserves under General von Sacken to come into line; but before they could arrive on the ground, the two gallant corps already engaged had decided the day.

The enemy were completely beaten near Möckern, driven out of this village, and compelled to quit every point of their position; the Allied cavalry broke into their masses of infantry, and sorely pressed them as far as Eutritsch and Gorlis, when night put an end to the pursuit. Marshal Ney had arrived as support, but came too late to renew the battle with any prospect of success; and, as General Langeron pushed on with vigour from Wetteritsch, Marshals Ney and Marmont caused their two corps to cross the River Partha at Schönfeld, leaving the villages of Gohlis, Eutritsch, and Mockau but weakly occupied, and taking up their headquarters at the manor-house of Schönfeld.

The Duke of Padua and General Dombrowsky had withdrawn their corps to Pfaffendorf, and a part of their troops occupied the suburbs of Leipsic. The trophies that fell into the hands of the dauntless Silesian Army on this day, consisted of 1 eagle, 2 standards, 43 pieces of cannon, 30 tumbrils, and above 2,000 prisoners. It was at a critical moment of this battle that the brave General von York put himself at the head of his cavalry, and rushing, with the overwhelming force of an imprisoned flood, upon the enemy's battery, charged and carried it, taking thirty pieces of artillery, with all their appendages, in the space of a few minutes. The invincible courage and intrepidity of the Prussian cavalry were never more eminently displayed than on this day.

The conflict was murderous in the extreme; but the advantages, so dearly purchased, paved the way to that victory of victories which afterwards crowned the Allied arms on the plains of Leipsic. General von Blücher's headquarters were, on the 17th, at Lindenthal, near Breitenfeld; General Langeron made a movement with his corps towards the right wing of the enemy, drawn up in the rear of Eutritsch.

There being every reason to suppose that the Silesian Army, in having so closely pressed upon the enemy's line, would be attacked in the course of this day by the united strength of Marmont's and Ney's corps, aided by reinforcements, the Crown Prince of Sweden was urged to hasten his march from Landsberg to Breitenfeld, to serve as a support. The Northern Army, in consequence, formed a junction with the left wing of the Silesian Army, late in the evening of the 17th.

******

The Northern Army, under the command of the Crown Prince of Sweden, had marched, in the morning of the 17th, from its position near Landsberg, and bivouacked at noon on the heights of Breitenfeld. It was pretty generally known at headquarters, that, when the Confederates resolved to renew the attack on the positions of Napoleon, near Leipsic, on the 18th, the Crown Prince of Sweden was adverse to the measure, and started many difficulties and objections. On this coming to the ears of our veteran General von Blücher, feeling anxious for the events of the day, he determined to talk to the prince himself, and therefore entreated Prince William of Prussia to accompany him to the crown prince, as he spoke no French, and understood the language but imperfectly. Accordingly, very early in the morning of the 18th, they proceeded to His Royal Highness's headquarters, at Breitenfeld.

Upon Prince William's opening the object of their visit, mentioning that the attack must at all events take place, and General Blücher's wish for his powerful and decisive co-operation; the crown prince, in a hurried and hasty tone, exclaimed:

"Do but consider that you have to act against the ferocious untameable spirit of a tiger! Reflect, that it is with Napoleon you enter the lists, who has never as yet lost a battle!"

Our veteran eagerly inquired what the prince said, and, on being informed, replied in his usual firm manner:—"Tell His Highness I shall attack the enemy wherever I find him, this morning, and shall beat him too; let who will support me. Delay is all we have to fear. Indecision can alone undo us."

The crown prince, however, still continued to state and repeat his difficulties and doubts: upon which Prince William of Prussia declared, in the name of the Allies, "That although they could not prevent His Highness from adopting those measures which he might judge most favourable to the issue of the campaign; yet, as the general attack was determined upon, they should, on his refusal to co-operate in this momentous hour, be obliged to leave His Highness no other troops to command than his own Swedes"

Hereupon the crown prince, with much warmth, replied:— "What is it you mean? How am I to construe this language?

Napoleon himself never dared to utter such abrupt remarks towards me, as Marshal of France, which Your Highness now thinks proper to make to me, as Crown Prince of Sweden."

Blücher, on these observations being explained to him, rejoined, with evident irritation and impatience:—"If His Highness is afraid—if he does not think himself strong enough, I'll let him have Longeron's corps (which he actually did); but by G— I shall make a greater impression on the foe, with my handful of men, than the prince, as I see, will with his tens of thousands. Procrastination will play the devil with us. Here, I observe, we may lose time. Let us be gone." As Blücher spoke these last words, the cannonade of the Bohemian Army was distinctly heard. The crown prince did attack, but his artillery was, by his tardy movements, still too much in the rear to be up in tune. (Related to the editor by Baron von K—n.)

✶✶✶✶✶✶

Lieutenant-General Wassiltschikoff, with a body of Cossacks and four regiments of cavalry, menaced the enemy's line between Eutritsch and Schönfeld; a heavy cannonade ensued; and the French having drawn up their cavalry on their right wing, they were instantly charged sword in hand, and driven with irresistible impetuosity into the rear of their own infantry, from whence they fled as far as the suburbs of Leipsic. Here they were overtaken, the major part of them cut in pieces, and the rest made prisoners. The enemy's masses of infantry remained immoveable, during this brilliant and bold attack in their rear, and only kept up an irregular cannonade.

The Prussian hussars brought back their prisoners and five pieces of artillery, in safety, to the main body, though galled in their retreat by a heavy fire of musketry. The enemy then made a retrograde movement behind the Partha, drawing themselves closer round the city of Leipsic. Thus, even the events of the 17th proved glorious to the Silesian Army. We will now revert to the operations of the Grand Army of the Confederates since the 15th.

The commander-in-chief, Prince Schwartzenberg, issued, on the 15th of October, the following order of the day to his troops, from his headquarters at Pegau:

> Brave warriors! The most important epoch of this sacred struggle is arrived. The decisive hour is striking: prepare for the fight! That tie which binds puissant nations together for one and the

same object, will be drawn closer on the field of battle. Russians! Prussians! Austrians! you combat for the same cause, you combat for the liberty of Europe, for the independence of your country, for the honour and immortality of your name.

One for all! All for one! Let this be your rallying cry, when rushing to battle. Be faithful to it in the decisive moment, and victory is yours.

Charles,
Prince of Schwartzenberg,
Field-Marshal.

This energetic appeal could not fail of exciting the greatest enthusiasm in the army, which eventually gave victory to the Allied arms, and liberty and independence to the Teutonic nation.

On the morning of the 16th, the Confederate Army took up the following positions: (See Map of the Battle of Leipsic.)

The 3rd Austrian corps, under the command of General Count Giulay, was posted on the left bank of the Elster, near Klein-Zschocher, and had orders to attack the 4th French corps, stationed near Lindenau.

The 2nd Austrian corps, under the command of General Count Meerveldt, was placed on the left bank of the Pleisse, having orders to force the passage of this river, in the rear of the enemy's right wing.

The Austrian reserves, under the command of the Hereditary Prince of Hesse-Homburg, were drawn up between the Pleisse and the Elster, near Zobigker and Prödel.

The Russian *corps d'armée* under the command of General Count von Wittgenstein, in conjunction with the first Prussian corps, under General von Kleist, took a position in the direction of Gröbern, Gossa, and Störmthal. The left wing of this combined corps was posted in the rear of the village of Gröbern, under the immediate orders of General von Kleist. Two divisions formed the centre, posted behind Gossa; and two divisions of Russian grenadiers, under General von Rajewsky, were drawn up as reserves in their rear.

The 4th Austrian corps, under the command of General Count Klenau, with a brigade of Prussians, under General von Ziethen, formed the right wing, and occupied Gross-Pössna. Those fine corps of Russian and Prussian guards, both foot and horse, with three divisions of Russian *cuirassiers*, formed the reserves of the whole Grand Army, and were drawn up near Magdeborn; the cavalry under the

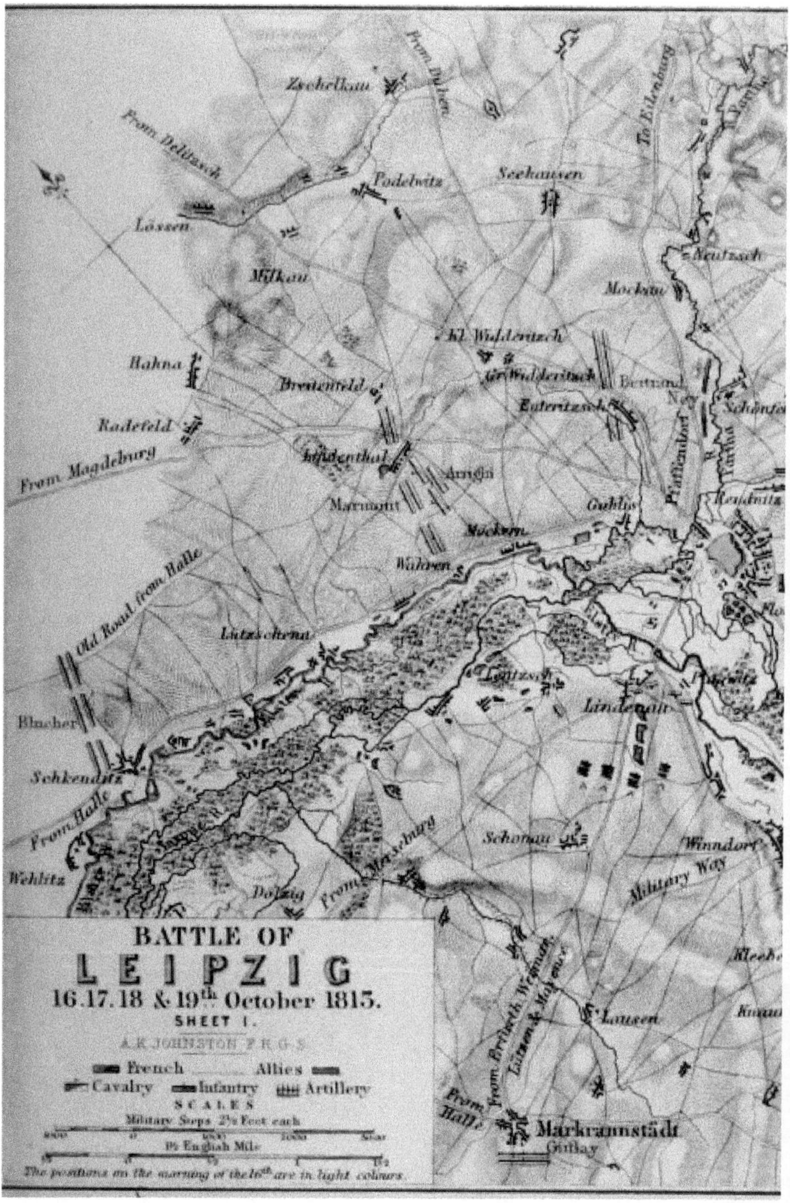

BATTLE OF
LEIPZIG
16.17.18 & 19th October 1813.
SHEET I.
A.K. JOHNSTON F.R.G.S.
French
Allies
Cavalry
Infantry
Artillery
SCALES
Military Steps 2½ Feet each
1½ English Mile
The positions on the morning of the 16th are in light colours.
Zschelkau
From Düben
From Delitzsch
Podelwitz
Seehausen
To Eilenburg
Lössen
Mölkau
Neutzsch
Mockau
Kl. Widderitzsch
Gr. Widderitzsch
Hahna
Breitenfeld
Bertrand
Radefeld
Euteritzsch
From Magdeburg
Lindenthal
Arrighi
Marmont
Gohlis
Möckern
Wahren
Old Road from Halle
Lützschena
Lindenau
Blücher
Schkeuditz
From Halle
Schönau
Windorf
Wehlitz
From Merseburg
Dölzig
Military Way
Lausen
From Halle
Märkranstädt
Giulay

Taucha
Tancha
Sommerfeld
Paunsdorf
Sebastiani
Sellershausen
Stuntz
Stötteritz
Guards
Probstheyda
Thonberg
LEIPZIG
Kellermann
Holzhausen
Zuckelhausen
NAPOLEON
Lauriston
Galgenberg
Wachau
Liebertwolkwitz
Kolm Berg
Seyffertshayn
Fuchshayn
Gr. Pösnau
Threna
To Rochlitz
Pahlen
Gossa
Mark Kleeberg
Crostewitz
Gruberm
Magdeborn
Russian and Prussian Guards
To Borna
Gaschwitz
Deuben
Rotha
Bohlen
Zeschwitz
Meerfeldt
Zwenkau
To Pegau
Engelsdorf
Kl. Pössenau
Albrechtshayn

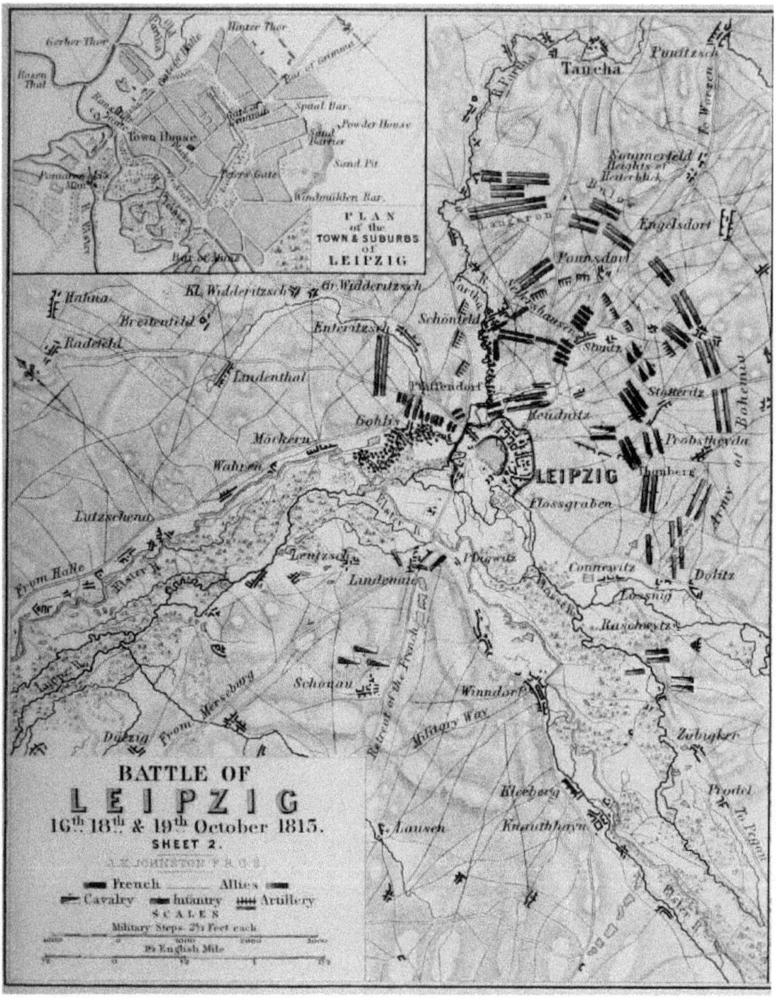

PLAN of the TOWN & SUBURBS of LEIPZIG
Gerber Thor
Hinter Thor
Town House
Spital Bar.
Powder House
Sand Pit
Peters Gate
Windmühlen Bar.
Tancha
Paunitzsch
Sommerfeld
Heights of Heiterblick
Engelsdorf
Paunsdorf
Kl. Widderitzsch
Gr. Widderitzsch
Hohna
Breitenfeld
Radefeld
Lindenthal
Euteritzsch
Schönfeld
Pfaffendorf
Gohlis
Möckern
Wahren
Reudnitz
Stötteritz
Probstheyda
LEIPZIG
Flossgraben
Army of Bohemia
Lutzschena
From Halle
Elster R.
Leutzsch
Lindenau
Plagwitz
Connewitz
Dölitz
Lössnig
Raschwitz
Schönau
Winndorf
Military Way
Retreat of the French
From Merseburg
Zobigker
Prodel
Kleeberg
Knauthhayn
Lausen
Elster R.
BATTLE OF
LEIPZIG
16th 18th & 19th October 1813.
SHEET 2.
A.K. JOHNSTON F.R.G.S.
French
Allies
Cavalry
Infantry
Artillery
SCALES
Military Steps. 2½ Feet each
English Mile

Grand Duke Constantin, and the infantry under the orders of General Count Miloradowitsch.

The whole of the Russian and Prussian troops were commanded by the general-in-chief, Count Barclay de Tolly.

The troops were all under arms at six o'clock in the morning, and the attack commenced at eight.

Lieutenant-General Count Kleist made the first movement, by advancing by Gröbern and Crosterwitz towards Markkleeberg, opening upon the enemy a smart cannonade, and brisk fire of sharpshooters. They were soon dislodged from the village, and, in spite of repeated attacks, he continued to maintain himself in it throughout the day. At the same time, the corps of the Prince of Würtemberg moved upon Wachau, attacked the village and the wood near it, carried them both, and forced the enemy to retire. The Prince of Gorczakow advanced from Störmthal upon Liebertwolkwitz, but arrived later on account of the distance. The right wing, under Count Klenau, marched by the way of Gross-Pössna, and took post upon the heights to the right of this village, menacing, by this movement, the flank of the enemy's position at Liebertwolkwitz.

The 2nd corps of Austrians, posted on the extremity of the left wing of the Grand Army, commenced likewise the attack, by opening a lively fire of riflemen, from the low woods on the left bank of the Pleisse; but the ground presented so many insurmountable obstacles to the bringing up of artillery, that the plan conceived by the Field-Marshal Prince of Schwartzenberg, could not be promptly executed.

Napoleon was not wanting in making his dispositions, on the first approach of the Confederate columns. The whole of the 8th corps, under Prince Poniatowsky, received orders to defend the village of Dösen, and the passages of the Pleisse, from Cönnewitz to Markkleeberg. Marshal Victor, with the 2nd corps, defended Wachau; and General Lauriston, with the 5th corps, the little town of Liebertwolkwitz. The whole of his guards were marched from Reudnitz to Probstheide, forming the reserves of his army. The 11th corps, commanded by Marshal Macdonald, advanced from Stötteritz towards Holzhausen.

The cannonade and fire of musketry continued with unabated fury, on both sides, from ten o'clock till near eleven. At this period Marshal Macdonald showed himself in advance before Holzhausen, and, in conjunction with General Lauriston, succeeded in forcing General Count Klenau to evacuate the position he had occupied; two divisions of the young French guards, under Marshal Mortier, having

PRUSSIA'S PEASANT SOLDIERS, 1813

been detached by Napoleon to serve as supports.

Count Klenau took up a fresh position between Gross-Pössna and Seifertshayn, and ordered a succession of attacks to be made on the wood occupied by the enemy: these posts were taken and retaken several times, with variable success; and on this wing the issue of the combat remained undecided, as, towards the evening, both parties had kept their positions. An attack of cavalry, under General Sebastiani, who, by dint of superior numbers, had forced the Austrian horse to retire, was repulsed by two regiments of Prussian *cuirassiers*, with their wonted bravery and dauntless intrepidity.

On the side of Wachau too, the enemy, aided by fresh troops, began to press forward about eleven o'clock. Napoleon had sent Marshal Oudinot, with the two other divisions of his guards, to this important point, as support for Marshal Victor, together with General Drouet, with the whole of his reserve artillery. These considerable reinforcements rendered it necessary for the Prince of Würtemberg to order a retrograde movement, his flank being thereby menaced; but he made a lively and obstinate resistance; and as General von Kleist had kept his position near Markkleeberg, he was promptly supported, some fortunate attacks held the enemy in check, and five pieces of artillery were taken from him.

Perceiving the advantages which the enemy had, in some measure, gained at this point, General Barclay de Tolly detached General von Rajewsky, with two divisions of grenadiers, and the third division of Russian *cuirassiers*, to the support of the Prince of Würtemberg. The attack of the *cuirassiers* proved unsuccessful, but the brave grenadiers stood their ground against the enemy with firmness, and the efforts of Napoleon to follow up his temporary successes proved ineffectual.

As soon as Prince Schwartzenberg was apprised that Napoleon was throwing the whole of his reserves upon Wachau and Liebertwolkwitz, and was straining every nerve to break through at these points, he immediately ordered up into line the whole of the Austrian reserves, under Prince von Hessen-Homburg, that were posted at Zöbigker. At the moment that the head of the Austrian reserve cavalry, under General Count Nostitz, was debouching in advance of Gröbern (about one o'clock, p. m.), the French dragoon guards and Polish cavalry, under General Letort, had already penetrated to the vicinity of Gröbern, and many of their battalions of infantry, drawn up in square masses, were following in close order.

General Count Nostitz, with inimitable promptitude, charged the enemy's cavalry, at the head of three regiments of Austrian *cuirassiers*, broke and dispersed them on all sides, cutting in pieces several squares of the French guards, or putting them entirely to the rout. The division of Bianchi had debouched out of Gröbern, in following the cavalry, and now advanced to Markkleeberg, where they relieved the troops under General von Kleist. General Bianchi cannonaded the flank of the enemy's advance, towards Wachau, repulsed them with heavy loss, and took eight pieces of cannon.

The enemy, on finding all his attempts to gain ground, at this point, frustrated, now turned into a new path of operations, by repeating his attacks upon the corps of the Prince of Würtemberg; for which purpose the corps of cavalry under General Latour-Maubourg, headed by Marshal Murat, was brought into action. The French infantry was much superior in number to that of the Russians, and there were only ten squadrons of their light cavalry on the spot. The enemy, favoured in part by the terrain, advanced to the charge with impetuosity, and were actually on the point of breaking through the centre of the Confederate Army, and cutting it off from the right wing, when the Emperor Alexander, ever at the post of danger, ordered, at this decisive moment, the regiment of Cossack-guards to charge the enemy. That charge was irresistible, the French horse were broken and dispersed, and 24 pieces of artillery, out of 26, lost but a few minutes before, were retaken.

Animated by these transient successes, the enemy's columns again pressed onwards to the left of Wachau; but the Russian grenadiers fought with unshaken resolution, vigorously repulsed every attack, and at last drove the enemy from off the field, at the point of the bayonet.

Towards three o'clock, p.m. the whole of the Austrian reserves had arrived at the different points assigned them, and the Russian and Prussian reserves, posted at Magdeborn, were drawn nearer. Prince Schwartzenberg now ordered a general movement to take place in advance, to put himself in absolute possession of the glacis of Wachau. The Russian guards and the division of Austrian grenadiers, under General Weissenwolf, were posted in the centre, to serve as supports wherever they might prove necessary, during this renewed attack. In the meantime, Napoleon was not remiss in reassembling his troops. He concentrated his cavalry at Liebertwolkwitz, and occupied the heights in front of Gossa, on which he planted a numerous artillery.

Towards five o'clock, some strong columns of the enemy's infantry attempted to take this village by assault; they had already entered it, but the Prussian brigade under General von Pirch, drove them out

CHEERING LÜTZOW'S FLAGS OF TRUCE IN LEIPZIG

again. The enemy continued to form fresh columns of attack, and advanced once more with fury to the assault. In the meantime, Lieutenant-general Jermoloff, at the head of the Russian foot-guards, had advanced to support the position, and the artillery belonging to the Russian and Prussian guards, were placed on an eminence, to the left of Gossa. Their fire was tremendous, and produced the greatest effects; the enemy lost an enormous number of men, were repulsed, and driven into their first position, while the Allies gallantly maintained themselves at all points in and near Gossa.

At the termination of this bloody conflict, the night was far advanced. Although the desperate and sanguinary charge of Murat had not been unsuccessful, and he actually did, in some measure, succeed in breaking the centre of the Confederate Army, yet it effected no material change in favour of Napoleon's positions, and the Allies could with confidence feel that no diminution of their relative strength was the result.

We have already observed, that General Count Meerveldt, on the extreme left wing, had encountered almost insurmountable difficulties, in executing his orders of forcing the Pleisse, with the intention of turning the enemy. An attack in the front of Cönnewitz was rendered impossible, by the enemy having broken down the bridges, and well lined the dams with infantry and artillery. Several attempts to pass the river, at Dölitz and Lössnig, had proved unsuccessful. Towards the evening, General Meerveldt succeeded in forcing a passage at the head of a battalion; but, being attacked by a great superiority of numbers, was obliged to fall back. On this occasion, General von Meerveldt was unfortunately taken prisoner, his horse being shot under him, and himself slightly wounded.

★★★★★★

The count was immediately hurried, though wounded and bleeding, into the presence of Napoleon. A series of abrupt questions opened the conference. Under the pretence of commiserating the count's situation, Napoleon liberated him on his word of honour, but likewise commissioned him to make Splendid proposals for an armistice to the Allied powers. The principal conditions were:

1. An uninterrupted retreat for his army over the Saale.

2. The evacuation of all the fortresses on the line of the Vistula and the Oder.

3. And then to negotiate for a peace.

★★★★★★

Thus, ended the battle of the 16th, on the right banks of the Elster and Pleisse. Pending these events, the corps under the command of General Count Giulay, posted, on the left bank of the former river, did not remain inactive. General Bertrand's corps had taken a position in front of Lindenau and Plagwitz. He was, however, so vigorously attacked by General Giulay, that he was obliged, at one, p. m. to evacuate Plagwitz, and soon after Lindenau, leaving two pieces of cannon in the hands of the Victors. Bertrand retreated behind the Kuhthurm, drawing up his infantry in squares, and keeping a brisk cannonade on the advance of General Giulay's corps, that now occupied the left bank of the Luppe, near Lindenau. Napoleon having sent strong reinforcements of cavalry, from the side of Leipsic, General Bertrand again moved onwards, and, after suffering a very heavy loss of men, carried the village of Lindenau.

★★★★★★

At this period of the battle, Napoleon sent off a courier to the King of Saxony, at Leipsic, with a note, written by himself, containing the following words:

Nous avons du succès; on m'attaque du côté de Lindenau, mais on se cassera le nez.

Napoleon.

The courier, who was nothing less than a German prince, much attached to Buonaparte, made many additions to the contents, during his audience of the king, so as almost to persuade His Majesty that victory was certain. The Duke of Bassano, who had accompanied the king from Dresden, was at this period continually with him, on pretence of imparting the most auspicious news of the battle; but, after the retreat of the French Army was in some measure arranged, his visits were discontinued, with excuses of ill health, and great fatigue.

On the morning of the 19th, the king sent Colonel Ryssel to the Emperor of Russia, with the offer of a capitulation, to save the city, at a time too, when the Duke of Padua demanded of the magistrates, with imperious threats, a hellish requisition of fifteen cwt. of pitch and tar, that he might set the suburbs on fire with greater celerity: had this been done, the conflagration would have been ascribed to the Confederates; but this base act of perfidy was prevented from perpetration, by the firmness of the magistrates, in refusing the delivery.

The Crown Prince of Sweden paid the king a visit, soon after he entered Leipsic, and a long, and, to appearance, very friendly conference, was interrupted by the report that the Emperor Alexander was riding towards the king's quarters. The emperor did alight in the square opposite, and the crown prince, after the exchange of a few compliments, proceeded to his hotel.

On the same evening, the Emperor Alexander had an hour's conversation with the Queen of Saxony alone, in her own apartment. The next morning the king returned the crown prince's visit, but had no conference whatever with the other three potentates, having only written a few lines to the Emperor of Austria, at Rotha. The King of Prussia, on the following day, caused His Majesty to be informed, he might choose any place of residence, more agreeable to himself, than either Leipsic or Dresden could possibly be.

******

General Giulay then took up his old ground, near Klein-Zschocher.

Such were the results of all those bloody combats that marked a circle of many miles in circumference, and of which Leipsic may be said to have formed the centre. It cannot be affirmed that they were altogether so favourable, or so decisive for the Allied arms, as the hopes of the most sanguine might suggest; yet Napoleon could by no means boast of a victory in any shape, although it must be confessed that the French troops fought, on this day, with singular bravery. Those momentary advantages, acquired by their courage, were however productive of no important consequences; for they did but lose again, in a few moments afterwards, what they had obtained by a horrible and inconceivable prodigality and wanton waste of human blood.

******

We may venture to state, from the authority of many officers, who have been eye-witnesses to the fact, that Napoleon, at all times after a battle, showed considerable asperity and ill-humour, whenever a regiment filed off before him, that had been in fire, and lost but few men. He would scarcely deign to look at it, or speak a word to the commanding officer; even though the regiment had been posted where it had had no opportunity to distinguish itself. If a regiment, on the other hand, had lost half its complement of men, he was instantly in good humour, did justice to the merit of the officers, and particularised them by name, even as low as captains. But, when he saw the remains of a regiment, returning out of battle, not exceeding the strength of a company, his transports seemed without bounds. He would graciously condescend to speak to some of the privates personally, generally ending with these expressions: "You are now worthy of me! Your regiment has experienced an enviable fate, which every brave soldier must wish for!"

✶✶✶✶✶✶

The heart of man must ever shudder at the recollection. The right wing of Napoleon's army had lost the important terrain of Markkleeberg. The centre of the Confederate Army had remained in possession of the position it had taken at the commencement of the battle. Marshal Marmont had also been completely beaten. Consequently, the Allies might boldly appropriate to themselves the palm of victory, and calmly leave the question to posterity, how far Napoleon could be justified in vaingloriously boasting to the world, that he had wrested it out of their hands, at a time when the battle was not even ended, much less decided.

The Crown Prince of Sweden, on finding that the movement of General Reynier towards Wittenberg had only turned out a simple demonstration, filed off his army from Halle to Landsberg. General Count Bennigsen, having left a considerable corps, under the orders of General Tolstoy, before Dresden, had put himself in march to join the grand Confederate Army, and was to arrive, on the 16th, at Colditz. General Colloredo, who had marched for the same purpose, in the direction of Freyberg and Chemnitz, could only reach Borna.

The Grand Army of the Confederates, in expectation of a general attack from the side of the French, was drawn up in order of battle, by break of day on the 17th. The outposts were, in many places, only a musket-shot's distance from each other. On the heights in front of Gossa, the enemy had formed large masses of infantry; and, in the vicinity of Liebertwolkwitz, a long line of cavalry presented itself. After some useless demonstrations, by marching and counter-marching his troops, Napoleon still showed but little inclination to attack at any point. Prince Schwartzenberg, being willing to wait the arrival of Generals Bennigsen and Colloredo in the line of operations, likewise, on his part, deferred the attack.

A grand council of war, at which Prince Schwartzenberg presided, was held in the afternoon, at the village of Sestowitz. It being reported that General Bennigsen could not reach Naundorf before the evening; that General Count Colloredo was in march from Borna; and that the arrival of the Crown Prince of Sweden, to support General von Blücher, was still uncertain; it was unanimously resolved to defer the attack until the 18th; it being taken into consideration that, on the morrow, the Army of the Allies would be reinforced by nearly 100,000 men, and thereby ensure with greater certainty the most brilliant results. The power of acting on the offensive had at least undergone no material alteration since the 15th; and a wise general could, without fear, adopt, for the present emergency, the reverse of that policy which might then have been thought advisable.

General Bennigsen effected his junction with the Allied forces, at Naundorf, in the evening; and General Colloredo took up a position near Gröbern, at about four o'clock in the afternoon. The Crown Prince of Sweden quitted Landsberg at two o'clock, a. m. on the 17th, and encamped with his whole army at Breitenfeld. General Winzingerode occupied Taucha.

In this manner Napoleon permitted the 17th of October to pass away in a state of inaction, that proved to him an irreparable loss of time. His motives appear the more inconceivable, as it may be presumed that he could not be ignorant of the approaching accession of strength which the Allies were on the point of receiving, and which, when once united, must eventually annihilate his army, already half beaten. It is equally beyond conception, why this great captain did not occupy the line of the Saale, on the 17th and 18th, when no obstruction whatever lay in his way.

The reinforcements which the Confederates had received, and the menacing attitude of their position, which threatened a vigorous attack on all sides, in the course of the following day, acted as powerful inducements for Napoleon to narrow the vast circle of terrain which his army occupied on the 16th and 17th, and indirectly forced him to take up a more concentrated position. He, in consequence, caused all the advanced corps to fall back in the night of the 17th, and, early in the morning of the 18th, posted his army as follows (See Map of the Battle of Leipsic.)

The 8th, 2nd, and 5th corps, under the special orders of Murat, took post near Cönnewitz; the right wing being commanded by Prince Poniatowsky; the centre, at Probstheide, under Marshal Victor; and the left wing, under General Lauriston, near Stötteritz. Several detachments were placed in advance of the line, occupying the villages of Dölitz, Dösen, and Zuckelhausen, and the shepherd's house at Meysdorf. Marshal Macdonald took up a position, with the 11th corps, near Holzhausen, keeping up a communication with the left wing of the army under Ney. The guards were drawn up in solid square masses, on the Thonberg, near the tobacco-mill, where Napoleon remained a great part of the day. The old guards formed four columns, ready to advance upon any four points that might be threatened. Marshal Oudinot was afterwards ordered to support Prince Poniatowsky with two divisions of the Young Guards, and Marshal Mortier was charged by Napoleon to guard the passes to Leipsic.

The Allied Army was under arms by break of day, occupying nearly their former positions, except that, on the right wing, the advanced-guard of the corps under General Bennigsen had taken post at Seyfartshayn.

As soon as it was reported to Prince Schwartzenberg, that the enemy had filed off from Wachau and Liebertwolkwitz, he immediately caused the necessary dispositions to be made for a vigorous assault. The whole of the Grand Army of the Confederates, under his command, was divided into three separate columns. The first column, under the command of General Count Bennigsen, was composed of his own corps, that of General Count Klenau, and the brigade of von Ziethen, and received orders to proceed from Seyfartshayn and Gross-Pössna, in the direction of Holzhausen.

The second column, under the command of General Barclay de Tolly, was formed of the corps of General Count Wittgenstein and Lieutenant-General von Kleist, having for reserves all the Russian and Prussian guards, and being destined to advance against the heights of Wachau. The third column, under the orders of General Prince von Hessen-Homburg, was composed of the divisions of Bianchi, Prince Aloys Lichtenstein, Count Weissenwolf, and the reserve cavalry, under General Count Nostitz; the corps of Count Colloredo forming its reserve. The division Lederer, from the 2nd Austrian corps, remained on the left bank, of the Pleisse, opposite Cönnewitz, as the third column advanced upon Dösen and Dölitz. (See Map of the Battle of Leipsic.)

The first column, subdivided into three divisions, began to advance at about eight o'clock, a. m. The corps of Russians, and the Austrian division under Bubna, filed off in the direction of Zweinauendorf, by which movement Macdonald's corps was out-flanked, and forced to retire to Stötteritz. General von Bennigsen, meeting with mere detachments to oppose his progress, advanced rapidly, and drove the enemy back to Mölkau. The 4th Austrian corps, under General Klenau, marched upon Holzhausen, and carried the village after a warm action. General von Ziethen's brigade, destined to keep up the communication between the corps of Bennigsen and Klenau, and the centre column, pushed forwards at the same time to Zuckelhausen, and took the village after some resistance.

The second column, commanded by General Barclay de Tolly, was assembled near Gossa; the Prussian corps, under General von Kleist, formed its advanced-guard. These generals began to put their troops in march about eight o'clock, but found Wachau deserted by the enemy. The village was occupied, and two brigades were advanced between Wachau and Liebertwolkwitz, that soon repulsed some detachments left there by the enemy. The brigade of von Pirch found the shepherd's house at Meysdorf still occupied by the French, who retreated on perceiving preparations were making for a serious attack. The reserve cavalry kept open the communication with the left wing and the third column. The corps of Russians under Count Wittgenstein followed close upon the rear of Kleist's corps, and the two corps drew up in battle array, not far distant from Probstheide. The Russian and Prussian guards took post as reserves near the brick-kilns, where they remained throughout the day.

It was towards two o'clock, p. m. that the two brigades, headed by Prince Augustus of Prussia, and General von Pirch, belonging to Kleist's corps, received orders to storm the village of Probstheide. This village formed, in some measure, the centre of Napoleon's position, and might, indeed, be accounted the key to it. No wonder, then, that Napoleon not only occupied it with a large force, consisting of the 3rd corps under Marshal Victor, and a part of the 5th, but likewise threw in from time to time considerable reinforcements from his guards in reserve. To carry this position, so defended, was certainly no very easy undertaking; The place itself was defended by more than 8,000 infantry; and batteries on both sides of the village, spread death and destruction all around.

But nothing appalled the gallant Prussians; and the two brigades above mentioned, stormed and carried it at the point of the bayonet. The French, backed by reinforcements, soon returned to the charge, and the Prussians were forced to yield to superior numbers, and retreat to the end of the village. A corps of the enemy attempted at this moment to take them in flank, but a regiment of West-Prussians repulsed them with loss. This advantage enabled the two brigades to storm and carry the village a second time; and for the second time, the enemy, by the mere force of numerical strength, again succeeded in driving the Prussians out of it. The brigades rallied at a short distance, in the most gallant manner, and, assisted by a detachment of Count Wittgenstein's corps, commenced a heavy cannonade on the solid masses of the enemy's infantry, debouching out of the village. Their loss was enormous; and every attempt the French made to advance was repulsed by a most destructive and murderous fire of grape-shot, that lasted till late at night.

The third column, under the orders of the Prince of Hessen-Homburg, advanced likewise about eight o'clock, a. m. on the right bank of the Pleisse, and took possession of the glacis between Dösen and Lössnig. The enemy's detachments in those villages were either dispersed or driven in; and this column then moved forwards in line with the second or centre column. The prince was wounded in Dösen, and the command devolved on General Bianchi. This general, being shortly afterwards hard pressed by the enemy, was supported by the corps under Count Colloredo, and the position was not only maintained, but the enemy repulsed to Cönnewitz.

Prodigious as were the efforts made on this day by the Confederate Army, to make an impression on Napoleon's line of positions, yet the conflict was marked by no particular feature. Striking vicissitudes on either side were not experienced, nor did any one bold manoeuvre turn the fortune of the day. But a series of regular assaults, bloody and obstinate, seemed to form the general character of the battle on this side of Leipsic,

Whilst the Allied Army were acquiring these advantages, the Silesian Army, under our veteran hero, and the Northern Army, commanded by the Crown Prince of Sweden, did not remain inactive; the latter being now much further advanced, the main attack was made by him. The Northern Army left their camp at Breitenfeld at eight o'clock, a. m. and filed off towards Taucha, where, following the dispositions laid down, they were to pass the Partha, in conjunction with General Langeron's corps, so as to unite their left wing with General Bennigsen's army.

The cavalry under General Winzingerode, and the corps of Lieutenant-General Bülow, that formed the extreme left wing, marched off in the direction of Taucha, General Baron von Pahlen made a most brilliant attack on the place, got possession of it, and made a battalion of Saxons that defended the town, prisoners. General Woronzow, with a corps of Russians, passed the Partha at Grasdorff. The corps of

General Langeron was to pass the Partha at Taucha; but General von Blücher, judging, by the position of the enemy, that there would be no difficulty in forcing the passage at Mockau, which step would much facilitate the debouching of the Northern Army by Taucha, gave orders to attack at that point. The enemy made but little resistance, and General Langeron's corps passed the Partha, and advanced upon Leipsic.

Marshal Ney was soon aware that his position behind the Partha was forced at all points, by the Northern Army moving forwards from Taucha, and immediately changed his order of battle, by posting the three corps under his command, in a line between Schönfeld, Sellerhausen, and Stüntz. The 7th corps was drawn up in two lines near Paunsdorf. The brigade of cavalry belonging to this corps, the light artillery, and a battalion of light infantry (all Saxons), as likewise a brigade of Würtemberg cavalry, under General Normann, were posted between Paunsdorf and Taucha. These troops were upon the point of being charged by the Russian cavalry, when they marched hastily forwards, the infantry shouldering their firelocks, and the cavalry sheathing their swords, and came over to the Allies.

The Saxon corps posted in Paunsdorf, no sooner heard of this event, than they took the same resolution; and although the Saxon general, von Zeschau, endeavoured to prevent them, yet the whole of the 1st brigade, consisting of eleven battalions of infantry, three squadrons of cavalry, and three complete batteries of heavy artillery, followed the noble example of their brethren in arms, and made the cause of the Confederates their own.

******

On the 18th, at Paunsdorf, one of Congreve's rockets fell before the front of a battalion of Saxons; but the *fusee* burning out by accident, before it burst, it produced no effect. Some of the men, on examining it, and discovering it to be one of the English rockets, of which they had heard such a terrible description, began to crack their jokes on this new-created harmless messenger; but in the midst of their merriment, a second happening to fall in the ranks, spreading destruction and dismay all around, the whole battalion, as if seized with a sudden panic, broke and dispersed itself instantaneously, nor could the officers, with all their authority and threats, collect and rally the men again, to bring them into the line. (From an eye-witness.)

******

General Platow received them with every mark of joy and enthusiasm, and detached some regiments of Cossacks, to keep the French horse in check, that endeavoured to impede the march of the Saxons and faithful Germans, on the right road of honour. The sovereigns of these troops were, no doubt, fighting on the side of France; but the love of liberty and independence, and a feeling of genuine patriotism, animated their hearts, and fired their imaginations, with the glory that would await them, if, in the hour of victory, their swords were found drawn for the deliverance of their adored country, and the downfall of the oppressor of mankind.

During these important events, that so unexpectedly promoted the success of the day, General Count Langeron had advanced upon Schönfeld, where he encountered the enemy prepared to meet him. A violent cannonade ensued: the village was carried at the point of the bayonet, after a bloody resistance, and the enemy, on evacuating it, set it on fire. The cavalry of the Northern Army was at last come into line, and effected their junction with the advanced-guard of Bennigsen's corps, and the Cossacks, under the Hettman Platow.

The French had evacuated Paunsdorf, on the Saxons having gone over to the opposite army, but it was now again occupied by their infantry and artillery. General von Bülow, supported by a Russian and Prussian battery, attacked the village with his usual impetuosity, and carried it with the most distinguished bravery.

Towards three o'clock, Marshal Ney debouched with his whole force, out of the villages of Sellerhausen and Volkmansdorf. The Crown Prince of Sweden ordered the Russian brigade of cavalry to charge the enemy, which was executed with the greatest courage and effect, the French being driven back into the villages already mentioned, after a considerable loss of men, and four pieced of cannon. These progressive advantages enabled the Northern Army to advance in several distinct columns, towards Leipsic. At this moment, the enemy showed heavy masses in the direction of Mölkau, and seemed to menace an attack on the flank and rear of the Allied troops.

It was Napoleon himself that attempted this manoeuvre. As soon as the disaffection of the Saxon and other German troops was reported to him, he detached General Nansouty, with the whole of the Imperial horse-guards, and 20 pieces of cannon, to take the advancing columns of the Allies in flank, while he himself proceeded in all haste with a division of his guards, to Reudnitz, to oppose General Langeron. General Nansouty, on debouching by Mölkau, supported by the infantry already posted there, found General Count Bubna ready to arrest his progress, this experienced general, whose position was near the right wing of Bennigsen's corps, having caused his troops suddenly to change their front; which manoeuvre forced Nansouty to halt, and forego his intention. The Prince of Hessen-Homburg was in the meantime dispatched with his brigade to the same point.

The Swedish artillery, by some unaccountable delay, not being up, the guns of the Saxon artillery that had come over to the Allies, were now turned against the enemy; they were supported by a battery of Congreve's rockets, and the French were repulsed on all sides, and Napoleon's designs completely defeated. General von Bülow had marched forwards from Paunsdorf, and, in spite of an obstinate defence, had dislodged the French from the villages of Stüntz and Sellerhausen. (*The Details of the Rocket System* by William Congreve: Leonaur 2021.)

Napoleon, from his post at Reudnitz, pushed forwards a division of his guards, to support Marshal Marmont, who now succeeded in forcing Count Langeron to retire from Schönfeld. But the crown prince, having caused the Swedish General Cardell to advance with twenty pieces of cannon, to maintain this threatened point, and at least to keep the enemy in check, General Count Langeron was enabled to retake the village towards the evening.

Our veteran hero, whom we left on the 17th at his headquarters near Lindenthal, promoted, by his dispositions on the 18th, the general good cause, and divided, by his well-directed operations, the forces and attention of the enemy. General von Sacken was directed to attack the suburbs of Leipsic, and the Rosenthal. General von York's corps formed on this day the reserve; but as General von Blücher observed that the enemy was sending off troops in his rear, on the road to Weissenfels, he, with his usual foresight and promptitude of action, detached General von York, with his whole corps, on the evening of the 18th, towards Halle, wisely considering, that on the left bank of the Saale, he might reach Merseberg and Weissenfels before the enemy.

Thus, ended the third day's battle, and the Confederate Armies bivouacked for the night on the victorious plains of Leipsic.

✶✶✶✶✶✶

During the heat of action on the 16th and 18th of October, there appeared in the afternoon of each day a most beautiful rainbow in the west, which, beaming in full splendour, spread its vivid arch over the field of battle. Could the pious observer of events, and the unprejudiced son of Christianity, be blamed in hailing the appearance, not only as a type and emblem of heavenly grace towards sinful man, but as a forerunner of victory in the good cause?

******

The Allied Armies, after the most obstinate combats, and therefore the more glorious, had surmounted every obstacle before them, and by bearing in from all sides, at one and the same moment, had established their united forces within a few miles, nay, within sight of the gates of Leipsic. All efforts of resistance on the part of Napoleon had proved fruitless, or had spent their rage in vain. To maintain himself for a few hours in Probstheide, Napoleon had sacrificed an enormous number of men, merely to undergo the degradation and shame of retiring discomfited and broken, under cover of the night, accompanied by no cheering prospects of ultimate success.

******

During the battle on the 18th, a private French hussar, belonging to Napoleon's guard of honour, was carried through the gate of Leipsic on a bier, accompanied on foot by an officer of very high rank. The unfortunate youth was covered with seventeen wounds. The officer endeavoured to procure him admittance into one of the hospitals, but in vain—they were all full. After passing along some streets, exciting the pity and commiseration of the bystanders, unable to afford or to procure relief, he arrived with his *protégé*, at the market-place, conjuring those near him, to show him to the house of a surgeon: the hussar, he said, was the only son of one of the richest and most ancient families in France, and he should have the cruel mortification to see him expire in his arms for want of surgical assistance: he offered 40 *Napoleon d'ors*, the whole contents of his purse, to anyone that would either show him the way, or procure him a surgeon; but such was the state of distress and confusion all around, that no one was to be found to attempt the gaining so high a reward!

******

It must, however, be admitted that he was not absolutely beaten out of the field; yet by awaiting the results of the next day, if the battle were renewed, he could hardly indulge the hope of making further resistance. Napoleon must now have been convinced, and convinced too late, of the necessity of a retreat, an operation which might have been performed under much more auspicious circumstances on the 16th and 17th. He no longer delayed retiring by the only road left open. In the evening of the 18th, he returned to Leipsic, and with Murat took up his quarters at an inn. A retreat was determined upon, practicable in the direction of Weissenfels alone; and consequently, during the night, the heavy baggage, a considerable part of his artillery and cavalry, and some of his guards, defiled by the road leading to that place; and the other corps followed as they came up in succession. The main body of Napoleon's guards remained in the vicinity of Leipsic, till the morning of the 19th, when they filed off through that place.

******

At a very early hour in the morning of the 19th, Napoleon's headquarters were at the Dutch wind-mill, to the right of Stötteritz. Seeing himself surrounded on all sides by a powerful enemy, his corps driven from position to position, and a total defeat almost inevitable, he here made the last preparations, and issued the last orders to cover and regulate, in some degree, the flight of his discomfited army through Leipsic. An adjutant of Marshal Murat, from whom we have this anecdote, was very near him at this crisis, and had opportunity to observe his most minute actions.

Rage and fury were but too visibly depicted on his countenance; he gave his orders in the most brief and hasty manner, and answered all questions with little more than monosyllables. After the audience to the numerous general officers, &c. had ended, Napoleon dismounted, and, to the surprise of every one present, threw himself, apparently in a fit of despair, on his face on the ground, and, with a convulsive motion of his hands and feet, seemed to strive to bury himself in the earth. A few moments elapsed, when, suddenly starting up, and again mounting his horse, he rode off at full speed towards Leipsic, to pay a visit to the King of Saxony.

******

On the 19th of October, in the morning, the victorious armies of the Confederates, headed by their gallant commanders, made every preparation to storm Napoleon in his last retreat; but the light troops soon reported, that the lines the enemy occupied the preceding night had been, for the most part, abandoned. No impediment obstructed the march of the Allied columns a moment, towards Leipsic. To ensure his retreat, Napoleon had confided the defence of the city to Marshal Macdonald and Prince Poniatowsky, whose troops were posted for this purpose close to the walls, and which, about nine o'clock, a. m.

were the only points they occupied.

The Grand Army of the Confederates approached Leipsic: an assault was determined upon, and a bombardment commenced. The Emperor of Russia and the King of Prussia had hardly joined the army from Rotha, when a Saxon officer, with a flag of truce, arrived, and, in the name of the city, begged for mercy. The messenger was received by the Emperor Alexander in person, who announced to him, that his request could not be granted; and the preparations for the assault were continued with alacrity, when a second flag of truce appeared from Marmont, with an offer to deliver up the rest of the Saxon troops, if the French Army might be permitted to retire unmolested, and the city spared a bombardment. Such proposals being only made to gain time, were instantly rejected: especially as the Allied troops had already penetrated into the suburbs, and the general attack had begun round the town.

General Baron von Sacken had advanced to the north side of the city, and, after a severe action, had taken the intrenchments in front of the Halle gate. A galling fire of grape-shot somewhat retarded his progress; but as soon as General Langeron, by order of General von Blücher, had filed off a body of troops for his support, through the meadows on the Partha, the enemy was forced to abandon the Halle gate, and the Russian soldiery entered as conquerors into the city.

Towards the east side of the place, the Northern Army commenced its operations. The Crown Prince of Sweden commanded Lieutenant-General von Bülow to attack and occupy the city. The gates were defended with obstinacy, but nothing could withstand the Prussian bayonet: the French gave way, and, in defiance of all their attempts to rally in the streets and houses, the intrepid Prussians became masters of the town on this side.

******

When the Prussians drove the French before them, in gallantly forcing their way, through the gates, into Leipsic, the inhabitants, in joyous exultation, threw bread and all kinds of refreshments out of their windows, to the hungry Prussians, who hardly stopped the impetuosity of their pursuit, to silence the calls of hunger, but devoured their morsels in the act of marching. One of these brave Prussians, with part of a loaf of bread in his hand, on which he was feeding with avidity, saw an unarmed Frenchman, crawling along before him, on whose countenance hunger and disease were frightfully depicted; he stepped towards him, and the poor object instantly fell on his knees, imploring quarter. The Prussian offered him his bread, saying: "There, take and eat; thou want'st it more than I do." In uttering these words, he marched forwards, and a few moments afterwards levelled his musket, and shot one of the flying French.

✶✶✶✶✶✶

The advanced-guard of General Bennigsen's army entered the city at nearly the same time, after a severe engagement in some of the avenues leading into the place. The immense quantity of baggage, artillery, and equipages of every description, that the French had relinquished on their tumultuous retreat, had choked up every street, gateway, and outlet; and the retreating troops were thus thrown into a chaos of confusion, while each sought his individual safety in flight.

Napoleon did not quit Leipsic till ten o'clock, a.m. only a few minutes previously to the entrance of the Allies. He escaped through the Peter's gate, and when he had passed the bridge at the extremity of the entrance, it blew up, and all the troops and materiel in the rear, were left to the discretion of the conquerors. The whole of the rear-guard under Macdonald and Poniatowsky, were either killed, wounded, or taken prisoners, by the Confederates. Towards noon, the French were driven from all points, and tranquillity was once more restored to the inhabitants of Leipsic.

✶✶✶✶✶✶

Some instances can be given of single acts of despair, that most forcibly mark the character of the French soldier.

During the irregular retreat of the French through Leipsic, on the 19th, a French soldier stood at the corner of a street, and, levelling his musket at a Swedish orderly dragoon, riding by at full gallop, fired, and missed him. The dragoon pulled up his horse, but in the act of cutting at the Frenchman with his sabre, the latter threw down his musket, dropped on his knees, and begged for quarter. The Swede was generous enough to give him his life; he had, however, scarcely turned round his horse, when the wretch took up his musket, loaded it, and, as the dragoon was galloping off, fired again at him, but luckily without effect.

Enraged that his generosity should have been so ill requited, the Swede soon overtook the runaway, who again implored quarters "No," said he, "we pardon soldiers, but no murderers: die thou must!" and, with a hissing stroke of his sabre, cut him down, never to rise more. (From an eye-witness.)

✶✶✶✶✶✶

A moderate calculation from an official source states the number of killed on the part of the French at 13,000. More than 30,000 prisoners, all effective men, fell into the hands of the Confederates, besides the 23,000 sick and wounded, found in Leipsic. The military trophies consisted of 250 pieces of cannon, 900 tumbrils and baggage-waggons, and 40,000 firelocks.

The Allied monarchs, except the Emperor of Austria, who arrived somewhat later, proceeding from different quarters, at the head of their guards, made a solemn entry into the city about one o'clock, p. m. and met in the great square of Leipsic, amid the joyous effusions of the delivered citizens, and the lively and unfeigned acclamations of the victorious soldiers. It was a moment of exultation that richly rewarded those who had suffered so many years of misery.

✶✶✶✶✶✶

The Emperor of Austria, the Emperor of Russia, and the King of Prussia, were scarcely assembled in the market-place, when General von Blücher approached the three monarchs to pay his respects. The Emperor of Russia, the moment he saw our veteran, dismounted to embrace him with the heartiness of the most intimate friendship, called him the deliverer of Germany, and presented him with a valuable gold-hilted sword, set with brilliants. The Emperor of Austria was profuse in his encomiums; and his grateful monarch did but look at him, but with a look that spoke the overflowings of his heart, with more eloquence, than the well-turned periods of language could have expressed. On the following day, the king promoted our hero to the rank of General-Field-Marshal.

✶✶✶✶✶✶

The unanimity of the Confederates, combined with an energy of co-operation that blended wisdom with promptitude, rendered the stupendous Battle of Leipsic such a brilliant exploit in arms as may ever seek in vain for a parallel.

Never had any field of battle, in modern history, been so inundated with human gore. But thus, and thus only, could the inordinate vainglory of Napoleon be for ever eclipsed, offering a memento appalling to nature, but truly beneficial to mankind. It will show to posterity, that, though daring enterprise may attain to vast dominion, it cannot be preserved at the expense of the rights and feelings of the van-

ALEXANDER MEETING THE PRUSSIAN AND AUSTRIAN SOVEREIGNS IN LEIPZIG

quished; and that though the oppressor, in the day of his prosperity, and in the haughty confidence of his might, may scorn the voice of the oppressed, yet power never can be supported by violence alone.

The results of this tremendous conflict of four successive days, in which the nations of Europe made so noble a struggle for their privileges as citizens, and their birthrights as men, were equal to the interests that were to be decided. The tyrant and oppressor of the age could now with agony exclaim:

> That game is lost, for which I played, to gain the empire of the world.

It was here firmly fixed, that the precepts of Christian morality should maintain their due influence over the civilization and improvement of the human race. Its effects restored religion to its wonted energies; and the wily serpent, whose pestiferous breath exhaled selfish atheism, and destruction to all moral order, had now cast his skin of infallibility, was sunk into hopeless bondage, and condemned to bite his chains, detested and abhorred.

Chapter 10
Blücher passes the Rhine

The immediate consequences of this stupendous and sanguinary Battle of Leipsic, this splendid and immortal triumph, that avenged the injured cause of mankind in so singular a manner, were nothing less than Napoleon's retreat in all haste to the Rhine; a retreat that soon degenerated into a disorderly flight. The corps of General von York, as part of Field-Marshal Blücher's Silesian Army, that had been detached, on the 18th, to the Saale, reached Halle on the 19th; and the rest of the army, under Generals Sacken and Langeron, followed the same route, on the evening of that day.

General von Blücher passed the Elster, in the rear of Skeuditz, and, pushing forward a column to Lützen, surprised a body of 2,000 men of the enemy, and made the whole of them prisoners. The corps of Sacken and Langeron now took the road to Merseberg, while that of von York filed off in the direction of Mücheln. A bridge was soon thrown over the Saale, and the main body of Blücher's army marched close on the heels of the flying French, towards the Unstrut. A part of Blücher's advanced-guard fell in with a convoy of Austrian, Prussian, and Russian prisoners, near Nebra, consisting of 200 officers and 4,000 privates, dispersed their *escorte*, and released the whole of them.

Our gallant indefatigable hero overtook the confused multitude of retreating French, on the 21st, near Freiburg, when attempting to pass the bridge over the Unstrut: a bloody conflict ensued, in which the enemy sustained a severe loss of artillery and men. Towards three o'clock, p.m. the French troops gave way, and fled in the utmost disorder over the bridge. Blücher's artillery thundered upon their masses of all arms, and made a most dreadful slaughter. His numerous cavalry charged at every opening, and cut in pieces all that made resistance. The passage over the bridge was actually blocked up by the crowds of fugitives, that attempted to pass.

The bridge broke down, and, horrible to relate, hundreds were precipitated at once into the flood beneath. It was a terrible sight. The number of men that here found their grave in the Unstrut was so great, that the current was obstructed, and the river overflowed its banks for a considerable distance.

Numerous bodies of Cossacks, under the Hetmann Platow, having joined the Confederate Army, their rapid marches, at this period, most essentially aided the operations of the Allies. They formed, under General Czernischeff, strange as it may appear, the advanced-guard of Napoleon's retreating army. They surprised Gotha on the 24th, and made above a thousand prisoners. They occupied Eisenach soon after, at the time that Napoleon had only reached Gotha.

Their services proved here of infinite value; and as light troops, to harass the enemy, intercept his supplies, beat up his quarters, scour the country, procure intelligence, and, above all, to prevent intelligence being obtained, no troops in modern warfare can be compared to them. Terrible, merciless towards the foe, mild and obliging in quarters, pious in their deportment, gentle and humane in their intercourse with strangers; who has ever passed at nightfall a Cossack bivouac, and unmolested stood listening to their evening hymns, that will not bear witness to the inoffensive character of this truly brave and honest tribe of untutored warriors? Their fame needs no eulogium!

******

In the tumult of the retreat through Leipsic, a Cossack, in turning the corner of a by-street, came suddenly upon a French foot-soldier, who, at the sight of the Cossack's pike, threw down his musket, and, falling upon his knees, begged for quarter. The Cossack dismounted, broke the Frenchman's firelock against the stones, and stripped him of his knapsack and bundle of moveables: it happened that a citizen of Leipsic saw the transaction from his house-door, and, to show his loyalty, brought out to the Cossack a bottle of brandy and a loaf of bread, just as he had finished his search about the person of his prisoner.

The Cossack smiled at the sight of the bottle, took it, and made signs that he wished for another; it was brought him; but, to the astonishment of his benefactor, it now appeared that he wanted it empty. His request was complied with; and he instantly poured the half of his brandy into it, broke the loaf into two equal pieces, and shared them both with his prisoner, making signs for him to eat and drink, while he did the same; and then, with a nod of thanks to the donor, he mounted his horse, and drove his prisoner before him.—Where is there an adherent of Napoleon and his principles that would have so acted?

******

Napoleon made rapid strides to reach Erfurt, where he paused a while, to organise and refresh his jaded troops. Blücher's army, in conjunction with Bennigsen's, followed close upon his rear, and caused him a daily loss of artillery, baggage, and prisoners. The road to Hanau was covered with the wrecks of his disorganised army. Near Gotha, Colonel Mensdorff, of Blücher's advanced-guard, had a warm affair with the enemy.

Field-Marshal Blücher, on reaching Eisenach, on the 26th, caused the place to be taken by assault, and occupied the road to Cassel. General von York encountered the enemy, when in full march through the Hörselthal, not far from Eisenach; he attacked him without delay, drove him from the ground, and carried the village of Eichrodt, by which operation he cut off the fourth French corps from the main body, and forced them into the Thuringian forest, whence they were obliged to reach Vach by a circuitous route. On the 27th of October, Field-marshal von Blücher's army passed the defiles of Eisenach, and pursued and harassed the enemy in all directions.

Here we have to lament the consequences of a foresight, however wise and laudable it might be thought, that formed a portal through which Napoleon actually reached the Rhine, with the shattered remains of his humbled followers and worthless Satraps. The Bavarian Army, under General Count Wrede, was known to be in march on Hanau, to intercept the French Army; and a very natural conclusion was drawn by Marshal Blücher, that Napoleon would, in all probability, direct the course of his columns on Coblentz, to cross the Rhine at that point, rather than throw himself, weak as he was, into the arms of Wrede. The supposition was an unfortunate one.

If our hero had followed up his march, Napoleon's total defeat and capture at Hanau could not, according to all human calculations, have been averted. But the Silesian Army changed its line of operations; and Napoleon, somewhat relieved from his apprehensions of being placed between two fires, hurried on to Hanau, regardless of those he left behind; as, upon reaching that place, he could, by his superiority of numbers, with safety enter the lists with Wrede.

In the beginning of October, Bavaria declared herself as the ally of

Austria, and, by this step, dismembered for ever the Confederation of the Rhine. General Count Wrede, a most distinguished warrior, was appointed to the command of the Bavarian Army in camp at Nymphenberg, to which a corps of Austrians was added.

★★★★★★

Memoirs of General Count Wrede.

This renowned general was born at Heidelburg, on the 29th of April 1767. He was destined for the profession of the law, and, after finishing his education at Heidelburg, was appointed counsellor of the court of justice at Manheim; being at the same time high bailiff of Heidelburg.

During the war of the French revolution, in 1794, he was a commissary of war for the Rheinpfalz, with the character of brevet-colonel in the Elector of Bavaria's service. The repetitions of jurisprudence had had, it seems, no charms for our general; and he, at this period of his life, turned his attention entirely to arms. His important occupations required his constant attendance at headquarters, which he continued to follow during the ensuing campaigns, until the year 1799, when he received orders from the Elector to organise a battalion of his own, for the purpose of protecting the Rheinpfalz.

At the head of this battalion, supported by cavalry and artillery, his spirit of enterprise had several opportunities of showing itself, by some fortunate expeditions against the French, by which he acquired the public thanks of his sovereign, and the esteem of his brother-officers. On the 19th of August 1799, the Elector of Bavaria appointed him a colonel of the general staff; and, on the 11th of December following, his Serene Highness invested him with the honorary military badge, as a gracious mark of his satisfaction for his distinguished services. In March 1800, Count Wrede was promoted to the rank of Major-General, and commanded a brigade of a body of troops, at that time in the pay of Great Britain. He headed his brigade at the battles of Möskirch, Neuburg, and in the unfortunate affair of Hohenlinden, with determined bravery and prudence.

When peace was concluded, he was appointed commander of the brigade in Suabia, having his headquarters at Ulm. In the year 1804, he commanded a corps of infantry, forming part of the Bavarian Army encamped at Nymphenberg; and, before the camp broke up, was advanced to the rank of Lieutenant-General.

In the war with Austria, which commenced in 1805, he commanded a division of the Elector's army, protected the environs of München, and subsequently advanced into Moravia. Napoleon made him grand officer of the legion of honour, and his sovereign, when peace was established, in 1806, invested him with the Grand Cross of the military order of Max. Joseph. The Bavarian Army having returned to their several garrisons, after the peace of Presburg, Count Wrede was appointed commander-in-chief of the province of Suabia.

The war against Prussia and Russia, which soon followed, afforded General Count Wrede many opportunities of distinguishing himself in a most signal manner, at the head of his division. The battles of Glogau, Breslaw, and Pultusk, bore witness to his intrepidity. On the return of peace, he again resumed his military command in Suabia. When the Congress was sitting at Erfurt, in 1808, he was intrusted with the command of the Bavarian Army, then in camp near Augsburg, which soon broke up, as the threatened hostilities did not take place.

France, by her ambitious projects, having again, in 1809, lighted up the flames of war against Austria, our general commanded the second division of the Bavarian Army, and fully justified, by his eminent services, that confidence which His Majesty the King of Bavaria and the nation had placed in him. At the Battle of Wagram, he received a dangerous wound. The excessive fatigues of this campaign, and the effects of his wound, induced our experienced general, at this period, to decline all public functions, and to retire to one of his estates, to re-establish his injured constitution. After a short interval of repose, His Majesty promoted him to the rank of General of the Cavalry, as a proof of the high esteem in which his great and meritorious services were held by his grateful monarch.

About the middle of February 1812, when the Bavarian Army took the field in the memorable campaign of Napoleon against Russia, the command of the second division was given to our general. At the bloody Battle of Pollozk, the Bavarian commander-in-chief, General Count von Deroy, being mortally wounded, General Count Wrede took upon him the command of the army. With the miserable wrecks of this fine corps of Bavarians, Wrede retreated over the Niemen and Vistula, and, under difficulties almost insurmountable, brought back the brave remains of his army, by his wise dispositions, in safety, to the frontiers, but breathing insatiable vengeance against the bloodthirsty author of all their calamities.

When the famous campaign of 1813 was opened, by the march of the Confederate armies into Saxony, a Bavarian Army of Observation was assembled in a camp near Nymphenberg. It consisted of nearly 25,000 men, mostly volunteers from the national guards, that had offered to serve in the line. General Count Wrede took upon him the command of this army on the 15th of October, now strengthened by a corps of Austrians. The army immediately left the camp, and, by a series of forced marches, reached Uffenheim, a distance of more than two hundred miles, on the 23rd, where headquarters were fixed. Here General Count Wrede received intelligence of the victory of Leipsic; on its being made known to the army, it became a spark that kindled into flame a thousand fires, that had till now been glimmering under the ashes.

An enthusiastic love of civil liberty burst forth throughout the ranks, and the same enthusiasm for the good cause proclaimed itself unanimously, as in the north of Germany. The march was directed on Würtzburg, which capitulated on the 26th; and the head of the columns reached the vicinity of Hanau on the 28th. The advanced-guard of Napoleon's discomfited army, on its irregular retreat to the Rhine, showed itself on the road from Erfurt. Our general lost no time in making his dispositions, both prompt and vigorous, to stop the enemy's progress. Several bloody encounters ensued: in one of the latter, our brave general was again severely wounded. When recovering from his wound in Hanau, the Emperor of Austria sent him the commander's cross of the military order of Maria-Theresa, accompanied by the following letter, written by himself:

> My esteemed General of the Cavalry, Count Wrede,   Fulda, November 2nd, 1813.
> The gallant deeds that have covered you and the Confederate Army under your command, with glory, have induced me to give you a proof of my grateful sentiments, by sending you the grand cross of the military order of Maria-Theresa. Most sincerely do I wish your speedy recovery from your dangerous wound, hoping that Providence will preserve for his country and the

cause of Germany, an officer at once so brave and prudent. Francis.

His Majesty the Emperor of all the Russias had sent our general, prior to this, the order of Alexander Newsky: on which occasion he received the following letter from the Russian cabinet minister, Count Nesselrode:

> General, Meinungen, October 30th, 1813.
> The emperor has directed me, as a mark of his particular esteem, and proof of his satisfaction at the great services which Your Excellency has so lately rendered the good cause, to send you the insignia of the order of St. Alexander Newsky. The distinguished talents of Your Excellency will most powerfully promote the further success of the Confederate Army; and His Majesty places the most unbounded confidence in your operations, and in the sentiments by which you are animated. I esteem myself peculiarly happy in being the organ of those flattering opinions which the emperor entertains towards you, and to offer you the assurances of my high esteem.
> Count Von Nesselrode.

In fine, all the Confederate princes were loud in their eulogiums on the conduct of Wrede. His energetic exertions to reach the enemy, his personal bravery, and the wise circumspection of his plans, gave birth to an admiration at once well-founded and general.

Having happily recovered from his wound, he crossed the Rhine at the head of his corps of gallant Bavarians, and forming part of the grand Confederate Army that entered France at the commencement of the year 1814, shared the glory of the victory of Brienne, on the 3rd of February. On the 13th, General Count Wrede attacked, in combination with Blücher, Marshal Victor, at Nogent, and, after an obstinate conflict, forced him to retreat.

A series of partial affairs now followed, and, on the 16th, the Bavarian corps directed its march to Sezanne, and, on the 17th, passed the Seine, after having formed a junction with Wittgenstein. Our gallant general and his corps, in sharing the fatigues of those eventful days between the 27th of February and the 31st of March, partook of the honour and glory, so dearly purchased, of entering Paris in triumph, as part of the grand Confederate Army. His grateful sovereign has since raised him to the dignity of prince of the realm.

✶✶✶✶✶✶

On the 15th of October, General Count Wrede put himself at the head of this Confederate Army, which did not exceed 30,000 men, to commence his operations against the common enemy. By a series of forced marches, he reached Würtzburg on the 24th of October, summoned the place to surrender, and, on refusal, commenced a heavy bombardment.

On the 26th, the place capitulated. General Count Wrede, without delay, continued his march on Hanau, where he arrived with his whole army on the 28th, in the morning.

The Austrian-Bavarian Army took up a strong position near the place; and, as the vanguard of Napoleon's retreating masses was in advance upon Hanau, General Count Wrede made the necessary dispositions to obstruct its progress, and delay its march. Some partial affairs only prepared the way to a most bloody and obstinate combat. The head of the first French column began to debouche on the 30th, about ten o'clock, a.m. out of the Pupperwalde and Lamboy-Wood. It was driven back with great loss.

✶✶✶✶✶✶

On the 30th of October, three hussars belonging to the imperial French guards, entered the village of Langendiesbach, and ordered the bailiff of the place to follow them to the emperor. The man refused, saying, that, in his absence, his house and barns would be certainly plundered. Two of the hussars then offered to remain on his premises, as a guard, if he would venture to accompany the other to the emperor's quarters: to this proposal the bailiff agreed. On arriving at Napoleon's bivouac, he found him seated on a bundle of straw, near a watch-fire, and a number of maps before him.

Without any introduction, Napoleon asked the bailiff (through an interpreter), whether he knew of any passable by-roads, by which the high-road through Hanau might be avoided. He answered in the affirmative. Horses were instantly ordered, and the bailiff was obliged to ride with Napoleon into the woods, and to point out every by-road and outlet in the neighbourhood. They were nearly five hours together. On his being dismissed, without any offer of a remuneration for his trouble, he begged Napoleon to let him have a *sauve-gard* for his village, in return for his local information; a gloomy scowl followed, but no answer. He repeated his request, and Napoleon sullenly remarked:

"Lefebvre has the necessary orders, he will take care of everything."

The bailiff, somewhat elated at this assurance, hastened back to his village. He found it (could anyone expect otherwise?) completely sacked and pillaged. And the two hussars, left in his house, had been the first to set the example, by emptying it of every portable article of value. Such are the proofs of the gratitude and honour of Napoleon and his satellites.

★★★★★★

Napoleon made a second attempt, which met with the same fate, and the French were repeatedly repulsed till near three o'clock, p.m. The French horse-guards now presented themselves, drawn up in a solid body, and, in spite of a heavy cannonade, debouched, then formed with great rapidity in three lines, and charged the Bavarian and Austrian horse; they were met with intrepidity, and repulsed; but at this moment a battery of French twelve-pounders, that had been planted in ambush, in the rear of the imperial horse-guards, opened a destructive fire on the flank of the Allied cavalry, and they were obliged at last to yield ground.

Napoleon had now opened himself a passage, and the first column of his troops, consisting mostly of guards, filed off on the road to the north of Hanau. General Count Wrede, having received reinforcements on the 31st, took post to the south of Hanau, having evacuated the place early the same morning: some brisk attacks followed, with various success, and Hanau was stormed by the Bavarians, towards three o'clock, p.m. with the view of cutting off some part of Napoleon's troops.

★★★★★★

A deputation from the magistrates and inhabitants of Hanau was admitted to an audience of Napoleon, in Pupperwalde. He was seated in the front of a tent, surrounded by a crowd of officers. Upon their being introduced, by one of his adjutants, Napoleon addressed them in a singularly abrupt and unceremonious manner;

"You are the deputation from Hanau? It is the worst city in Germany. The citizens have received the Bavarians and Austrians with every mark of exultation and joy. I know I cannot force them to love the French; but, methinks, common tense should have told them to show at least more attachment to France, than to Russia. The one is much nearer to afford succour. and help, when necessary. But, however, as a punishment, I bombarded the town last night. Has the fire done much damage?" On being answered in the affirmative, he replied, "It was my intention to have burnt at least half the city about your ears." And then turning to Augereau, who stood near him, demanded, "What he could say in favour of Hanau?" The marshal, in his answer, gave some praise to their former conduct.

"*C'est bon,*" replied Napoleon; "*je sais que les magistrats sont de brave gens, mais la bourgeoisie est de la canaille*:—for this time, let their present punishment suffice." And they were then dismissed.

★★★★★★

General Count Wrede was wounded in gallantly leading on his troops to the assault. During the night, the rest of the French columns took the road to Francfort (Frankfurt). The loss, on both sides, was very severe. General Wrede, in his attempt to arrest Napoleon's career to the Rhine, showed the most invincible courage, in maintaining this very unequal contest. The attempt was crowned with glory, as he suffered no positive defeat, and yet kept Napoleon at bay for two days, disputing with him every foot of ground; and only by the overwhelming force of numbers, did the enemy open his road to Francfort, and General Wrede find himself unable to stop his further march to the Rhine.

Napoleon halted not at Francfort, but pursued his march to that river, in the direction of Mentz, where he crossed it on the 7th of November. It was the last battle which Napoleon fought in Germany to save himself; and his influence and dominion over it were thus for ever destroyed. The dawning prospect of better times seemed already to indemnify the Germans for so many years of misery; and the scum and filth of the French nation, that had been raised to the top, by the force of their vices, and by such talents as they devoted exclusively to purposes of immoral tendency, had received a chastisement, that, if it did not promote repentance, at least humbled them in the dust.

In now casting a retrospective glance over the operations of the grand Confederate Army, subsequent to the Battle of Leipsic, and preceding the passage of the Rhine, we do but pursue the thread of our narrative.

Napoleon, to secure his retreat from Leipsic, had destroyed every bridge over the Elster, and the numerous small arms of that river, and the Luppe, between Leipsic and Lindenau, and was thus able to remain in the latter place till near three o'clock, p. m. of the 19th of October. The extraordinary efforts of the Allied Army, during the last six days, had produced, it cannot be concealed, such a general state of exhaustion throughout the troops, that not only the impediments thrown in their line of march by the enemy, but the absolute necessity of some hours of repose to the men and horses, obliged them to halt for a while in Leipsic and its environs.

Their light troops alone continued, without intermission, to harass and distress the flanks of Napoleon's disorganised masses, and prepare obstacles for their future movements, which only a war like the present could render possible. Naumburg was occupied by a corps of Austrians, and a strong column advanced by the way of Pegau, to press on the left flank of the enemy, and to prevent their concentrating themselves behind the Saale. The Northern Army pursued Napoleon's right flank, in the direction of Querfurt, Artern, and Sondershausen, detaching strong corps towards the Weser.

The headquarters of the grand Bohemian Army were at Weimar on the 24th, continuing its march parallel with the left flank of Napoleon's forces, whose advanced-guard, composed of his Young Guards; his centre column, of the wrecks and remains of all his other corps; and his rear-guard, that covered the retreat, of his old guards, were incessantly exposed to the bold attacks of the Cossacks on all sides. His retreat was of a description that almost exceeds the limits of possibility. Clouds of light cavalry were advanced before him, breaking up the roads, destroying the bridges, and removing every article of human sustenance. The route of his troops was marked with an hourly loss of men and warlike stores. He reached Hanau on the 29th, and the Rhine a few days afterwards.

General von Blücher had, for very cogent reasons, directed his line of march from the vicinity of Eisenach to Coblentz, on the 28th of October. The intelligence of Napoleon's retreat on Mentz soon reached him; he entered Francfort on the Maine, at the head of his gallant army, and, on the 30th of December, issued the following proclamation:

> Brave Warriors of the Silesian Army!
> Your gallant progress, from the Oder to the Rhine, has torn provinces out of the hands of the enemy which he had formerly subdued. You are now to pass the Rhine, to force the enemy to accept of peace, who can ill brook the having lost, in

NAPOLEON AT WEIMAR

two campaigns, his conquests during nineteen years.

Soldiers! I need only point out the path of glory to the victors on the Katzbach, near Wartenberg, Möckern, and Leipsic, to be sure of the result. But it is here incumbent upon me to impose on you new duties. The inhabitants of the left bank of the Rhine are not inimical to our cause. I have promised them safety and protection of property; I have done it in your name. You must keep this promise sacred. Bravery confers honour on the soldier; but obedience and discipline form his brightest ornaments.

Blücher.

The Rhine seemed, as it were, to form a kind of barrier to the further operations of the victorious Allied Armies at the end of October and the beginning of November, particularly for the centre and left wing; and, during the whole of November, no serious preparations were made to pass this river with the main body. Mature deliberations, in the meantime, on the part of the august Allies, produced a well-digested plan of future operations, which, towards the middle of December, was put in execution, with a harmony and unanimity, blended with a general enthusiasm, that gave fair promise of the most brilliant results to the arms of the Confederates.

At the commencement of the new year, 1814, all the corps of the Confederate Army had passed the Rhine.

******

An official statement of the strength of the Allied Armies and corps that took the field at the opening of the campaign into France may not be unacceptable to our readers.

Countries.	Numbers.	Generals.	Armies.
Bavaria	36,000	Wrede	Grand army.
Hanover	20,000		
Brunswick	6,000		
Oldenburg	1,500	Duke of Brunswick	North army.
Hanse Towns	3,500		
Mecklenburg-Schwerin	1,000		
Saxony	20,000		
Weimar	800		
Gotha	1,100	Duke of Weimar	North army.
Schwarzburg	650		
Anhalt	800		
Hesse-Cassel	12,000	Prince of Hesse	Silesian army.
Berg	5,000		
Waldeck	400		
Lippe-Schaumburg	650		
Nassau	1,680	Duke of Coburg	Silesian army.
Coburg	400		
Meinungen	300		
Hildburghausen	200		
Mecklenburg-Strelitz	600		

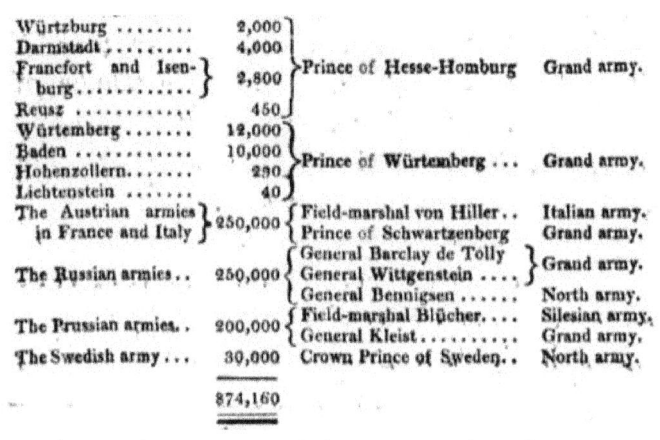

Würtzburg	2,000		
Darmstadt	4,000		
Francfort and Isenburg	2,800	Prince of Hesse-Homburg	Grand army.
Reusz	450		
Würtemberg	12,000		
Baden	10,000	Prince of Würtemberg	Grand army.
Hohenzollern	290		
Lichtenstein	40		
The Austrian armies in France and Italy	250,000	Field-marshal von Hiller	Italian army.
		Prince of Schwartzenberg	Grand army.
The Russian armies	250,000	General Barclay de Tolly	Grand army.
		General Wittgenstein	
		General Bennigsen	North army.
The Prussian armies	200,000	Field-marshal Blücher	Silesian army.
		General Kleist	Grand army.
The Swedish army	30,000	Crown Prince of Sweden	North army.
	874,160		

N. B. The English Army, including Spaniards and Portuguese, under the Marquis of Wellington, the auxiliary Corps of Danes, the Neapolitans, and the Army of the Netherlands, are to be added to the above number.

******

The Grand Army, under the command of Prince Schwartzenberg, consisting of the corps of Colloredo, Lichtenstein, Giulay, Crown Prince of Würtemberg, and Wrede, as likewise the whole of the Russian and Prussian reserves under General Barclay de Tolly, directed their march through the western part of Switzerland, passed the Rhine, and moved onwards into Alsace, towards Langres and Chaumont, after leaving behind them the necessary detachments to blockade and besiege the several fortresses which they had left in their rear.

Field-Marshal von Blücher began to pass the Rhine, by Kaub, Bacharach, and Coblentz, with his Silesian Army, on the 1st of January 1814. General von York's corps had the honour of leading the march, and was the first that crossed the Rhine. In the night of the 31st of December 200 men, of the regiment of Brandenburgh, landed on the left bank of the Rhine, and, after a trifling resistance, drove in some of the enemy's outposts. About ten o'clock, a.m. nearly 4,000 men, infantry, had crossed the river in barges. Bacharach and Oberwesel were taken. The bridge of pontoons at Kaub was ready the same day, and the corps of General Langeron, and the main body of the army, followed on the 2nd of January. General Sacken crossed the Rhine, with his corps, at Manheim, and General St. Priest at Coblentz.

Marshal Blücher issued the following proclamation to the inhabitants of the left bank of the Rhine:

I have led the Silesian Army over the Rhine, that the freedom and independence of nations maybe established, and peace acquired.

The Emperor Napoleon has incorporated Holland, a part of Germany, and Italy, with the French empire; he has declared that he would not give up a single village of these conquests, even if the enemy appeared on the heights of Paris.

It is against this declaration—against these principles, that the armies of all the European powers are on their march. Will you defend these principles? Well, then, enter the files of Napoleon; try the chance of battle against that just cause which Providence so evidently protects. If not, you then find protection with us. I shall defend your property.

Let every citizen, every peasant, remain tranquilly in his dwelling—every magistrate at his post, and continue, without interruption, the employments of his office. But from the moment the Allied troops occupy a place, all connexion with the French empire must cease. Whoever acts against this ordinance commits treason towards the Allied powers, will be brought before a court-martial, and be punished with death.

Von Blücher.

On the left bank of the Rhine,
January 1, 1814.

It was now that France experienced all the disadvantages resulting from an unsettled, tyrannical government, and that all her power and all her strength had been employed merely for the purpose of acquiring conquests, that had neither secured her boundaries, nor rendered actual invasion impossible.

But before we proceed further, we think it necessary to call the attention of our readers to the minor operations of the extreme right wing of the Confederate Army after the Battle of Leipsic.

The Crown Prince of Sweden, (see note following), at the head of the Swedish Army, and two divisions of Russians and Prussians, directed his march, from the victorious plains of Leipsic, towards the Weser, and arrived at Hanover on the 25th of October, pushing forwards his left wing towards the Ems. He halted with his army a few days, to refresh his troops, and to give Denmark an opportunity of making overtures.

★★★★★★

BLÜCHER'S PASSAGE ACROSS THE RHINE

Memoirs of the Crown Prince of Sweden.

Charles John Bernadotte was born on the 24th of June 1763, at Pau, near the foot of the Pyrenean mountains. His father had attained considerable eminence in the law, and gave his son a liberal education. On reaching manhood, he gave way to his favourite propensity, and chose the profession of arms; and his first campaign was made under Rochambeau, in America: he was there taken prisoner by the British forces. When the French revolution broke out, we find him, in his twenty-sixth year, in the regiment of Royal Marines. He became a Staunch republican; and, having distinguished himself during the subjection of the Low Countries, he was made a General of Division.

He gave singular proofs of his conduct and bravery at the Battle of Fleurus, 1795, and at the crossing of the Rhine in 1796, being at that period attached to the army of General Jourdan. His division blockaded Mentz for some time; and had, afterwards, a considerable share in the success of the battle of Neuhoff. General Bernadotte was detached, with his division, to strengthen the army of Buonaparte in Italy, which circumstance gave rise to a very intimate acquaintance between these two personages. Napoleon ordered him to take Gradiska, which he accomplished.

After the Battle of Rivoli, Buonaparte sent General Bernadotte, with the colours taken from the enemy, accompanied by a strong recommendation to the Directory, in favour of the general. He was received in Paris with distinguished and very flattering marks of respect; and was thereupon appointed *commandant* in Marseilles. Soon after the peace of Campo-Formio he repaired to the Austrian capital as ambassador from the French republic. The displaying of the three-coloured flag before his hotel, caused a vehement popular commotion in Vienna, and General Bernadotte was induced to retire to Rastadt, to await the decision of the Directory.

On the breaking out of a new war, General Jourdan was appointed to the command of the army intended to act against the Archduke Charles, and Bernadotte was intrusted with one of the wings. This army was soon obliged to repass the Rhine. General Bernadotte was now placed at the head of the war department. The Directory, a short time after, commanded him to resign his place in favour of Mallet-Mureau, and to repair again to the army. It appears that this abrupt conduct of the Directory gave considerable offence, as Bernadotte made immediate application for his dismission, which was granted him, with a pension; and he retired from all public affairs to his estate in the country.

Ties of relationship attached him to the family of Buonaparte, his lady being the sister of the wife of Joseph Buonaparte, eldest brother of Napoleon. The Army of the West was intrusted to his command; and, at its head, he contributed to the destruction of the faithful royalists at Quiberon Bay. The peace of Luneville being ratified, he resigned his command to General Laborde; and was on the point of proceeding to the United States, as ambassador, when hostilities again broke out between England and France. In the year 1804, the First Consul sent him to Hanover, where he succeeded General Mortier in his command, and, by the mildness of his measures and suavity of his manners, he made himself universally esteemed by the Hanoverians.

The year following, the First Consul declared himself Emperor of the French, and invested Bernadotte with the dignity of Marshal of the Empire. He assisted at the Battle of Austerlitz. During his stay in Germany, in 1806, Napoleon created the marshal a prince, as Prince of Ponte-Corvo, at the same time that Talleyrand was made Prince of Benevente. The prince distinguished himself at the Battle of Jena, and at the affair of Lübeck, against General von Blücher. From the year 1807, to 1809, he commanded the Army of Observation in the north of Germany.

At the head of the Saxon troops, he took part in the Battle of Deutsch-Wagram. When peace was signed, he retired, in 1810, to his estates, at Lagrange la Prevôte, near Melun; from whence he was called to inherit the throne of Sweden, by the unanimous voice of the Swedish nation. As Crown Prince of Sweden, he powerfully assisted in the deliverance of Germany, which must ever be remembered with gratitude by the nation.

★★★★★★

Meanwhile Marshal d'Avoust, (see note following), who had been suffered to entrench himself up to the ears in Hamburgh, had taken up a strong position between the two Hanse towns of Lübeck and Hamburgh.

★★★★★★

Memoirs of d'Avoust:

It is the part of the biographer to relate stubborn facts; he is obliged, not only to detail the virtues, but the deceit and cruelty of individuals, their ambition and avarice, their meanness and violence. The task may be useful, but no one will have the hardihood to say, that it is, in the latter case, a grateful one; for the man, whose duty it is to point out an individual, as an instance of unexampled moral turpitude, to the inquisitive world, must be conscious, not only of the utility, but of the feelings of abhorrence, arising from his exertions. Each sentence he pens presents to his view some horrid, monstrous, and diabolical trait of character—some feature, stamped with the appalling image of a black and callous soul: greatness, found without generosity—valour, without mercy—and wisdom, without virtue. The subject of the present memoirs is such a portrait. The mass of authentic anecdote, dispersed throughout this chapter, portrays, in striking colours, his prominent features.

D'Avoust has drawn down upon himself the eternal hatred of all good Germans, in a much higher degree than any other of Napoleon's *Satraps*. The origin of this deadly hate may be traced to his persecutions of German authors, (see note), his avowed contempt of everything relative to the Teutonic nation, his eager inclination to discover, in the most private connexions, imaginary conspiracies against France; and, above all, the unnatural severity with which he at all times executed Napoleon's decrees.

Note:—Mr. Becker, an admired German writer, and Councillor of the Court, at Gotha, was arrested, conveyed to Magdeburg, and thrown into a dungeon, in direct violation of the rights of nations. The Duke of Weimar endeavoured to procure his release, and caused representations of his innocence to be made to Marshal d'Avoust, to which he returned the following brutal and insolent answer, in a letter still extant, in which, after a positive refusal of liberation, he proceeds thus: "And, besides, the Germans are altogether a stubborn people; and they will hardly become tame and docile, until I have made some striking examples, by hanging up, on one tree, a German prince, a man of letters, and a merchant, as a warning to the rest!—"

A few minute particulars concerning the life of this man, will no doubt prove acceptable to our readers.

D'Avoust, Duke of Auerstädt and Prince of Eckmühl, was born at Annou, in Burgundy, and is descended from a noble family. His father had more than once exercised the functions of an ambassador. He was killed, by accident, on a shooting-party, leaving his son an orphan of tender years. At a suitable age, young d'Avoust was placed in the military school at Brienne, where he imbibed the first rudiments of his knowledge of military tactics. It is singular that Napoleon was formed at the same school.

At what period d'Avoust first entered the army, and obtained a commission, we are unable to say; but we find him, in the year 1785, as second lieutenant in the Royal Champagne regiment of cavalry.

When the revolution broke out in France, the greater part of his brother-officers emigrated. D'Avoust's mind seemed, however, adapted for the scenes of the revolution; and, although exposed, as a royal officer, to some vexations, he declared himself a staunch republican. In the year 1790, d'Avoust was appointed commander of a battalion of volunteers of the Yonne, was attached to the Army of the North, and was present at all the affairs of Dumourier's campaign.

When Dumourier deserted the cause of the republic, and came over to the Austrians, it was d'Avoust that made the daring, but frustrated attempt to prevent, him, and take him prisoner as a traitor. He was made a general in 1793, and served in the Army of the Moselle. He soon afterwards passed the Rhine under Pichegru; was left to defend Manheim, and taken prisoner in the place. Upon being exchanged, he again passed the Rhine, with a division, in 1797. Peace was made; and d'Avoust accompanied Napoleon into Egypt as General of Brigade in the corps of Dessaix.

After the convention of El Arisch, he embarked, with Dessaix, for France, and landed at Toulon. He was immediately called to Paris by Napoleon, and received the command of the cavalry attached to the army in Italy, and finished the campaign under Brune. In the tenth year of the republic d'Avoust was appointed commander-in-chief of the grenadiers belonging to the Consular guards. When Napoleon styled himself Emperor of France, he was made a Marshal of the empire. He commanded a *corps d'armée* at the Battles of Austerlitz and Jena, and in that of Deutsch-Wagram. Subsequent to the peace of Tilsit, he commanded a body of troops in Germany, having his headquarters at Erfurt, from whence he took up his residence in Hamburgh, on being appointed General Governor of the Hanseatic Departments.

He commanded a corps under Napoleon in the famous campaign into Russia, and returned to Hamburgh in May 1813, to become the instrument of Napoleon's rancorous malice and vindictive thirst for revenge. We need not enter into arguments to prove the true character of d'Avoust; his inhuman acts cry aloud to the uttermost corners of the earth, and leave an impression on the minds of every good Christian, that is difficult to describe, but very sensibly to be felt.

★★★★★★

After the denunciation of the armistice, a corps under General Wallmoden, and a division of Swedes under General Vegesack, in the whole about 20,000 men, had been left in Mecklenburg-Schwerin, to observe and keep d'Avoust in check. The strength of d'Avoust's corps, including from 10,000 to 12,000 Danes, might be moderately estimated at 32,000 men. He had, therefore, a considerable superiority of numbers. In the course of the month of August, d'Avoust penetrated to Schwerin, (see note 1 following), the capital of the Dutchy, and bivouacked his army on strong ground near the lakes. Here he remained, for some time, inactive. (see note 2 following.)

★★★★★★

1. When d'Avoust arrived at Schwerin, the capital of the Duchy of Mecklenburg-Schwerin, he expressed himself much surprised to find that all the authorities and opulent inhabitants had left the place. He sent for Mr. Rôder, chamberlain of the court, and gave him to understand what miseries awaited the country when deserted by its magistrates, and bid him repair to the reigning duke, and tell him, that if he did not immediately send the bailiffs of the crown baillages, and other members of the civil power, to perform the functions of government, he would make mayors of his hussars, and lord-lieutenants of his *gens-d'armes*. "My first step," he added, "will be to order the conflagration and destruction of all the duke's palaces, castles, and moveable property of every description."

The duke, however, very properly disdained returning any answer to such brutal threats, more worthy the commander of a body of vandals, than a prince of polished France. D'Avoust, on the whole, treated Mecklenburg with some lenity, and an outward show of moderation, but in doing so, he was actuated only by his own private and selfish views; and these were, that Napoleon had actually promised him the dukedom of Mecklenburg-Schwerin, with an increased extent of frontier.

At a conference which Mr. Bülow, grand-marshal of the court of Mecklenburg, had with d'Avoust, during his present occupation of the duchy, the latter mentioned, in a haughty, supercilious manner, that the Emperor of France had already, at a conference, on the 27th of April, with the Duke of Weimar, at Erfurt, previous to the Battle of Lützen, fixed the fate of Mecklenburg's duke, by speaking of him in these terms: "He has ceased to be reigning duke: I shall give his territories to another more worthy of my confidence. He was the first German prince to desert the Confederacy of the Rhine. I shall trust him no more."

It was remarked, as rather extraordinary, that, regardless of the above-mentioned threats, the duke's residences, castles, domains, gardens, &c. were particularly spared, and carefully kept up, by d'Avoust during his stay in the duchy. He made very detailed inquiries concerning their number, their value, and the revenues of the duke's private property and estates; the peasantry of which latter were less pillaged than the others. To obtain the necessary information he did not scruple employing the vilest vagabonds—people who, under the government of the duke, had been guilty of embezzlements of the worst description. A man, in particular, of the name of Susemihl, a name branded with every attribute belonging to the character of a traitor, became one of his most intimate counsellors. (Related to the editor by Baron von K—n.)

2. In the month of August 1813, the headquarters of d'Avoust were at a favourite hunting-seat of the duke's, called Frederick's-Thal, near Schwerin. Many petty dilapidations and robberies were committed by his suite, to mention which, would be doing them too much honour; but that the public may know the man, we will here relate one of those numerous acts of pitiful peculation and rapine of this satellite of Napoleon, as being done under his own immediate eye and direction.

In the banqueting saloon hung those four well-known English caricature prints, by Rowlandson, of the Fox-chase and the Fox-hunting Dinner. They seemed to strike d'Avoust's fancy mightily, and he gave express directions to one of his adjutants to have them taken out of their frames, carefully rolled up, and sent to Hamburgh: these orders were immediately put in execution. (Related to the editor by Baron von K—n.).

★★★★★★

A division under General Loison was advanced to Wismar. General Wallmoden and General Vegesack occupied Neustädt and Rostock, near which latter place some partial advantages were obtained over the enemy. The intelligence of the complete defeat of Marshal Oudinot at Gross-Beeren, reached d'Avoust about the latter end of the month, and he forthwith made a retrograde movement with his army in the night of the 3rd of September, and, by a forced march, reached the line of the Stecknitz, near Ratzeburg. His retreat did not escape the circumspection of General Wallmoden, whose light troops, consisting of the volunteers of Mecklenburg, the Hanseatic cavalry, the Hanoverian sharp-shooters, and the free corps of Reiche and Lützow, pressed hard upon d'Avoust's rear-guard, and took from it above a thousand prisoners, besides a considerable quantity of baggage and stores.

General Wallmoden pursued the enemy, and took position at Boitzenburg. D'Avoust threw a corps of about 9,000 men, under General Pecheux, over the Elbe, with the view of making a diversion on the side of Magdeburg. General Wallmoden having received early intelligence of this intended movement, passed the Elbe at Dömitz, with a part of his army, and, after a warm affair at Görde, on the 16th of September, completely beat Pecheux, taking from him 1,800 prisoners, 8 pieces of cannon, 12 tumbrils, and much baggage. The shattered remains of this corps afterwards found their way back to Hamburgh, by the route of Lünenburgh. D'Avoust, with a singular obstinacy, still remained immoveable in his position on the Stecknitz till the month of November.

The hopes of the Crown Prince of Sweden, in regard to the politics of Denmark, were not realised; and, consequently, towards the middle of November, his advanced-guard of 6,000 men put itself in march from Hanover, to join General Wallmoden at Boitzenburg, and his Highness crossed the Elbe, with the main body of his army, near the same place, on the 30th of November. After forming a junction with General Wallmoden, His Highness made the necessary dispositions to assault the almost impregnable position of d'Avoust behind the Stecknitz; and a corps was ordered, as a diversion, to cross the Elbe at Geesthacht, and thus to threaten d'Avoust's direct communication with Hamburgh. This detested adherent of Napoleon found himself in jeopardy, and in all haste evacuated the line of the Stecknitz, retreating behind the Bille, or, more properly speaking, throwing himself and his army into the devoted city of Hamburgh.

The crown prince pursued him till under the walls of Hamburgh, and, leaving a corps of observation before the place, directed his march on Lübeck, which place opened its gates to him on the 6th of December. The auxiliary corps of Danes, attached to d'Avoust's army, filed off from the Stecknitz towards Segeberg and Rendsburg. The crown prince detached a corps to observe their operations, which marched by the way of Neumunster. Some well-contested affairs took place, and the Danes made good their retreat to Rendsburg on the 15th of December, after a very severe and bloody action, in which much bravery was shown on both sides.

The Prince of Hesse, who commanded the Danes, now offered terms for a cessation of arms; they were agreed upon; and an armistice, till the 29th of December, was concluded. Meanwhile General von Bennigsen had arrived before Hamburgh with his army of Russians and Poles, and the crown prince being relieved, retraced his steps towards the Weser and the Rhine. Hamburgh was now strictly blockaded on all sides; and the brutal d'Avoust had free scope to exercise his monstrous passion for devastation, and the sight of human misery in all its gradations.

******

1. When the Russian Army was on the point of investing Hamburgh, d'Avoust issued an order, commanding all owners of horses of every description to provide themselves with forage for six months. As soon as this was complied with, at an enormous expense, another mandate appeared, ordering that all horses, not belonging to the garrison, should have their throats cut, which was immediately put in execution; and the forage collected by the citizens, was then seized upon by d'Avoust, under the pretence of its now being useless.

2. The inhabitants were commanded by d'Avoust, upon pain of expulsion, to provide themselves with six months provisions, with an assurance, publicly announced, that private property would, in every event, be respected. Hardly had eight days expired, before a new regulation, in two separate ordinances, appeared, by which each member of a family was bound, under penalty of exile, to deliver fourteen pounds weight of provi-

sions into the French magazines!

3. A very eminent physician of Hamburgh, on venturing to make remonstrances to d'Avoust, concerning the converting his house into an hospital, at half an hour's notice, stating that it was the only relic of his property still left untouched; that his books, his physical apparatus, his anatomical collection, &c, could not be moved in so short a space of time, and would inevitably be destroyed by the lawless soldiery; d'Avoust answered, in his usual brutal manner: "How, Sir! your property? Where can you have property? (And then, laying hold of a button of his coat, added,) Not even this button can be called your property; it belongs to the emperor. You must turn out of your house within half an hour. Begone!"

******

The fate of Hamburgh will form, for ever, an epoch in the history of French principles, when describing their effects, and the actions of their propagators, well calculated to incite every well-wisher of his native country to hold them in utter detestation. D'Avoust was general-governor and commander-in-chief. (See note 1 following.) His preparations for defence were upon a large scale, and he appeared determined to defend himself to the very last extremity. His acts of oppression exceed all human conception. (See note 2 following.)

******

1. At a conference which d'Avoust had with one of the Senators of Hamburgh, soon after his reoccupation of the place, he casually remarked, that he should only punish the criminal.
"Who may they be?" inquired the Senator.
"The rich," he rejoined, scoffingly.
The General of d'Avoust's *état-major* observed, in the course of a conversation with the editor, "that the city had shown a furious enthusiasm at the sight of the Russians, for which the inhabitants would, in return, have the pleasure of seeing their pockets turned inside out." To this the general added a remark, which at that time had much point; "As to the English," he said, "they had accustomed themselves to travel too much on the continent; they would, in future, have less liberty and opportunity."

2. The rigorous measures adopted by d'Avoust against the personal interests of the citizens of Hamburgh, can with difficulty

be defended by any kind of sophistry; and the state of men's minds in the north of Germany could not but serve to render every action of this satellite of Napoleon detested. D'Avoust, in his subsequent defence, seems to lay much stress on his asserting that "he defies anyone to prove his having done an action unbecoming an officer and a man of honour;" or, in other words, confesses he was only a subordinate instrument in wore powerful hands. But can mercy and forbearance be less necessary to an officer in obeying the orders of his sovereign, than to a private citizen? No sovereign ever issued mandates to make war upon private individuals.

We will allow d'Avoust every advantage to be derived from the basis on which he founds his innocence and exculpation—we will not even dispute his right to seize his means of defence wherever they were to be found, either in the bank, in the houses of the citizens, or in their lives and property. The honour or dishonour of executing cruel mandates to their utmost extent, instead of modifying them by the laws of humanity, we will leave to be determined by that diversity of opinion which must necessarily exist, and only from plain, unvarnished, and authentic facts, venture to mark his character with those blots of atrocity and inhumanity, which, when once fixed, it is not, nor ever can be, in his power to efface.

His master's orders were to defend the place, and to complete its fortifications. A glacis of sufficient extent from the outworks was a main object, the obtaining of which must have appeared necessary from the first moment of his re-entering the city. A good engineer knows the space required according to the nature of the ground; consequently, the suburbs, villages, and houses lying in the way of forming such a glacis could be ascertained on the first survey of the outworks by the general of engineers, and reported accordingly to the commander-in-chief: that such reports were made, are facts that cannot be controverted; but it would ill have suited the thirst for vengeance that rankled in the heart of this cat's-paw of despotism, towards the inhabitants of a corner of Germany so recently in a state of the highest enthusiasm at the transient recovery of their freedom, to have shown them any marks of mercy and forbearance.

Instead of a general warning to the inhabitants of all the suburbs and villages, that the site of their houses, grounds, and gardens would, or must, form the glacis on this or that side of Hamburgh, they were deceived and cajoled into a belief of safety, that their property might become an easier prey to Napoleon's plundering hordes; and d'Avoust could glut his malicious animosity at the sight of individual distress, and the elegant retreats of the brave citizens of Hamburgh a prey to the flames. The French re-entered the city on the 30th of May 1813; and it was only in December following, in the middle of winter, that the orders for burning and destroying were issued, with a specious notice of forty-eight hours' time to quit, but which was never in any instance observed.

We will here relate the events at Hamm, a large village, full of country-seats, and beginning close to the out-works on the east side of Hamburgh, as a counterpart to what passed on the north and west sides, and leave the question to be decided by our readers, whether d'Avoust did act the becoming part of an officer and a man of honour towards the citizens of Hamburgh and its vicinity.

In the second week of December an adjutant from General Gengoult brought the mayor of Hamm an order, that it was Marshal d'Avoust's will to have every house in the village of Hamm, to the number of forty, as far as the church, burnt and levelled to the ground; but that the inhabitants were to be favoured with forty-eight hours' time to remove their property: several of these houses were then full of fugitives and property saved from dwellings burnt prior to this, it being the fourth time, within the last fortnight, that the mayor had to announce such heart-rending tidings to the parish; and, dreadful to relate, hardly thirty hours were elapsed of this prescribed time, before a swarm of pioneers, with their firebrands, burst, before break of day, into the houses like furies, and, turning a deaf ear to all the mayor's remonstrances, devoted to the flames, or pillaged, the beds, clothing, and property of many a widow and helpless family. The church and churchyard became their asylum. The monstrous barbarity of setting fire to houses before the expiration of the forty-eight hours so solemnly granted, and before the inhabitants had left them, induced the mayor to write a letter to d'Avoust, of which the following is an extract:

Monseigneur,   Hamm, Dec. 13, 1813.

The officer who brought the order for burning all the

houses as far as the church, assured me, that you had graciously been pleased to grant to the poor sufferers a respite of forty-eight hours, to enable them to remove their property. It is a painful task for me to announce to you that the respite has not been attended to, the pioneers having, by break of day this morning, set every dwelling on fire, although the respite granted expires not before three o'clock tomorrow morning. The remaining inhabitants of Hamm beseech you, in the most pressing manner, to inform them how far the burning of their houses may yet extend, as they only demand time and notice to remove their effects. I entreat to be favoured with a word of consolation on this head, that I may communicate it to the distressed parishioners.

B——, Mayor."

General Gengoult undertook to deliver the letter; but, instead of an answer, he next day showed the mayor a letter from General Loison, containing very pointed praises for his having merited the thanks of Marshal d'Avoust, for the punctuality and celerity with which his orders had been executed. The mayor received no answer whatever to his letter. But, on the 23rd of December, General Gengoult gave him a verbal assurance in the name of Marshal d'Avoust (thus we save our honour; we let others act the hangman's part—we are innocent), that he was authorized to announce to the inhabitants still occupying houses in Hamm, it was his (the marshal's) intention not to devote any more of them to the flames.

Two days afterwards, however, came the order to cut down all the trees within two hundred and fifty yards of the present line of posts; and, on the 15th of January 1814, d'Avoust sent an order that every remaining house in Hamm should be burnt the same evening; so that only two houses were left standing in this beautiful and romantic village, once studded with the tasteful edifices and gardens of Hamburgh's opulent merchants, and extending, in a straight line, nearly two miles and a half in length from the outworks of Hamburgh.

The country-seats, houses, barns, and stables last set on fire were full of fugitives, with effects and property of every description that had been saved from earlier conflagrations; there was, however, no time, no means to save an article, the whole was consigned to the flames, and, like a troop of parish paupers, the population of Hamm were turned out into the high road, in the midst of a very severe winter, to seek a shelter—to seek a morsel of bread; and we may say, driven to speechless despair at the sight of many a household relic, treasured up for years in a family, feeding the flames of the watch-fires of their infuriate persecutors.

It may be advanced in extenuation, that d'Avoust's means of defence required these barbarous measures, or were strengthened by them; but the sequel proves the falsity of such assertions, and places the act in a more glaring light of atrociousness and malignant personal revenge. On the 26th of January 1814, at an early hour in the morning, the Russians attacked, with three columns, the French line of posts in Hamm, drove them in with a trifling loss, and the whole of the French in Hamm, who had retreated to the church, consisting of nine officers and three hundred men, were taken prisoners; a very natural consequence, by the first attack, as, according to military tactics, the position of Hamm, with regard to the outworks of Hamburgh, is only a defile to be defended by sharpshooters; for, when the enemy is in possession of Wandsbeck, it affords no offensive position, because it can always be assaulted from the commanding grounds on the left flank.

★★★★★★

Nothing seemed sacred to him. The private property of the citizens, placed in the bank, was greedily seized upon. Thousands of industrious families were reduced to absolute beggary and starvation. He converted an opulent, populous city into a desert, and smiled, with horrid joy, when viewing the ruin, he had caused. The inhabitants that remained in the place, were exposed, every hour, to acts of diabolical tyranny. A look was sufficient to cause anyone to be thrown into prison—spies swarmed in almost every house—women were forced to dig in the trenches—the innocent were shot without mercy, for the most trifling offence. To conclude: d'Avoust, it will be seen, laughed to scorn all religious institutions, all moral precepts.

★★★★★★

After the bank had been completely gutted by d'Avoust, of silver coin and bars, to the value of nearly £700,000 sterling, he refused paying the salaries in arrears (not exceeding a few hundreds) due to the clerks and bookkeepers, many of whom, with their families, were thus reduced to a state of actual want. Mr. Pehmöller, one of the worthy bank-directors, commiserating their forlorn situation, was induced, on the 19th of April, to obtain an audience of d'Avoust, to make representations of their distresses. This unfeeling marshal answered Mr. Pehmöller's very pathetic description of their misery in the following terms: "He had but one object in view, to which all others must become subservient: his peculiar situation demanded this of him, and that was, to defend the place to the last extremity.—Economy was requisite in making use of the funds he had taken. Nothing but a general peace could induce him to leave the city; the enemy would never force him to evacuate it. In this state of things, the persons belonging to the bank had done much better to have quitted the town. He should give no order for their being paid their arrears." And then, waving his hand, the conversation ended. Mr. Pehmöller had no other consolation to soften the pain caused by such diabolical apathy, than the conscious feeling of having done his duty. One of these families was afterwards found in a state of absolute starvation! Everyone must be seized with horror on reading the tales of woe caused by d'Avoust's inhuman orders to clear, in a few hours, the public hospital for the insane and infirm, near Hamburgh. The sacred rights of humanity were thereby most barbarously violated with bitter scorn and derision. If anything were wanting to fill up the measure of d'Avoust's crimes, here "nothing that is devilish, accursed, and horrid, could be added. The shrines of Christianity had been beastly insulted by drunken soldiery; infants murdered at the mother's breast; but here the poor insane wretch—the squalid idiot—the melancholy maiden—the raging madman—the blind, and bedridden—were tumbled indiscriminately together, into the open fields, in the midst of winter, and left exposed to hunger, cold, and a miserable death, the sport of bantering *gens-d'armes*, the object of every species of ill-treatment; and their fits of convulsive laughter, weeping, cursing, and praying, were alike permitted to be the soldiers' scoff and mockery! Most of them, near five hundred in number, of both sexes, passed the night in a field covered with deep snow, without the least shelter; and more than thirty were found dead the next morning!

★★★★★★

CHAPTER 11

Battles of Brienne and La Rothière

The corps of Russians, under General Count von Wittgenstein, reinforced by the troops of the Grand Duke of Baden, had passed the Rhine at Fort Louis, and, after blockading the fortresses of Strasburg, Landau, and Schlettstadt, continued their march, by the way of Zabern, towards Joinville.

General Count St. Priest ordered General Bistram, with his brigade, to attack the intrenchments which the enemy had thrown up opposite the Lahn, and, after a slight resistance, they were carried. Upon this, General Bistram advanced towards Coblentz, took it by assault; and 7 pieces of cannon and 500 prisoners fell into his hands. General von Hünerbein drove the French out of Rheinbellen and Waldalgesheim, and marched into Kreutznach on the 2nd of January, in the evening: General von York now followed with the whole of his infantry.

A division of the enemy, under General Riccard, which occupied the banks of the Rhine, from Mentz to Coblentz, endeavoured to make a stand at Zimmern, on the Hundsrück. General Count von Henkel marched in that direction, burst open the gates in the night, stormed the place, and made above 200 prisoners in the several affairs.

General Count von Sacken concentrated his troops near Manheim. The French had erected a strong palisaded work, mounted with four guns and two howitzers, on the other side of the Rhine, opposite the influx of the Neckar into that river. General Sass was sent over with a detachment, in boats, and carried the works by storm. The *commandant*, 7 officers, 300 privates, and the artillery, remained in the hands of the victors. General Count von Sacken now directed the march of his corps to Frankenthal and Worms, detaching General Prince von Curland, with his brigade, in the direction of Alzei, to open a communication with the corps of von York and Count Langeron.

He found a small body of the French posted at Alzei, which he dispersed, making a lieutenant-colonel, 5 officers, and 120 men prisoners. In the meantime, Major-General Karpoff had charged eight squadrons of the enemy's cavalry at Mutterstadt, and dispersed them on all sides. Three lieutenant-colonels, 22 officers, and 198 dragoons, were on this occasion taken prisoners. General Count von Langeron occupied Bingen, on the 3rd of January, and drove the enemy into Mentz. During these three days, 13 pieces of cannon and 1,500 men were taken from the enemy.

The Silesian Army spread itself over the terrain between the Moselle and Manheim, and pushed forwards in the direction of Metz and Nancy. The greater part of Langeron's corps remained to blockade and besiege Mentz; and several other detachments of the Silesian Army undertook to observe the fortresses of Luxemburg, Thionville, Metz, Verdun, and Longwy. The army was in consequence much weakened; but on the other hand, it was considerably reinforced by the junction of the Prussian corps under General von Kleist.

The following corps were at this period placed under the immediate command of Field-Marshal Blücher:

1. The 1st Prussian corps under General von York, and the Generals of Division, Charles von Mecklenburg, von Horn, and von Hünerbein:

2. The 2nd Prussian corps, under General von Kleist, and the Generals of Division von Klüx, Prince Augustus Ferdinand of Prussia, and von Pirch:

3. The Russian corps, under General Count Langeron, von Sacken, and Tscherbatoff;

4. The Saxon corps, under the Duke of Weimar and General von Thielman.

The two following corps joined soon afterwards:

5. The 4th corps of German troops, consisting of Hessians, under the Prince of Hesse:

6. The 5th corps of German troops, consisting of detachments from Berg, Waldeck, Lippe, Nassau, Coburg, Meinungen, Hildburghausen, and Mecklenburg-Strelitz.

Forming, in the whole, an effective army of 150,000 men, well provided with every appendage to take the field.

Marshal Blücher issued the following proclamations; the one to his soldiers, the other to the French, on entering their territory;

> Field-Marshal von Blücher to the 2nd Prussian Corps, and the 4th and 5th German Corps.

> The Allied monarchs are satisfied with the Silesian Army: they have proved this, by doubling its strength, in adding to its files the brave soldiers of the 2nd Prussian corps, who fought: under the eyes of the august monarchs at Culm, and in the bloody conflict of Leipsic: and you, honest Hessians! who never denied your German character, nor failed in being faithful to the princes born in your country; and you, warriors of the fifth German corps, who never lost sight of your name, even in the ranks of the enemy, although composed of several tribes, yet are you firmly united by the same sentiments, the same abhorrence of foreign dominion, that has so long oppressed and degraded you. Soldiers! I feel myself most highly honoured in being your commander. The Silesian Army of 1813, receives you as brethren—as worthy members, with whom they will joyfully share everything. The Silesian Army of 1814, will continue to pursue the path of honour. And you, Germans! led by your hereditary princes, be assured that it will become my first care, my highest pride, to let the arrogant enemy feel the force of your arms, that he may confess—whatever success wily craft may have formerly had—that the ancient Teutonic bravery still lives in us, and that by your heroic deeds a lasting peace may be secured.

To the inhabitants of France, the field-marshal issued as follows:

> Frenchmen! do not let yourselves be deceived by scandalous reports, spread abroad by the evil-minded. See in the hosts of the Confederate sovereigns, the friends of humanity, whose only enemies are the enemies of peace.
> Your relations, your friends, your brothers, your children, prisoners in a foreign land, unite their wishes with ours, for the attainment of a peace, whose first benefit will be for them to return to the bosoms of their families.
>
> von Blücher.

In the cities of Worms and Speier, General von Sacken's corps found hospitals of the enemy, and, a quantity of military effects. On the 3rd of January, General Lukofkin had a brilliant affair of cavalry near Neustädt.

Marshal Marmont was posted on the 5th, with his corps, near Kaiserslautern, and passed the Saar, near Saarbrück, on the following day, after being joined by the corps of Generals Durutte and Riccard, who had retreated from Hundsrück, in the direction of St. Wendel.

The enemy broke down the bridges over the Saar, and occupied all the passes. They were briskly pursued by von Sacken's corps towards Saargemünd; a number of prisoners were taken, and another military hospital fell into their hands at Zweibrücken. General von York's corps advanced upon Saarlouis and Merzig, by the way of St. Wendel. Colonel Count Henkel entered Triers on the 6th, and more than a thousand sick and wounded, and a quantity of muskets, fell into his hands. The enemy were pursued to Luxemburg. It seemed his intention to hold a firm position on the Saar, so as to gain time to provision his fortresses, and reorganise his new levies.

A part of Langeron's corps marched as reserve towards Saarbrück. Marshal Blücher fixed his headquarters, on the 9th of January, at St. Wendel. In the course of the day, Major-general Karpoff pushed over a detachment of Cossacks to the other side of the Saar near Saargemünd, obliged the enemy to evacuate the place, and began to re-establish the bridge. In the meanwhile, General von York had caused another bridge to be thrown over the Saar, near Becking, and on the 10th, passed it at the head of his cavalry; but the enemy had deserted all his positions, and retreated to St. Avold. Towards noon, the bridges at Saarbrück and Saargemünd were ready, and the light troops of both corps penetrated as far as Forsbach. On the 11th, the enemy's advanced-guard were still at St. Avold, but on the appearance of a battalion of Prussians, they precipitately fled towards Metz. General von York pursued them on this road, leaving a brigade to blockade Saarlouis, and detaching another to Thionville and Luxemburg.

The retreating enemy were overtaken, and driven, sword in hand, to the gates of Metz. Sacken's corps now advanced to Nancy and Pont-à-Mousson. The cavalry of the advanced-guard reached the latter place on the 13th of January. The enemy, however, made no stand at any point; he evacuated the line of the Moselle on the 14th, retiring to Toul, and Major-General Prince von Curland presented the keys of the city of Nancy to General Count von Sacken. The rapid march of the Silesian Army, after the passage of the Rhine, was but little expected by the enemy. Our veteran field-marshal paused not a moment, but pursued his course with a numerous and well-appointed cavalry without intermission towards the Meuse.

The field-marshal removed his headquarters on the 16th from St. Avold to Nancy.

The grand Austro-Russian Army advanced into France from the south towards the north-west, and Blücher's army from the north-east towards the south; and the two armies formed a junction on the 15th of January, between Langres in Champaigne and Nancy. The headquarters of Marshal Blücher were still at Nancy on the 17th, and those of General Count Wrede at Charmes. The enemy had withdrawn himself over the Meuse, but still occupied Toul with infantry and artillery. General von Sacken advanced by the way of Pont-Vincent.

Field-Marshal Prince von Schwartzenberg having reported to our veteran hero that Langres was taken, and the enemy driven at all points over the Meuse, he ordered Toul to be stormed from the side of Woid. The dispositions were made: the enemy did not, however, wait the attack, but surrendered at discretion to General von Lieven. General von Sacken's corps marched in advance, to clear the Meuse of the enemy, and General Langeron occupied Toul, as reserve.

General von York's cavalry were posted before Verdun. The corps of General von Kleist marched upon Metz. Two of General von Sacken's columns filed off in the direction of Ligny and Joinville. In the afternoon the enemy debouched out of Ligny, with a force of about 2,500 horse, and, after cannonading the cavalry under General Wasiltschikoff, retired, on seeing that not a foot of ground was yielded to him. Ligny was stormed and carried on the 23rd, by order of our veteran Marshal, by the division of Prince Tscherbatoff; and on the 25th, the French were driven out of St. Dizier, and pursued on the road to Vitry, by the same general, who continued his march to Brienne on the 20th, to form a junction with the other part of Sacken's corps. St. Dizier was kept occupied by General Lanskoy, with 800 dragoons, to await General von York's corps coming up from St. Mihiel.

During these unimportant marches and advances, Napoleon had left Paris for the army on the 25th, and arrived at Chalons on the 26th, in the evening. He here commenced an attempt to act on the offensive with an army of 80,000 men, by proceeding to Vitry. Being, no doubt, informed, that Prince Tscherbatoff had filed off from St. Dizier, he seized the opportunity of attacking General Lanskoy at that place with a force of 25,000 men, who was, in consequence of such numbers, obliged to make a retrograde movement to Joinville. But no sooner was this event reported to our veteran hero, than he made his dispositions with his usual foresight and vigorous promptitude. Having removed his headquarters from Nancy to Toul on the 28th, he drew in General Lanskoy's detachment, concentrated the corps of General von Sacken, and a division of Langeron's corps, under General Olsufieff, near Brienne, pushed detachments of cavalry in advance towards Arcis and Troyes, which the enemy had occupied with infantry; and in this position awaited the development of Napoleon's further operations.

The 4th corps, under the Prince of Würtemberg, and the 3rd, under General Count Giulay, were in position near Bar-sur-Aube; the former spread itself towards Thil and Doulevent, to form a junction with the 5th corps, under General Wrede, which corps, as well as that under General Count Wittgenstein, were ordered to arrive at Joinville on the 29th. General Giulay extended his corps in the direction of Vandamon, and General von Kleist's corps was to pass the Meuse by St. Mihiel on the 2nd of February, to support the corps of General von. York. The remaining corps of the Grand Army were on the march to Bar-sur-Aube, but which they could not reach before the 1st of February.

In this state of affairs Marshal Blücher saw himself, at the moment, under the necessity of depending solely upon his own strength and the good countenance of his troops.

Napoleon's intentions were very obvious, being no other than to attempt cutting off Blücher from the main army, or to push him, by manoeuvring, so far aside, as to have it afterwards left to his own individual choice which army to attack singly to the greatest advantage. But here, again, the military talents of our hero shone forth in all their native splendour. To effect a march upon Nancy was everything to Napoleon, and none but those movements which our veteran so coolly and intrepidly performed, could have placed so great a barrier in Napoleon's way.

They secured Blücher's communication and junction with the Grand Army, and the enemy was unable to follow up his first plan of operations. General von York in the meantime remained standing with his corps between Nancy and the Marne, to observe Metz, and the occurrences that might take place in that quarter. Thus situated, Napoleon was compelled to follow the movements of the Silesian Army. With the main body of his troops, consisting of the corps of Marshals Victor and Marmont, the major part of his guards, and the brigades of cavalry under Generals Milhaud, Grouchy, and Colbert, he moved on to Vassy on the 28th, and pushed forwards, by the way of Montierender, towards Brienne on the 29th of January.

It was impossible for the field-marshal to judge what the real intentions of Napoleon were; whether to attack, to manoeuvre, or only to make demonstrations. At all events, however, he continued to concentrate his forces round Brienne. General von Sacken's corps, which had marched to Lesmont, now returned, and General Count Pahlen, who had joined, at this juncture, the Silesian Army, with the advanced-guard of Count Wittgenstein's corps, covered this movement of Sacken's, in the morning of the 29th of January, and at the same time observed the deploying of the enemy's forces.

Some important dispatches of the enemy happened to fall into the hands of Blücher, on this day. They contained orders for Marshal Mortier, who was still in position at Troyes, with a part of the guards, to leave this place, and the Aube, and to post himself on the right wing of the French Grand Army. It was therefore clear, that Napoleon intended to unite the whole of his forces. This induced Blücher to attempt approaching the Confederate Army still nearer, as a complete junction could not take place at Bar-sur-Aube before the 1st of February, and a secure position at Trannes, which extended to Maisons, where the Prince of Würtemberg was preparing to post himself on strong ground, offered him many peculiar advantages.

Our hero was upon the point of making this movement, when the enemy advanced with numerous strong columns upon Brienne. This event instantly changed his plan of operations, and as it was near three o'clock, p.m. he determined to accept battle, although he well knew the numbers of the enemy were much superior to his own.

Brienne le Château is quite an open place, with no walls, composed of wooden houses, and lying at the foot of a hill, on which the castle or manor-house stands; a rising ground stretches itself from thence towards Lesmont; but, on the side towards Montierender and Trannes, the face of the country forms an extensive plain.

The corps of General Olsufieff still occupied Brienne, and that of Sacken was drawn up in columns, on the road from Brienne to La Rothière.

A considerable body of the enemy's cavalry began to debouch in front of General Count von Pahlen, and made it necessary for him to retreat on Brienne, in order not to entangle himself with such superior numbers. The enemy pushed on the right wing of his mass of cavalry to the foot of the heights, with the view of out-flanking him, to prevent which, General Count von Pahlen marched, with his division, through the town, and joined General von Sacken. In the meantime, Napoleon proceeded to attack Brienne, with columns of infantry, supported by a numerous artillery; he commenced a brisk cannonade, and set the town on fire in several places. These movements were made from Napoleon's right wing, the cavalry of which, after Count Pahlen's retreat, remained inactive. On his left wing few cavalry were posted.

The gallant General Olsufieff succeeded in repulsing all the furious simultaneous attacks of the enemy. His Russians fought with their wonted intrepidity, and every attempt of the enemy to lodge himself in the place proved of no avail.

Napoleon, who was in the field, here committed a fatal and unpardonable error, in the disposition of his troops. General Count von Pahlen having retreated, and Napoleon's mass of cavalry, on his right wing, becoming, of course, useless, it was highly incumbent on him, as a good general, to have filed them off to his left wing, where alone they could prove of service, and be disposable. But this he did not do; and this egregious error did not escape the vigilant eye of Blücher, who instantaneously gave orders to execute one of those bold, decisive, and grand movements, by which doubtful contests are decided.

Our hero commanded the cavalry of General von Sacken's corps, and the cavalry brigade under Count Pahlen, to act in conceit, and to throw themselves upon the enemy's left wing. His commands were obeyed with precision and alacrity. The close of evening favoured the secrecy of their approach; the Russian dragoons rushed to the attack, charged, and overthrew whole columns, cut in pieces all that made resistance, and pursued the fugitives towards the town, sword in hand. The whole of the enemy's left wing was broken and dispersed, and twelve pieces of cannon taken from them. A noble emulation seemed to fire the Russian cavalry, and, if possible, they surpassed themselves.

The enemy, however, from the points of his right wing, continued to renew his attacks on the place, with fresh troops; but they were again repulsed. During the night, the French found means, from the side of the castle, through an unoccupied pass, to get possession of a part of the town. But the corps of General von Sacken advanced, and stormed the place at eleven o'clock at night: the whole of the town fell a prey to the flames, the Russians kept possession of it, and only a few French riflemen occupied the castle. The troops fought with that ferocious animosity which generally accompanies night attacks, and the loss of the French was immense.

Marshal von Blücher postponed his intended march upon Trannes till the following day, and kept Brienne occupied with a detachment of cavalry.

On the 31st of January, the enemy advanced his reinstated left wing, and, towards noon, pushed on his columns of infantry to Brienne, and commenced a heavy cannonade upon the Russian cavalry, posted behind the place; upon which the latter drew back slowly into the position of Trannes.

Napoleon now followed with his whole army, which he drew up in two lines, his right wing leaning on Dienville, his centre on La Rothière, and his left wing on La Gibrie.

General von York had, on the same day, advanced upon St. Dizier, attacked and carried it, forming, at the same time, a junction with General Count von Wittgenstein's corps.

The enemy deployed a great body of his cavalry in front of the position of Trannes, in the morning of the 31st of January, with the intention, most probably, of ascertaining the exact strength of the Confederate forces. He occupied the wood of Beaulieu, being the only point from which the Allied position could be attacked to advantage. The strong ground at Maisons was taken up by the corps of the Prince of Würtemberg, in the course of the day, by which occupation he formed the right wing of Field-Marshal Blücher's army. General Count Guilay posted his corps, as a support, between Bossancourt and Arsonval. General Barclay de Tolly collected the Russian and Prussian guards in reserve, between Colombe and Bar-sur-Aube, to be able to support any threatened point.

The corps of General Count Wrede having been concentrated between Joinville and Mussec, on the 30th, was, in conjunction with General Count Wittgenstein, to have attacked Vassy on the 31st; the dispositions were already made, and the Bavarian-Austrian Army was in march, beyond Joinville, on the morning of the 31st of January, when the report was made that Count Wittgenstein had carried it in the night. This circumstance, added to the advance of Napoleon to Brienne, determined General Count Wrede to direct his march to Soulaines, where the enemy had posted from 5,000 to 6,000 men; but they did not wait the result of an attack, the place being evacuated at midnight.

It was resolved to make a general attack upon the whole line of the enemy, on the 1st of February. Prince Schwartzenberg placed, for this purpose, the corps of Count Giulay, the Prince of Würtemberg, and the reserves of Russian grenadiers, under the immediate command of Marshal Blücher, independently of his own army. With these gallant and tried troops our hero was to commence the onset, the dispositions being entirely left to his judgment.

Marshal Blücher determined to make the attack at noon, in three columns. The Prince of Würtemberg had orders to break up from Maisons, and to arrive at Eclance at twelve o'clock, to attack Chaumenil from this point. General Baron von Sacken was to attack La Rothière, and Count Giulay, Dienville. The Russian grenadiers were drawn up as reserves.

The battle commenced by the Prince of Würtemberg attacking, with his corps, the wood in front of Eclance, while La Rothière was assaulted in a grand style, by General von Sacken's infantry. The cavalry of this corps charged that of the enemy, though superior in number, but were at last obliged to fall back on their infantry.

Having been reinforced, they renewed the charge with undaunted bravery; a severe conflict ensued, which lasted some time with sanguinary obstinacy; the French were driven from one rallying point to the other, and finally broken and dispersed, with a terrible loss; their infantry were put into disorder, some batteries charged sword in hand, the field of battle was cleared of the enemy entirely, and thirty-two pieces of cannon formed part of the trophies so dearly earned, by the firmness, discipline, and courage of the Russian cavalry in particular. It may be said, that from this moment the battle was won, although Napoleon still occupied Dienville, La Rothière, and Chaumenil.

A brigade of Russian grenadiers was sent, by Marshal Blücher, to reinforce the Prince of Würtemberg; and General Barclay de Tolly moved in advance to La Rothière, with the reserves of guards under his command.

At this period of the battle, our hero put himself at the head of the columns that were intended to force La Rothière. He led them personally into fire, with the animation and energy so conspicuous in his actions, when the hour of emergency and danger calls them forth. A Cossack was shot dead, close to him. But the place was carried, and the enemy dislodged out of it, at the approach of night. Nature seemed to have aided in rendering this combat most grievously painful. A dreadful fall of snow hid, at intervals, the columns from each other, and the wind drove it in the faces of the troops with such violence, that it was utterly impossible for them, at times, to fire in steady platoons.

Our hero was present everywhere; he executed his dispositions himself, fearlessly exposing his person. His chivalrous example electrified his troops to an uncommon degree, and great was the increase of his fame on this glorious day. How admirable was the coolness he displayed, in leading, arranging, and heading the grand assault upon La Rothière and Chaumenil, which he, with so much foresight and penetration, had deemed the most important points to be gained; although the enemy, by way of a demonstration, pretended to threaten the flank of the Confederate Army; yet no artifice could mislead the judgment of our experienced captain and commander.

The instant the enemy began to fly from La Rothière, the Prince of Würtemberg pushed on his troops from Petit Megnil, fell upon their right flank, and took five guns. The French still obstinately occupied the houses in La Rothière, and defended each like so many forts. Napoleon, at the head of his guards, stormed the town three times successively; but all his attempts were in vain. Russian grenadiers maintained the place, and the fame of their ancient glory

******

We have had opportunities of remarking, that the Russian possesses, in an eminent degree, nearly all those qualities. that are accounted necessary to form a good soldier. Obedience, devotion, patience, courage, bodily strength, and a good constitution, are in no nation of Europe so generally to be found as in the Russian. They may be reproached with the want of cleanliness, by the superficial observer, because, when in the field, the niceties of their dress form their least care; yet, whenever a clear spring presents itself, they never neglect to bathe themselves, even in the severest weather.

But in no situation incident to a soldier's life, is the Russian so much superior to the Frenchman, as in an hospital. A hospital full of sick and wounded Frenchmen is a den, where despair, melancholy, and base dejection brood in gloomy silence. That of Russians, on the contrary, is a scene of cheerfulness and merriment. A Russian is resigned, but it is a resignation intermixed with a grateful sense of God's mercies, while a Frenchman's resignation degenerates but too easily into selfish despair.

A total neglect of every measure of cleanliness is always evident amongst the French in such a state, while the Russians occupy themselves with nothing else. The latter have a custom in their hospitals which may not be unworthy of imitation, as being preferable, in many instances, to wetting the floors, when cleaning them, which is this: fresh sand is regularly spread over the floors, half a foot thick, every morning, and a large quantity of pine or fir branches, chopped small, is then strewed over the surface, which affords a fragrant and refreshing effluvium, that overpowers, in some measure, those unpleasant smells that arise, and seems to clear and rarefy the foul air engendered from the steam of perspirations so general in crowded hospitals, and which so often prove contagious.

★★★★★★

In animating his troops, Napoleon several times exposed his person; he strained every nerve, and fought like an exasperated tiger, to boast of having gained the first victory over the Confederates on the French soil, and to restore the lost confidence in the fortune and omnipotence of his arms.

During these important events, General Count Wrede had advanced, with the 5th corps, from Soulaines to Brienne. His advanced-guard, under General Hardegg, made such an impetuous attack on the enemy, that their junction with the corps at Chaumenil was completely prevented. General Count Wrede, with the view of co-operating with the corps of the Prince of Würtemberg, stormed the village of Chaumenil, without loss of time, at the point of the bayonet, and carried it. Napoleon soon perceived that he had thereby lost an important point of his line of operations; and, by ordering up the artillery of his guards, endeavoured, by a heavy and murderous cannonade, to dislodge the Bavarians out of the place.

But his sanguinary efforts proved fruitless, when coming in contact with Bavarian intrepidity. They bravely stood their ground. The Bavarian Colonel Diez, with a brigade of cavalry and a regiment of Austrian dragoons, seized a favourable moment, and throwing himself on all sides at once, on the enemy's square masses of infantry, that covered their batteries, succeeded in breaking them, and hotly pursued the flying foe till night was far advanced. A battery of sixteen pieces of cannon was taken, sword in hand.

The right wing of Napoleon's army still kept its ground at Dienville. Count Giulay here exhibited much gallantry and resolution; he advanced at the head of his troops to the assault six several times. Repulses and rallies trod close on the heels of each other, but the well-known steady coolness of Austrian bravery overcame every obstacle; and, by the sixth assault, near twelve at night, the place was carried with a dreadful carnage. It was about this time that Napoleon made the last, but fruitless, attack upon La Rothière; and the trumpet of victory was now sounded at all points, in honour of the Allied arms.

Grand and glorious were the trophies that graced the martial deeds of the gallant Confederates on this day.

******

The next morning, by break of day, the intrepid field-marshal, on finding the enemy had relinquished the field of battle, rode down the front of the Russian columns, at the head of his numerous staff, and paid due honours to these illustrious corps, who had behaved in so distinguished a manner, and omitted nothing to show that he knew what it was, to be well served, by acknowledging their merit in the strongest terms. As he approached the several divisions, he addressed the troops and officers in the most emphatical manner, in nearly the following words:

> Brave comrades in arms! I shall thank your emperor for having done me the honour to, command such excellent soldiers! This honour, and this pleasure, will accompany me to the grave!

The commanding officer explained these words in the Russian language to the troops, and shouts of transport rent the air. The trumpets sounded victory, and every eye glistened with joy and rapturous delight. It was an ecstatic scene.

******

Our hero had to boast of having taken from Napoleon, in the field, 73 pieces of cannon and 12,000 prisoners, including two generals and a proportionate number of officers.

The Emperor of Russia and the King of Prussia had placed themselves in the centre of the Confederate Army, between Trannes and La Rothière, and animated the troops by their presence.

Napoleon was several times in danger of being taken prisoner by the Cossacks. His troops fought desperately, and their obstinate defence, under Marmont, Mortier, Victor, Colbert, and Grouchy, fully proves what exertions Napoleon made to step forth as victor from the combat. But he was beaten. Blücher, the gallant and the brave, the Marshal *Forwards* of the day, beat Napoleon, and forced the stubborn tyrant to fall back discomfited, with the main body of his army, from Lesmont to Troyes.

******

During the Battles of Brienne and La Rothière, the army had to struggle with many privations. Its veteran chef shared them with evident cheerfulness. For several days nothing was served at his table but boiled potatoes, of which he partook in a manner that endeared him to his troops.

Firm and intrepid, and at all times affable, jocose, and in high spirits, whether in a shower of balls or m a shower of rain, whether sleeping on straw or on the bare ground, whether in a storm or in sunshine, no man certainly ever showed a greater equality of temper, steadiness of character, ardour, and zeal, than Blücher did at this period.

Silent and attentive, sitting before a watchfire, smoking his pipe, he would listen to the counsel and opinions of his staff officers, and at last give his judgment for and against, with his own peculiar energy and decision. Over-scrupulous considerations never had any weight with him, and what he had once determined upon, he executed, at the head of the advance, fighting and commanding sword in hand.

******

Napoleon made good his retreat by two routes. With the main body, he took the road by the way of Lesmont towards the Seine, along which river Schwartzenberg's corps, on the other side, endeavoured to fall on his rear. The reserves, under Marmont, posted on the heights of Brienne, to cover his retreat, were ordered to march on Vitry. Every day, at this period, was marked by an affair of outposts, at once bloody and disadvantageous to Napoleon.

That our readers may be the better enabled to comprehend the subsequent occurrences, and operations of the several conflicting armies, we previously lay before them the following observations.

The line of those operations which were carried on by the belligerents, might be compared to a triangular figure, of which Paris formed the point, and a line drawn from Cologne to Geneva, the basis; the north side, from Cologne to Paris, found protection from the emancipated Low Countries, assisted by Great Britain; and the south side, from Geneva to Chambery, should have been protected by Switzerland, but this country did nothing whatever for the furtherance of the good cause.

It was therefore necessary that the Confederates should divide their strength, that they might cut off the south of France from Italy, and make threatening movements in the rear of the viceroy, but at the same time to advance upon Lyons, to obstruct a concentration of Napoleon's forces on the Seine.

The Silesian Army, under Blücher, and the Grand Army, under

Schwartzenberg, were to come in contact with each other on the Marne. The one drew his reinforcements from Brussels and Liège, and the other by the way of Basle.

The Crown Prince of Sweden formed, with his Northern Army, the last link to the chain. He had, however, exclusively of his Swedes, a considerable body of troops, under Generals Bülow, Winzingerode, and Czernischeff, which he had marched, in November, towards Holland, and that now, in conjunction with the Dutch Army, and the Saxons, under the Duke of Weimar, joined the right wing of the Silesian Army, and took part in the principal combat.

It must here be obvious to everyone, that the line from Geneva and Basle to Paris was the weakest and the longest, in the rear, and in the wings of the Grand Army; that is, it was the most distant from its supports. The corps of Bubna and Simbschen were evidently too weak. The line from Düsseldorf or Cologne, to Paris, acquired, by Holland and the sea, a much greater degree of safety. The support was nearer. The number of fortresses did, to be sure, in some measure render communications and advances somewhat difficult; yet the enemy, under Carnot and Maison, could only act on the defensive.

On the other hand, Augereau, in the south of France, having at his disposal all the forces of the country, could act on the offensive; in which case, the fortresses were of infinite service to the success and continuation of his operations.

Consequently, if the forces of Austria should be broken through, between Basle and Paris, much might be lost. It is this very circumstance, maturely weighed, which fully explains the slow advances of Prince Schwartzenberg.

Marshal Blücher was compelled to advance with all possible celerity. If he were beaten (and this could only be possible in front, or on his right wing, near which the Grand Army stood), he could fall back without difficulty on the Northern Army, recover his losses, and recruit his strength.

But Schwartzenberg was so peculiarly situated, that he could be beaten in front, on his left wing, and in his rear; and if the enemy should succeed in throwing back Blücher's army more to the north, he was actually surrounded on all sides. After the bloody combats in February, he was therefore cautious of not advancing too rashly. He kept his eye upon Lyons, upon Mentz, and upon Basle; and could, by so doing, under the pressure of unfavourable events, be prepared for acting.

This was the reasoning, and these were the reflections of the commander-in-chief. There is just as little foundation for blame, in the measures adopted by Prince Schwartzenberg, as in the more active conduct of our veteran hero. Blücher must march forwards—he must advance—he must bid open defiance to the enemy.

Chapter 12

Blücher Marches His Army on Paris

It is certain that Napoleon laid down the plan of his operations, upon the basis of the review drawn up at the end of the last chapter. It was his intention to break off the right point or corner of the Confederates' triangle of operations, in his desperate attacks upon Blücher's army forming that point, and then to destroy the left point under Schwartzenberg and Bubna. But three times was he forced to recoil, from Blücher's gallant resistance; twice did Schwartzenberg humiliate him; and, from Lyons to Geneva, Napoleon failed entirely. The course of the events will afford a copious theme for explanation.

Marshal Blücher, after his signal victory at La Rothière, proceeded onwards, in conjunction with General von York's corps, to Paris. On the 3rd of February General von York conducted his attack on the united corps of Macdonald and Arrighi, and the divisions of cavalry under Sebastiani and Excelmans, with so much address, that he drove them back on Chalons-sur-Marne, and summoned the town to surrender. This being refused, he stormed the suburbs of the place, on the side of Vitry, and set the town on fire, in four places, by a shower of shells which he threw into it. A deputation from the inhabitants came out of Chalons, with the permission of Marshal Macdonald, and entreated that hostilities might cease.

It was afterwards arranged with the marshal, that all the stores and magazines were to remain in the place, and neither be moved to the rear, nor in advance, and that the town should be delivered up in its present state. The victorious Prussians marched into it on the 6th of February. But the marshal, after consenting to these conditions, did not scruple immediately to violate them, by causing the stone bridge over the Maine to be blown up, notwithstanding the representations of the inhabitants. General von York, however, in spite of this breach

HOW THE ALLIED TROOPS MARCHED INTO PARIS.

of faith, passed the river, and followed up his pursuit of Macdonald towards Paris. The gallant conduct of General von York, on these two days, was very conspicuous, and afforded his troops an opportunity of distinguishing themselves in the several attacks. Meanwhile Prince Schwartzenberg, with the Grand Army, kept in a line, and in the same direction with the Silesian Army, along the banks of the Seine.

The two armies were separated, most probably, to procure themselves easy means of subsistence; but they were near enough to each other to act conjunctly if necessary.

Napoleon having received reinforcements out of Spain, succeeded in throwing himself between the two armies, with a force of at least 100,000 men, and in such a position, that he had it in his power to press hard upon the right and left of the Confederate Armies, as best suited his views.

The army of Blücher, on its march to Paris on the 10th of February, occupied a line which extended from Vertus, where Blücher and Langeron had their headquarters, by the way of Champaubert and Château Thierry, to La Ferté-sous-Jouarre, on a plain of nearly sixty miles in extent. It was this circumstance that rendered Napoleon's attempt to break through it but too successful. General Alsufieff was posted at Champaubert with 4,000 men of Blücher's army, where he was assailed by Napoleon on the 10th, and obliged to relinquish the position he had assumed, with severe loss. He himself was taken prisoner. Generals von York and von Sacken formed a rapid junction in this precarious situation; but, with all their heroic exertions on the 11th, they could not force their way from Montmirail to join Blücher, on the shortest route, and from whom they were in a manner cut off. They, in consequence, withdrew over the Marne on the 12th, near Château Thierry, and marched upon Chalons.

Marshal Mortier followed hard upon them, and crossed the Marne on the 13th February. In the meantime, our veteran hero, with the corps of Kleist and Langeron, had, with the most strenuous efforts, repulsed Marshal Marmont from Etoges on Montmirail. Napoleon, having received notice of this bold and unexpected advance, that favoured the operations of Generals von York and Sacken, hastened back by a forced march in the night of the 13th, with his guards, and divisions of cavalry, from Château Thierry, whither he had followed Mortier, and formed a junction with Marmont.

His great superiority of cavalry enabled Napoleon, after an obstinate and bloody conflict, to surround Blücher's army; which event he vainly regarded at the time, as productive of the total defeat of the field-marshal. But, instead of this, our hero, with the greatest energy, foresight, and presence of mind, formed the main body of his army into square *phalanxes*, braved with dauntless valour the gathering storm, and fought his way, at the head of his invincible Prussians, in the direction of Vertus to Chalons, under a constant fire of musketry and charges of cavalry.

A retreat of this kind was accompanied with considerable difficulty, as the contest was with superior numbers, and everything was to be effected by the good countenance of the troops alone. The following minute particulars of this unexampled retreat may not prove unacceptable to the reader. The scene in which our hero happened to be principally occupied, was equal to the scope of his abilities, and it may be also said, that it was worthy of his talents.

Marshal Marmont, in pursuance of his orders, made a retrograde movement, on the 14th, out of the village of Fromentières. Our veteran commander, who had bivouacked during the previous night, near Champaubert, determined on following him. The enemy retreated as far as the village of Joinvilliers, at which place a considerable mass of the enemy's cavalry was observed to have been posted. In the heat of pursuit, six pieces of Prussian artillery, that were too far advanced, fell into the hands of the French. But the Prussian cavalry, under General Ziethen and Colonel von Blücher, a son of the field-marshal, charged instantly, with furious impetuosity, the enemy's horse, that were endeavouring to secure their booty, repulsed them with loss, and retook the guns.

From the intelligence obtained from the prisoners, it was ascertained that Napoleon had just arrived on the field with his guards and a considerable body of cavalry, having made a fatiguing forced march during the night from Château Thierry. Meanwhile Blücher's infantry kept advancing upon the village, in columns and battalions, on the open grounds from both sides of the high road that led through the place. The enemy's horse, strengthened by reinforcements, soon returned to the charge, penetrated the weak advanced-guard of Blücher's army, and fell upon the infantry drawn up in columns on the plain.

This movement and manoeuvre of Napoleon was, however, foreseen by our hero. The columns having been previously formed into square *phalanxes*, they received the tumultuous charges of the enemy's horse with unparalleled firmness, stood their ground as if rooted to the spot on which they were posted, and kept up an unremitting and destructive fire of musketry from all sides on the advancing enemy.

To the right of the village six of the Prussian squares were attacked at one and the same instant, and were all equally successful in driving back the daring adversary. Blücher's cavalry having again rallied under the protection of the infantry, the French, instead of being the assailants, now found themselves attacked in their turn; the murderous fire of the Prussian infantry had thrown them into disorder, and the charges of the Prussian horse were attended with the most brilliant success. Napoleon, however, still continued to bring fresh troops into action, and large bodies were observed in motion on both flanks.

Two battalions of Blücher's advanced-guard, that had already penetrated into the village, had scarcely time to form into squares; and a large portion of them were either killed or wounded. The cavalry of the field-marshal's army did not exceed 1,100 effective men, while the enemy showed at least from 5,000 to 6,000 horse in the field: no acts of bravery could counterbalance so great a disproportion of numbers, in an arm so very essential in the open country wherein our hero was now posted. To prevent the serious consequences that might eventually result from further resistance, the field-marshal resolved to withdraw himself from a position exposed to such an unequal combat, and gave orders that the infantry should put itself in march, formed in alternate squares and columns, with the artillery placed between the open spaces that separated each column.

Numerous bodies of sharpshooters, with divisions of cavalry, covered the flanks and rear: and in this order the retreat began. The country round the line of operations was without enclosures of any kind, and only intersected here and there with spots of underwood, which caused the movements of the enemy's cavalry to be less exposed to the observation of the Allies. To render success more certain, the infantry carefully avoided throwing themselves under cover, and, by proceeding along the high road in firm columns, could keep the enemy more effectually in check, and ensure their own safety from being endangered by the numerous bodies of cavalry that now hovered around them. A continual succession of attacks and repulses followed each other, at short intervals, from the village of Joinvilliers to half way between Champaubert and Etoges, being a distance of nearly twelve miles.

Every column and every square was charged or attacked in turn, and exposed to the enemy's galling fire. The Prussians, nobly supported by their Allies the Russians, were not backward in returning their fire with steady precision. Marching, loading, and firing alternately, and yet preserving the most perfect order, the most exact discipline—

no hurry—no confusion—their retreat more resembled the evolutions of a review, than the strenuous efforts of a handful of brave men, headed by an adored chief, to extricate themselves, by dint of personal courage and resolution, from the toils which a wily enemy had spread for their destruction. The French cavalry, in the heat of charging, often precipitated themselves between the Prussian columns, and their disorderly retreat soon attested the success of the Confederates' bayonets. Several heavy and regular charges were attempted by Napoleon, whenever the terrain offered a favourable opportunity, all of which were ultimately repulsed with heavy loss.

Towards sunset it was observed that the enemy had succeeded in turning the flanks by a bye-road, and throwing himself across the high-way, in front of Blücher's advanced-guard, between Champaubert and Etoges. It was Napoleon's obvious intention to block up the field-marshal's line of march entirely. The masses of cavalry were numerous, and not only occupied the road itself, but the open country on both sides of it.

It is not to be denied, that the emergency of the moment was great, and big with event.

Our veteran hero saw himself actually surrounded on all sides. To the sudden, but vigorous resolves of the gallant Blücher, the troops were indebted for their safety, their honour, and their glory; and these were no other than to force his way, at the point of the bayonet, through every impediment, without loss of time. It was evident that nothing but delay could prove vitally dangerous to the field-marshal. After ordering up his artillery in advance, that began a heavy cannonade upon the enemy's horse, the columns of infantry continued their march, although incessantly galled on all sides by the French riflemen; and, when within musket-shot, opened a regular fire in platoons upon the cavalry that opposed their progress.

The enemy's cavalry could not withstand such undaunted resolution, assisted by an enthusiasm that rendered the most desperate enterprise easy to such warriors. They were obliged, after a severe loss, to relinquish the high road to Blücher's army, and to content themselves with partial attacks on the flanks and rear of the Prussians. The columns and squares, posted advantageously on the flanks and rear, were attacked, but none of them were either broken, put into disorder, or obliged to yield ground to the enemy, sooner than their line of march demanded it.

As night approached, the cavalry in advance was attacked again by infantry; but the march of the army continued without interruption towards Etoges. The troops, on entering the village, were fired upon by the enemy, posted in the houses and gardens. In driving the French out of the place, the divisions under General von Kleist and General von Kapzcewitz particularly distinguished themselves; they cleared the village of the enemy, opened a passage for themselves and the remainder of the army, and, covered with glory, bivouacked for the night on the heights of Bergêres.

Marshal Blücher's loss, on this memorable retreat, may be computed at 3,500 men killed, wounded, and taken prisoners. Napoleon's object was to crush the whole corps: his means of offence were more than double to those of Blücher; of cavalry he had three times the number; and yet, with this decisive superiority, he achieved but little. Nor ought it to be omitted, that the effects of the enterprise, instead of proving disastrous to the general cause, were, on the contrary, calculated to abate the energy of the French troops, and destroy all confidence in themselves.

Blücher's artillery was more numerous, and much better served, than that of the enemy; and the dreadful chasms it at times produced in the hostile cavalry, by a well-directed cross-fire, must have occasioned an enormous sacrifice of men on the part of the French.

The glory of the Prussian and Russian arms was not only supported by the able, gallant, and meritorious conduct of the troops engaged, but they acquired fresh splendour at this important and critical *sera*, by their intrepid resistance against a powerful and adventurous enemy.

The happy union and perfect harmony which was preserved between the Prussian and Russian forces, and the wonderful exertions of wisdom and policy in their heroic commander, must be reflected upon with singular satisfaction, by every well-wisher to the good cause.

Victory might be said, although retreating, to follow their standards, and to carry along with her a series of successes through an extended variety of attacks of difficulty and danger.

The excellent dispositions of General von Gneisenau, who directed the movements on the high road, and the conduct of General von Ziethen, and Prince Augustus of Prussia, did not a little contribute to the success of the retreat. Their regular co-operation proved of the most signal service.

These operations having been happily effected, Marshal Blücher determined upon taking up the position at Chalons; while this movement presented a singular advantage, by ensuring his junction with the other corps of his army. Generals von York and Sacken had, according to intelligence received, occupied Rheims, and General Winzingerode was only two or three marches from that city; these corps formed, in consequence, a junction, to their mutual gratification; and, on the 17th of February, the whole Silesian Army was again in line in the vicinity of Chalons.

★★★★★★

At this time, when the field-marshal had made good his retreat to Chalons, to form a junction with the corps of General von York, Sacken, and Winzingerode, and the Confederates, by the affair at Montereau, were thrown into a temporary consternation, our veteran wrote the following very laconic, but sheering words to the Emperor of Russia:

> Let not anxiety, for a moment, plant a wrinkle on Your Majesty's brow; for I shall catch him (meaning Napoleon) at last.
>
> Blücher.

(The Original German,)

> *Eure Majestät mögen Sich kein graues Haar wachsen lassen, ich werde ihn doch schon am Ende fangen, Blücher.*

(Imparted to the editor by Baron von K—n.)

★★★★★★

The commander-in-chief permitted his brave companions in arms to enjoy a day's repose on the 18th of February; but, on the next day, again put his army in motion, advanced on the 21st to Mery, and joined the corps of General Count Wittgenstein, posted in that neighbourhood. The enemy assaulted Mery on the 22nd. Every necessary disposition was made to defend the town, and the bridge over the Seine. But a variety of unforeseen impediments occurred; a terrible fire broke out in the high street, the artillery was obliged to be withdrawn, and the town evacuated. It was re-attacked by the Allies on the 23rd, the French driven out of it after a desperate resistance, and the place maintained.

In the meantime, Napoleon had seen himself forced to direct the whole strength of his army on the Seine, in order to check the progress of the Confederates under Prince von Schwartzenberg. Marshal Victor and General Oudinot, although reinforced considerably by detachments from Spain, found themselves too weak to act on the offensive against the Grand Army of the Allies under Schwartzenberg.

The latter had left Troyes on the 10th of February, stormed Nogent and Sens on the 11th, and driven the enemy over to the left bank of the Seine on the 14th. General Count Wrede, at the instigation of Blücher, forced the passage of the Seine in the night of the 12th, at Nogent, towards Provins; and the Prince of Würtemberg, Generals Bianchi and Giulay, near Bray and Montereau.

General Count Wrede and General Count Wittgenstein forming, with their corps, the extreme advance of the Grand Army, were posted near Nangis, on the 15th of February, not being more than forty leagues from Paris; the detachments of Platow and Hardegg occupying Fontainbleau on the 17th. General Count Wrede was on the point of executing the orders of the Prince von Schwartzenberg, to advance upon Sezanne, in the rear of Napoleon's line of operations, when he was obliged to halt.

It seems Napoleon had hastened back again, by another forced march, in the direction of La Ferté sous Jouarre, and, falling suddenly, with an overwhelming superiority of numbers, on General Count Wittgenstein's corps, had compelled him to pass over to the left bank of the Seine. During his pursuit, Napoleon fell in with the Prince of Würtemberg's corps near Montereau, whose detachments had already occupied Melun. The prince defended himself with signal bravery and obstinacy for several hours, but, after a great effusion of blood, was obliged to fall back. Napoleon marched onwards by the way of Nogent, and took possession of Troyes, which, by virtue of a convention, had been previously evacuated by the Allies.

Before farther progress could be made, the energetic conduct of our intrepid Veteran prevented any fatal consequences ensuing from Napoleon's ephemeral successes. Blücher's movements were rapid and well digested; and his support rescued the Confederates from an unpleasant situation, the consequence of some mischances, for which no one can in the least degree be censured. Blücher's affair with the enemy, by Mery, on the Seine, on the 21st, in which he maintained his position, materially prevented General Count Wittgenstein's corps from suffering a severe check, and covered, in a great degree, the retrograde movement of the Prince of Schwartzenberg, which he was making along the Aube, as far as Columbey, to the north-west of Chaumont, where he arrived on the 25th of February.

******

The manly and independent spirit of Marshal Blücher could ill brook silence when military operations were about to take place, which did not exactly coincide with his own judgment. The retrograde movement of the Grand Army to Columbey was not made with his concurrence; and in his lively zeal for the good cause, he presented the following forcible remarks, drawn up with his own hand, both to the Emperor of Russia and King of Prussia:

> It has been reported to me by Colonel von Grollman, that the Grand Army is to make a retrograde movement. I think it my duty to lay before Your Majesty the unavoidable, disastrous consequences that must ensue from such a step.
>
> 1. The whole French nation will be under arms, and that part which has declared itself for the good cause, will be ruined.
>
> 2. Our victorious army, flushed with success, will become dispirited.
>
> 3. Our retrograde movements must be made through a country, where our troops, urged by want, will deprive the inhabitants of their last morsel, and drive them to despair.
>
> 4. Napoleon will thereby recover from the shock which our rapid movements have caused him, and regain the opinion of the nation in his favour.
>
> That your Imperial Majesty has permitted me to act again on the offensive, claims my most unfeigned thanks. I can promise to myself the most brilliant success, if Your Majesty would be graciously pleased to issue positive orders that the corps of General von Winzingerode and General von Bülow may obey my directions. In cooperation with these generals I shall march forwards to Paris, and shall be as little afraid to meet Napoleon as any of his marshals, if they should oppose my advancing.
>
> Permit me to express to your Imperial Majesty the satisfaction I shall feel in fulfilling Your Majesty's commands and wishes at the head of the army intrusted to my care.
>
> Mery, Feb. 22, 1814.   Blücher.

★★★★★★

The field-marshal had acted in direct conjunction with the grand Confederate Army but a few hours, when he ordered his to move forwards, and after repulsing Marmont, who endeavoured to stop his progress, or to interrupt his plan of operations, he crossed the Aube, directing his march to La Ferté Gauchery, and consequently towards Paris. His principal object was to unite his forces with those of Generals Bülow, Woronzow, and Winzingerode, formerly attached to the army of the Crown Prince of Sweden, but who were now pressing forward with alacrity into the scene of glorious action, towards Rheims and Soissons. The field-marshal's army would then be strengthened to 100,000 men.

And with this army, animated with enthusiasm, and intoxicated with victory, he proposed to undertake the bold and decisive march—direct on Paris, from the north side; by which manoeuvre Napoleon would be rendered unable to face and make head against both Schwartzenberg and Blücher, with the whole of his army, without leaving the one or the other an open field of action, on which he could carry on those operations that must ultimately prove fatal to Buonaparte. This movement of the field-marshal's upon Meaux, which would cut off the enemy's communication with Paris, and which caused great apprehensions in that capital, forced Marshals Mortier and Marmont to evacuate La Ferté sous Jouarre; and the commander-in-chief passed the Marne, without any obstruction, on, the 28th of February.

The reports of this march had scarcely reached Napoleon, before he broke up with the flower of his army from Troyes, on the 27th of February, in hopes of striking a deadly blow against the plans and views of the Allies. He left behind him a trifling force of 30,000 men, to observe the Prince of Schwartzenberg, whose army might be estimated at this period at 80,000.

Napoleon crossed the Marne on the 1st of March; but, to his great vexation, General von Bülow was already in possession of Soissons; by which circumstance all the single corps that were to form Blücher's army, and come under his command, could be united in this central and very important position.

Soissons was a point of singular importance; and the junction of the several corps was formed in the following manner:

On the 26th of February General von Bülow undertook an expedition from Laon against La, Fere. The covering of his right wing, and the security of his supplies, rendered the occupation of this fortress of great moment; and, consequently, General von Thümen was detached with his brigade against La Fere, and a necessary number of howitzers to bombard the town. The brigade advanced upon the place, and this highly valuable and meritorious officer displayed his usual zeal. After throwing, shells into the body of the town for a few hours, and then summoning it to surrender, the *commandant* capitulated, and General von Thümen marched in, at the head of his troops. The possession of the place was, in every point of view, of great importance; but, under the present circumstances, it proved a most severe loss to the enemy, as it contained a grand arsenal for the artillery in all its branches: more than a hundred pieces of brass cannon were found within it, as well as immense stores of every article appertaining to an artillery-train.

The certain intelligence of Field-Marshal Blücher's intended advance upon Paris having reached General von Bülow, he again put his corps in motion on the 1st of March towards Soissons, after leaving a small detachment in La Fere; and, at the same time, General Winzingerode moved from Rheims by the way of Fismes.

General von Bülow arrived before Soissons on the 2nd of March. This town is surrounded with ditches filled with water; and a high stone wall, flanked by towers, renders the place secure against a *coup de main*. The garrison consisted of from 1,200 to 1,400 men, mostly Poles, the best troops which Napoleon had at this time in the field, and they were well provided with artillery.

The opening of a communication with Blücher rendered the possession of the place absolutely necessary; but the attempt to take it by main force might have cost the Allies several thousand men. In consequence of this consideration, after the town had been briskly cannonaded, articles of capitulation, very honourable to the garrison, were proposed by Generals Winzingerode and Bülow: they were accepted by the *commandant*, upon Captain von Martins, who was intrusted with the negotiation, making some successful representations concerning the hopelessness of relief; and he was permitted to march out, at the head of the garrison, with the honours of war.

The necessity of occupying this town was even more pressing than the possession of La Fere. The weak corps of General von Kleist was already thrown back on the road from Soissons, on the 2nd of March; and on the 3rd, the day after its occupation, the main body of the Silesian Army arrived in its vicinity to assume a position.

Chapter 13
Victory of Laon

In this march of the field-marshal, from Mery to the heights of Soissons, of such a novel and critical nature, the gallant hero displayed his accustomed foresight and judgment, and conducted it in a most able and judicious manner. Notwithstanding the celerity of the movement, the utmost regularity was preserved, and no one untoward circumstance took place.

It was towards the evening of the 4th of March that the complete union of all the corps was formed, composing an enterprising army of 100,000 warriors. Blücher immediately directed Soissons to be occupied with 10,000 men, belonging to General von Langeron's corps; and the main body of the army assumed a position behind the Aisne. Meanwhile Napoleon had marched, in all haste, upon Fismes, made a booty of some baggage left in the rear, and occupied Rheims; by which operation he cut off all communication between the corps of General St. Priest, the Grand Army under the Prince of Schwartzenberg, and that of Blücher;

But the field-marshal had penetrated the probable manoeuvres of his adversary with precision and ability. He had sacrificed willingly all his communications, and, in case of necessity, meant to trust to the strength of the Netherlands. It was not the development of Napoleon's plans that urged him to act, but the execution of his own deep-laid operations. To establish a footing on a new line of offence, presents a spectacle of a movement of an army, never surpassed in the military annals of the world, and is a circumstance of glory that, in itself, would immortalise the name of Blücher.

During the 5th of March, Soissons was kept occupied by two Russian corps, and the field-marshal appointed Lieutenant-General Rudczewicz to be governor of the place. The army still bivouacked behind the Aisne.

The operations of the enemy commenced on the 6th. He endeavoured to obtain possession of the suburbs of Soissons by a heavy cannonade. His attacks were repulsed by the bravery of the troops and the able dispositions of the governor, and, although they were continued till night, yet the French gained not a foot of ground.

On the afternoon of the same day Napoleon had succeeded in getting possession of the ferries at Berri-au-Bac, and pushed forward his troops to Corbeny. General von Winzingerode sent a division to Crannes to oppose his progress; and the army was drawn up on the heights between L'Angegardien and Crannes, so as to make front against the enemy, and to act upon the offensive by the way of Crannes, if necessary.

Towards noon, on the 6th of March, the enemy's columns began to deploy from Berri, and to advance more to the right. The Field-Marshal von Blücher immediately ordered his army to advance upon the high ground running in a straight line from Crannes, to be able to debouch into the plain from that place. But Napoleon had already occupied Crannes with his guards, and had filled the woods and defiles with sharp-shooters, so that some considerable difficulties presented themselves in debouching the army.

The glacis was also too confined for a body of 80,000 men to act upon with effect; and, it being reported that an enemy's column was on its march, by the way of Corbeny, towards Laon, the field-marshal determined, at seven o'clock in the evening, to detach General Winzingerode, with 11,000 men, mostly cavalry, and a due proportion of horse-artillery, with orders to march off to the left, to intercept the enemy in the direction of Corbeny, on the road to Laon, and to act immediately on the offensive.

General von Bülow was likewise detached to occupy the position of Laon, and thereby to ensure his communications with the Low Countries.

When it was reported to the commander-in-chief that General von Bülow occupied Laon, he directed the Generals von York, von Kleist, and von Langeron, to move towards Fethieux, to serve fcs supports to General Winzingerode. The corps of General Winzingerode still remained drawn, tip on the glacis near Crannes. General Sacken's. corps formed his reserve. The field-marshal had calculated that the detached cavalry under General von Winzingerode could arrive near Fethieux before break of day, and that the infantry would reach the same point in time for his support. But, unhappily, the whole of these complicated movements could not be executed with that precision so necessary for their taking effect.

Some difficulties occurred to General von Winzingerode in crossing the River Cette, which detained him and the corps that followed. General von Kleist fortunately surmounted every obstacle; and, although he was detached ten hours later, yet he arrived before General von Winzingerode in the position at Fethieux. Meanwhile Napoleon impetuously attacked the corps of General Winzingerode with the whole of his forces. According to previous instructions, General von Sacken, who commanded the right wing, retired slowly, and in the finest order, from height to height, keeping up a brisk and well-directed cannonade upon the enemy.

The exertions of the French were particularly directed to turn, if possible, General von Sacken's position, and to press him hard by their superiority of cavalry. In this action, a favourable result was deemed of such importance by Napoleon, that several of his marshals performed the duties of generals of brigade and division, and Victor and Grouchy were wounded. This obstinate combat ended with the day, without Napoleon having succeeded in breaking through, or making any impression on the line of the Allies, whose troops made a most noble stand against a superior force, without losing a single piece of cannon or a prisoner. Indeed, it is barely possible to do justice to the gallantry and steadiness of the Russian artillery and cavalry on this day, which will thereby be ever conspicuously memorable in the annals of this war.

In the course of the night, General von Sacken also withdrew into the position of Laon, in which the Field-marshal had determined battle should be given. Under these circumstances, as Soissons was destitute of every article of sustenance, it was in consequence evacuated by General Rudczewicz.

The whole of Blücher's army was concentrated behind Laon on the 8th of March. The corps of General Bülow occupied the town and the glacis. The corps of Langeron, Sacken, and Winzingerode stood to the right, and those of von York and von Kleist to the left.

Two battalions of infantry, belonging to York's corps, kept possession of the village of Athies; the 2nd and 8th brigades, under Prince William of Prussia, stood in the first line; the 1st and 7th brigades in reserve.

Towards evening the enemy advanced upon the road from Soissons, and forced the advanced-guard of the field-marshal's army upon Chiny. Early in the morning of the 9th, under cover of a very heavy fog, a body of the enemy's infantry drove in the outposts, and carried the villages of Semillv and Ardon. But about eleven o'clock, a.m. as the fog began to clear away, the field-marshal directed the corps of General von Winzingerode to act on the offensive. The two villages were retaken, and Winzingerode's right wing repulsed the enemy to Lasnicourt.

About three o'clock, p.m. it was reported to the commander-in-chief that the enemy were in advance, in strong columns of all arms, supported by a numerous artillery, from the side of Rheims. As the combat on Blücher's right wing had happily taken a favourable turn, and no important operation was to be expected from this side, our veteran hero was naturally led to expect that Napoleon intended his principal attack should be made on his left. The safety of Blücher's left wing was indeed of the utmost importance.

The cavalry in reserve was intrusted to the command of General von Ziethen; he passed the brook near Athies, and took up a flanking position towards the cavalry of the enemy, which threatened to turn the left wing on the first favourable opening. On the right wing the corps of General von Bülow acted entirely on the defensive.

Marshal Blücher now ordered the corps of von Sacken and Langeron to advance to the left as reserves to the corps of von York and Kleist, directing General von York, as soon as these reserves were come up, to assail the enemy by a sudden and general movement forwards. It had begun to grow dark as the reserves arrived. Generals von York and Kleist, prompt in the execution of orders, redoubled their pace in advancing upon the columns of the enemy's infantry. The first attack fell to the lot of Prince William of Prussia, leaving the burning village of Athies a little to the right.

The attack of Prince William was supported on this side of the village by General von Horn with his usual gallantry; he stormed, at the head of his troops, an enemy's battery with such rapidity, that only one round was fired before the whole of it fell into his hands. Meanwhile General von Ziethen executed so admirably those manoeuvres with which he was intrusted, when he had turned the right flank of the enemy, that the defeat of Napoleon was thus rendered complete. General von Kleist commenced his attack along the low bushes lying in his front, so as to concentrate its effects with that of the other corps on the high road from Rheims.

These operations were happily effected, notwithstanding a variety of impediments occurred, both from the nature of the ground, and the desperate resistance made by the enemy. The commanders, however, performed the service committed to their care with much precision, ability, and courage.

The enemy was on the point of occupying Athies with several heavy columns, when he had to meet the attack of Prince William. All firing was strictly prohibited, and the bayonet only was to be used. The troops pressed forwards with unloaded arms, rushed upon the enemy, and charged with fixed bayonets; the effect produced by such gallant conduct was such as might have been expected; they forced the French to retire in confusion, and the Allied battalions still moved onwards, regardless of a most terrible and continued discharge of grape. But a short time, however, elapsed, and General von Kleist had completely repulsed, and thrown into disorder, the whole of the masses of the enemy's right wing, as likewise the corps of Marmont and Arrighi. In the mean, time, General von Ziethen had charged the rear of the enemy, sword in hand, and put them entirely to the rout; and a conflict the most severe, was terminated most gloriously for the Allies, leaving in the hands of the victors forty-six pieces of cannon.

The bold and well-directed manner in which Prince William forced the enemy to fly from the high woody grounds near Athies, paved the way to victory. The heavy fire of musketry poured down upon them from the heights, could not for a moment arrest the progress of his troops, who undauntedly stormed the eminence, eager to close with the foe.

The good fortune and bravery of the Prussians prevailed in this memorable night attack, notwithstanding the multitude of obstacles opposed to their success. The defeat of the enemy soon became general, and he fled in the greatest disorder and confusion. General von Ziethen, at the head of his cavalry, and supported by four battalions of infantry from the corps of Prince William and General Horn, pursued the French, and occupied the defile from Fethieux to Maison-rouge.

General von York continued, after surprising Marmont's corps, to follow up his advantages, till late in the evening, taking a great number of prisoners.

******

Marshal Marmont's corps was here completely taken by surprise. They were in bivouac, and busily employed in preparing their suppers. The Prussian cavalry approached through bye-roads, silent as death, followed by a battery. The infantry, covered by a wood, got close upon them. The Frenchmen could be very plainly seen lying round their watchfires. A terrible cannonade and volleys of musketry now suddenly opened upon them. The bugle-horns of the Prussians were heard from all sides. The terror, confusion, and flight of the French baffle all attempts at description. It proved a bloodless hunting-party for the gallant Prussians. Everything was left behind: the whole of their artillery, baggage, horses, and waggons, fell into the hands of the Confederates. Marmont was driven, with the shattered remains of his cavalry, to the Maine; and General von York returned from the pursuit, to fall again into line with the field-marshal's army, now threatened with another attack at Laon from Napoleon.

★★★★★★

In the meantime, Napoleon still stood in his admirable position before Laon. He attempted on the 10th to repeat his attacks upon the centre and the right wing, under Bülow and Winzingerode. But the field-marshal anticipated the enemy's intentions, by issuing orders to General von Winzingerode to fall on the enemy's left wing, while General Langeron was to watch his movements; Napoleon's offensive operation proved, therefore, unsuccessful. The ground afforded every advantage to Napoleon, and by keeping up a severe cannonade and fire of grapeshot, he held the front of Blücher's line in check, till the close of the evening, when he again renewed a general attack. He caused the suburb Semilly, on the road to Soissons, lying at the foot of the hill on which Laon stands, to be assailed by some battalions of infantry.

This suburb was occupied by Bülow's corps, and he defended it with unexampled spirit and coolness: he resisted the impetuosity of the French infantry, repulsed every repeated attack, and the enemy were at last compelled to retreat at all points. It is very probable, that the attack was only a feint on the side of Napoleon, to prevent, if possible, the total destruction of Marmont's corps.

This twofold victory, which the veteran field-marshal gained over Napoleon on the 9th and 10th of March, near Laon, cost the Allied Army but an inconsiderable number of men, while the loss of the French may be moderately estimated at 18,000, in killed, wounded, and prisoners.

Napoleon's retreat was made in the most disorderly manner, and was the only step he could take, to prevent his complete discomfiture. He left all his wounded men behind him, in his flight towards the Aisne: the light troops of Blücher's army pressed hard upon his rear, and caused him a great loss in men and *matériel*.

This was the second grand battle, in which victory was wrested by our veteran hero from the iron grasp of Napoleon on the French territory.

The great and unremitting exertions which the army had made during the last four days, and the unusual fatigues they had undergone, rendered it absolutely necessary that it should now have some repose, and, consequently, all the advantages that might have been derived from briskly following up the pursuit of Napoleon, the Allies were, at the moment, obliged reluctantly to forego. A pause, therefore, ensued in the operations of Blusher's army, which lasted nearly eight days.

The field-marshal's conduct and continued activity during this memorable battle gained him the admiration of the whole army, exalted in an eminent degree the honour of his country, and gave pledges of his being ranked amongst the most illustrious officers of the age. His merit can scarcely be equalled; his exertions, personal courage, and ability contributed much to the success of the combat, and to enhance that character of military fame, to which his former services had so justly entitled him.

The only affair of importance which took place immediately after the Battle of Laon, was the occupation of Rheims. On the 12th of March, General Count St. Priest attacked that city, carried it, and took about 1,000 men prisoners. The enemy, with superior force, appeared before the place on the 13th. General Count St. Priest supported the unequal contest with great bravery, but was at last obliged to give way, with such a disparity of numbers under his command: he himself was wounded. A part of his corps withdrew to Chalons, and another in the direction of Berry-au-Bac, to join the Silesian Army.

We will now draw the attention of our readers to the operations of the Confederate Armies.

The Crown Prince of Sweden, having been relieved in Holstein, and in the blockade of d'Avoust in Hamburg, by General Bennigsen, put his army in march towards the Rhine, on which he arrived on the 10th of February. The crown prince's army advanced from Cologne towards the Low Countries, and reached Liège on the 26th of February, where the prince fixed his headquarters. His advanced-guard under Generals Woronzow and Stroganoff, were detached to join Blücher, But an inactivity now showed itself in the further operations of the Swedish Army, the cause of which is enveloped in a veil of mystery, even to this day. The Swedish Army was cantoned on the Meuse; the headquarters remained in Liège, and, by some unaccountable fatality, it was bereaved of sharing the honour of those glorious days that so soon followed each other in quick succession.

After the affair at Bar-sur-Aube, between the French and Confederate Armies, the former retired towards Troyes on the 25th of February, and took up a position in front of the town, between the Aube and the Seine. Generals von Wittgenstein and von Wrede briskly attacked the enemy in their strong position on the 3rd of March, took the villages in the centre by assault, and drove the French in great disorder into Troyes. A number of cannon and prisoners fell into the hands of the gallant Confederates: Troyes was assailed and parried on the 4th, for the second time, and the general-in-chief, Prince Schwartzenberg, fixed his headquarters in the place on the 6th of March.

A column was pushed forwards in pursuit of the enemy, who retreated on the road to Nogent. Meanwhile the Prince of Schwartzenberg took up strong ground with his army in the direction of Sens.

The Prince of Würtemberg was on the 8th again in occupation of Montereau, that had once cost him such a number of brave men.

The Hettman Platow, at the head of a very numerous body of Cossacks, scoured the country in all directions between the Seine and the Marne, kept up the most advantageous series of intelligence concerning the different corps of the Confederates, and harassed the enemy at all points, depriving him of his convoys of provisions, and isolating him even in the midst of his own provinces.

Napoleon was now reduced to play a desperate game. After the unfortunate battle at Laon, he threw himself, as if in despair, on the Confederate Army, now standing on the Aube, only leaving a moderate corps to observe the Marne. He found his opponent drawn up ready to receive him, between Plancis. and Arcis, his forces concentrated, and on strong ground. He crossed the Aube on the 20th of March, and, in the afternoon, passed through Arcis, at the head of 40,000 men; here he was instantly attacked by the Prince von Schwartzenberg, who repulsed him with heavy loss, taking from him 11 guns, and 400 men of his imperial guard.

The Congress at Chatillon was dissolved the same day. The Prince of Schwartzenberg, not satisfied with the partial advantages of the 20th, continued his attack on the 21st, and drove him through the town of Arcis. To cover his retreat, Napoleon occupied the place with a large body of troops till the morning of the 23rd, when, having come out of the defile which had served to protect him the day before, he was briskly attacked in the plain by a division of Russian guards, defeated, and had twenty-three pieces of artillery taken from him.

Napoleon found himself repulsed and driven back by the Prince of Schwartzenberg; but still obstinately bent on executing his plan, of keeping this army and that of Blücher separated, he seemed to think no sacrifice, no hazard too great, to obtain his purpose: and he now hastened towards the Upper Marne, to take firm footing on the Meuse.

Prince Schwartzenberg, however, was not to be deceived by this manoeuvring march of Napoleon, but proceeded to detach a corps to strengthen the communications on the Saone and Rhone, towards the south. Another corps, under Wittgenstein, of about 10,000 men, mostly cavalry, followed Napoleon, step by step, to observe him, and, with the main body, the commander-in-chief marched straight across the country, towards the Marne, to join Blücher, who was advancing from that river, and, by this daring manoeuvre, to cut off Napoleon at once from Paris.

During these operations, Field-Marshal Blücher, after his army had enjoyed that repose so vitally necessary, commenced acting again on the offensive.

The corps of Generals von York and von Kleist were directed to advance upon Fismes. General Winzingerode occupied Rheims. General von Sacken's corps marched towards Vally, and that of General von Bülow in front of Soissons. The main body of Blücher's army passed the Aisne on the 19th of March, at Berry-au-Bac and Pontavaire.

On the 22nd, the corps of von York and von Kleist pursued their route upon Château Thierry.

The corps of Langeron, Sacken, and Winzingerode concentrated themselves at Rheims during the 23rd; and General von Bülow kept Soissons blockaded.

The Grand Confederate Army stood near Vitry on the 24th, at the moment that Field-Marshal Blücher had arrived with his army in Chalons and Rheims.

The two Allied Armies now formed a complete junction in the very rear of Napoleon's position; a combination, to frustrate which, Napoleon had in vain exerted all his talents and all his physical endeavours. His grand manoeuvre accordingly proved abortive, and was for him only the forerunner of great disasters, while it was preparing fresh triumphs for the gallant Confederates.

It was now determined that the two armies should make a combined forced march upon Paris, give up all communication with the Rhine, and, by this energetic but judicious measure, produce the most brilliant effects for the good cause.

The march of Prince Schwartzenberg's army on Vitry contributed to mask the intentions of the Allies, of turning to the right about and proceeding to Paris, when joined by Blücher.

General Wittgenstein's cavalry kept the rear of Napoleon's army upon the alert, and served to prevent the corps of Marshals Marmont and Mortier from joining him.

In the interim, Napoleon, after the affair at Arcis, had retired on Vitry. Fearful of fighting a pitched battle with Schwartzenberg, who seemed too much prepared for him at all points, Napoleon hoped, by this sudden flank march on Vitry, to cause the Confederates some apprehensions concerning their communications in the rear, and by their dispositions, in consequence, to keep them open, enable him to draw them still farther from Paris. On the 22nd, his own headquarters were at Obcomte, between Vitry and St. Dizier, spreading his army in the direction of Joinville, Ligny, Bar-le-Duc, Chaumont, and Langres; in which position he remained till the 24th of March.

According to all the rules of military tactics, after the grand union of the two armies, no other measure was to be expected than the giving Napoleon battle: it was, indeed, what he had prepared himself for, during the last two or three days; but instead of this the Confederate forces no sooner came in contact, and shook hands upon their happy meeting, than they instantly began their steady, daring march upon Paris.

The corps of Marmont, Mortier, and Arrighi, had followed the army of Field-Marshal Blücher, with the intention of keeping him on the Aisne; and when Napoleon made his retrograde movement on Arcis, they were on march between Vitry and La Fère Champenoise, to join him. Marmont pushed forward a corps, in the night of the 24th of March, upon Vitry, without knowing that it was still occupied by the Confederates, having supposed that they had followed the movement of Napoleon.

The Prince of Würtemberg and General Rajewsky, with their several corps, the Russian reserve cavalry of the guard, and a part of Blücher's cavalry, fell in with Marmont's corps, charged and broke it, the remains retreating to La Ferté Gaucher, on the road to Paris. A very large and complete artillery-park fell, on this occasion, into the hands of the Allies. The two divisions of Pactod and Amey were surrounded, and, after a warm affair, the whole of them were taken prisoners near La Fère Champenoise. The Emperor Alexander and the King of Prussia happened to be present at this engagement.

There is not, perhaps, in the history of modern campaigns, a stratocratic manoeuvre upon a grander scale to be found, than that which the Confederates had now put in practice, by interposing themselves between Buonaparte and Paris. The boldness of this memorable operation of the Allies, evidently unnerved Napoleon's whole system, overturned the basis of his plans, and placed him in the state of a mariner endeavouring to steer his vessel without a compass.

He faced about, it is true, making a feint of marching, by the way of Bar-sur-Aube, direct to Paris; but, as if stunned and confounded, instead of proceeding on the line of the Marne, to throw himself on the rear of the Allies, and to offer battle, whatever it might cost him, he made a flank march from the Marne to the Aube, and from thence behind the Seine, and by this short-sighted and bewildered measure hastened in a superlative degree his own downfall and destruction.

Field-Marshal von Blücher, at the head of his Silesian Army, entered Etoges on the 25th of March, and pressed forwards by the way of Montmirail towards Meaux.

Marshals Marmont and Mortier drew back to Sezanne. Generals York and Kleist, having arrived the same day at Montmirail, detached a body of their cavalry on the road to Sezanne, and broke up by break of day on the 26th, to cut off the enemy in the direction of La Ferté Gaucher. They found La Ferté occupied, soon dislodged the enemy, and established themselves in the place. The French fled towards Coulomiers, closely pursued by the Prussian cavalry and a brigade of infantry; they were overtaken near that town, charged, and dispersed; and 300 prisoners, together with a number of tumbrils, were taken from them.

The Silesian Army reached Meaux on the 27th, in the most perfect order and regularity. In the afternoon the rest of Marmont's and Mortier's corps appeared on their march from Sezanne to Coulomiers. The powerful and well-directed artillery of York's and Kleist's corps, which opened their fire upon the French columns, as they marched in advance down the road, forced them to file off from the high-way, and to throw themselves into the bye-roads towards the Seine. If the Allied cavalry had happened to have been on the spot, the remainder of these two French corps would have fallen into their hands, or have been cut in pieces.

Between La Ferté Jouarre and Meaux, an attempt was made by a body of 10,000 national guards to impede the march of Blücher's army. They put on a good countenance, and seemed determined to dispute the further advance of the Allies; but the brave General von

Horn being detached to charge them at the head of his brigade of cavalry, executed his orders with such celerity, courage, and firmness, that one of their masses of infantry was entirely broken up and cut in pieces, the rest put to the rout, and the French general who commanded them taken prisoner by General von Horn himself.

The corps of Marmont and Mortier, being now completely deranged, retired at all points, ou the 28th of March. When making good their retreat through Meaux, they blew up an immense magazine of gunpowder, without any previous notice to the inhabitants, and then pursued their retrograde march to Claye. The corps of York and Kleist came up with the enemy at this latter place, and after a desperate conflict, which lasted till late at night, they succeeded in dislodging the French, and occupied Ville-parisis and Montsaigle.

During these operations, the Silesian Army defiled over the bridges of the Marne, near Triport, which had been re-established, notwithstanding the enemy's cannonade.

It was on the 29th of March that the grand Confederate Army began likewise to defile over the bridges near Triport and Meaux. The preconcerted union of Schwartzenberg's and Blücher's army was now fully accomplished, in order of battle. The Confederate Army pursued the high road to Paris, while the Silesian Army filed off on the road from Mery to that capital.

Marshals Marmont and Mortier had advanced, by forced marches, with the shattered remains of their corps, by the way of Melun towards Paris, and had taken position in front of the wood near Landy; they were attacked by the advanced-guard, and driven back upon Pantin. The grand headquarters were at Bondy on the 29th: in the meantime Blücher pushed forwards two principal corps to the right, in the direction of Mory, Drancy, and St. Denys, to reach Montmartre.

The French had taken position in front of the heights of Montmartre, under cover of some hasty intrenchments they had thrown up, and lined with 150 pieces of artillery; their line extended to the villages of Pantin, Romainville, and Belleville. The enemy's force consisted of about 8,000 regular troops, and 30,000 national guards. The canal, and the nature of the ground altogether, rendered his position a strong one, particularly as the Allied cavalry had no extent of terrain to make a charge. In the interim, Napoleon had issued orders to defend the capital to the last extremity, being himself, as he announced, on his march to relieve it.

Field-Marshal Blücher's conduct, under the difficult circumstances in which he undertook this memorable march on Paris, may be accounted a master-piece of discretion and firmness. The bold measures of the field-marshal, the splendid feats he performed, his well-chosen commanding positions, his energy of action, and the efficiency of his dispositions on the field of battle, all alike point him out as a military hero, not only worthy of the wonder and admiration of the age in which he lives, but of future generations.

Preparations for a general attack on the enemy's position at Montmartre were vigorously carried on, during the 30th of March. It was the plan of the Allies, that the Grand Confederate Army, under the Prince of Schwartzenberg, should assault the heights of Romainville and Belleville, while the Silesian Army was ordered to carry those of Montmartre.

Marshal Blücher made the following arrangements with the several corps of which his army was composed. General Count Langeron's corps formed his right wing, and those of von York and Kleist his left. The corps under the command of General Winzingerode remained in reserve, and that under General von Sacken was still in position near Meaux. General von Bülow covered Soissons. Our veteran General directed Count Langeron to take Audervilliers, to blockade St. Denys, if it would not submit, and to advance with his main body towards Clichy, for the purpose of attacking Montmartre from this side. Generals von York and Kleist were ordered to assault Montmartre from the routes of La Villette and La Chapelle.

The Confederate Grand Army began their attack upon the enemy's lines at Pantin, at five o'clock, a.m.; that of the Silesian Army did not commence till near eleven, a. m. at which time Romainville and Pantin had been already carried by the Allied Army. The enemy still occupied Ferme le Rouvroy with infantry, supported by a battery of eighteen pieces of cannon, very advantageously planted.

The advanced-guard, under Major-General Katzeler, carried the place itself, but could not debouch out of it, until the enemy's battery was first silenced. The artillery necessary for this operation did not arrive on the ground till near three o'clock, p.m. along with Winzingerode's corps, whose operations were favoured by the corps of York and Kleist filing off to attack in conjunction with Count Langeron. The reserve of grenadiers, and a brigade of guards appertaining to the Grand Army, and supported by six battalions, under Prince William of Prussia, had just made an attack from Pantin towards Paris, forcing the enemy's battery near Villette to draw back its right wing, as the reserves and the artillery of von York's and Kleist's corps came into action, and thereby enfiladed the whole of the French battery.

The enemy retreated instantly into Villette; but again, faced about, and, although hard pressed, endeavoured to charge with a large body of cavalry, supported by infantry and artillery. It happened that the cavalry of York's and Kleist's corps had begun to form at Ferme le Rouvroy, and two regiments of Prussian hussars boldly met the enemy's charge, repulsed them with heavy loss, threw themselves upon their infantry, and put the whole to rout, taking their guns sword in hand.

Four battalions belonging to General Woronzow's corps, taking advantage of the favourable moment, stormed La Villette at the same time, and the enemy fled in the greatest confusion, leaving their artillery and *matériel* in the hands of the victors: they were briskly pursued to the very barriers of Paris. On the road from Pantin, the guards had likewise penetrated to the barriers, from that side. The whole of the enemy's positions were, in this manner, either turned or stormed, about half past three o'clock, p. m. when the firing ceased on both sides.

Flags of truce now appeared, to entreat a suspension of hostilities, as the City of Paris would submit. They were conducted to the august sovereigns, who had arrived hear the barriers, and an armistice was granted for four hours, to afford time for the French forces to defile into Paris.

Imagination can scarcely form an idea of two situations more opposite to each other, than that of one army, flushed with a series of continued victories, and another, depressed with the mortifying reflection of unvaried discomfiture. The one rushes on with the cheerful confidence of certain conquest; the other proceeds with a reluctant diffidence, resulting from a humiliating retrospection of experienced defeats.

During these events, the corps of General Langeron had continued its movement, those of York and Kleist kept up a brisk cannonade, and advanced upon Montmartre. The village of La Chapelle was already carried, and the assault upon Montmartre upon the point of being attempted, as the intelligence of the armistice reached them. But Count Langeron being at a greater distance, his infantry had already stormed the heights of Montmartre, on that side, and taken twenty pieces of cannon, before the report arrived.

Prince Schwartzenberg and the veteran Marshal Blücher were now at the head of their respective armies, in positions, from which they could cannonade at their pleasure the city of Paris. The whole of the barriers were delivered up to the Confederates in the course of the evening, and on the following morning, the 31st of March, the capital of the French Empire was in the hands and at the mercy of the Confederate monarchs. At seven o'clock in the morning, the whole of the French regular troops, under Marshal Marmont, evacuated Paris, in virtue of a convention entered into for that purpose.

The glorious trophies of the 31st of March consisted of 70 pieces of artillery, 3 standards, and 500 prisoners.

Scarcely were the issue of the battle at La Fère Champenoise and its consequences known to Napoleon, when, on the 27th of March, after pushing aside the two corps of Winzingerode and Czernischeff, he hastened from Bar-sur-Aube to Troyes, and, on observing that Paris was lost to him, he proceeded in the direction of Sens to Fontainbleau; where, on the 4th of April, he issued his last order of the day. Thus, ended the plans he had formed for the welfare of Europe, the subjection of Russia, and to remain master of both Germany and Italy.

But it must not be forgotten, that Providence achieved the work, which it took (entirely upon itself, that its hand might be visible to all. The German nation has in particular to hail the hour of its deliverance, with unceasing sentiments of pious gratitude. It has recalled it from a state of bondage to the bright certainty of future honour and happiness, and prevented the diffusion of those principles which directly tended to destroy all property, subvert the laws and religion of a country, and to introduce the wild and ruffian system of rapine, falsehood, espionage, base tyranny, and impiety.

✶✶✶✶✶✶

> The following anecdote, which we have from an authentic source, is here introduced, that our readers may form some faint conception of the extent to which espionage was carried, under the reign of Napoleon.
>
> It happened that Fouché and the Prince of Benevento, and that too in the presence of Napoleon, fell into a dispute concerning a transaction, of which each of them could have acquired a knowledge only by their several spies. They grew warm upon the subject; Fouché maintained that his intelligence of the affair was alone authentic, adding:
>
> "I am so well served by my spies, that I can tell you, prince, the name of every person that has entered your house, and whom you have seen, both today and yesterday, where you saw them, and how long you stayed with them."
>
> "If," replied Talleyrand, "if, there be any merit in such kind

of espionage, I value myself upon being your superior in that point; for I not only know what has passed in your house, but what is to take place tomorrow. I know every dish you have had upon your table for this week past, and what has been ordered for the ensuing: even your *tête-à-têtes* are not—"

Here Napoleon's patience seemed to be exhausted, for he interrupted all further reply, in his usual abrupt manner:

"Hold your tongues, both of you! You are a couple of *polissons*; but I alone can determine which is the greatest!"

Fouché was formerly a professor at Nantes, and was a master at the excellent institution of the Oratorion, so useful to education. At the time Napoleon Buonaparte returned from Egypt we find Fouché minister of the police under the Directory. He took an active part in the revolution of *Brumaire*, and betrayed the Directory. He was dismissed in 1802, but having been the principal instigator of Georges's conspiracy, he once more came into favour, and returned to the ministry. It was Fouché who urged and goaded Buonaparte on to the murder of the Duke d'Enghien, that Buonaparte might also stain his hands with the blood of the Bourbons, as himself had already done, in voting for the death of Louis the Sixteenth.

In the year 1810, he sent a confidential person, Mr. Ouvrand, to London, for some private purposes. Ouvrand returned to France, was thrown into the prison at Vincennes, and Fouché was again in disgrace. Being appointed governor of Rome, by Napoleon, he received, on the road to that city, an order from his master to retire to Aix, in Provence, as into a kind of exile, for having steadily refused to deliver up to him the whole of his secret correspondence as minister of the police. When Napoleon was unfortunate, he was recalled; but Cambacères, who is his sworn enemy, and Savary, who was afraid of losing his place, having caused fresh suspicions of his fidelity to arise, he was sent into Italy with an honourable mission, but which was nothing less than another exile. He returned to Paris when Napoleon Buonaparte abdicated the throne for the first time.

★★★★★★

Their Majesties the Emperor Alexander and the King of Prussia put themselves at the head of their victorious guards, and made their glorious triumphal entry into Paris, between ten and eleven o'clock,

a. m. of the 31st of March. It was one of those grand spectacles that occur but seldom during the course of many centuries. They were escorted and surrounded by all their distinguished generals, and endless files of heroes formed their train. The gazing multitude saluted them as they passed with reiterated acclamations of

"*Vive l'Empereur Alexandre!*"
"*Vive le Roi de Prusse!*"
"*Vive Louis XVIII!*"
"*A bas Napoleon! La paix! La paix!*"

The Allied monarchs proceeded through the suburb St. Martin, across the Boulevards to the Place of Louis the Fifteenth, and from thence to the Champs Elisées, (Elysées), where their respective troops defiled in the most perfect order before them.

St. Denys capitulated on the 31st of March, All the military trophies which had been previously taken from the Allies, were found in Paris, or in the Dome des Invalides, from which latter place they were taken away by detachments of Russian and Prussian guards, on the 1st of April.

Napoleon had, in the meantime, halted at Fontainbleau. His marshals and princes renounced their obedience to him, and appeared in Paris, to await their fate from the decisions of the august Allied monarchs. Upon this important occasion it was seen, that the marshals, who had hitherto acted as a united and formidable body, for the meretricious glory and unjust aggrandizement of France, not only took part with the Confederates, but almost immediately accepted posts under Louis the Eighteenth. Many were pleased to observe that:

> The matter in issue was, in fact, whether a good, just, and liberal constitution was or was not to be maintained in France; whether the wild ideas of universal conquest, and of theory, were to overwhelm the wholesome maxims of established practice and well-founded experience; and whether those laws, under which Europe had flourished for such a series of years, were to be rendered null and subverted by a tyrant, unsanctioned by the people, at the head of a hated stratocracy, and the dread and abhorrence of neighbouring nations.

As Frenchmen, nearly and deeply interested in the real welfare of France, the marshals seemed to hasten to convince the world, that the happiness of the French people was their sole object. They were eager to announce, that they held the principles and the system of their former *Sultan* as treasons towards France, and incompatible with the peace of Europe. On this great, this solid basis, the august Allies listened to their arguments of secession, and believed and trusted their promises and protestations. It was a critical period. To have done less, would have cast an. odium on the noble and generous conduct of the Allies; and to have done more, would have implied a want of wisdom and sound policy.

The Silesian Army combated for the freedom and independence of Germany, during a campaign of seven months and a half, in which it fought six pitched battles, three single-handed, and three in conjunction with the Grand Allied Army; was concerned in eight bloody engagements and numberless skirmishes, took 48,000 prisoners from the enemy, and could reckon amongst its glorious, unexampled, and immortal trophies, 421 pieces of cannon, with a proportionate number of tumbrils, &c. &c. It was composed of the best strength of the Prussian nation; and the veteran Blücher led into the field a host of heroes, worthy of the great Frederick, the names of their fathers, and heirs of their glory. Nor was this faithful people less backward in making voluntary sacrifices at the shrine of loyalty; the mother offered her son and her jewels; the father his horse, his sword, and wealth; the youth his life; and the infirm their blessings!

Field-Marshal Prince Blücher, as forming part of the suite of his august monarch, arrived at Dover on the 6th of June 1814, on his way to London, which he reached the day following.

His Royal Highness the Prince Regent honoured our veteran with a valuable mark of his esteem, by presenting him, in public, with his miniature, set in diamonds, to be worn round his neck, suspended by a blue riband.

During his popular and interesting stay in England, which filled the whole country with conversation, and attracted the curiosity of the public, in a manner that was seldom or never witnessed, all ranks were eager to show their admiration of Blücher's heroic deeds, to signify their pleasure at the sight of the gallant veteran, and to express their satisfaction at being honoured with the visit of so famed a general.

He may be considered as one of the brightest members of that profession which has humbled the vain-glory of a feverish enthusiastic people, and taught the doubting world, that deeds in arms, aided by honour and justice, mercy and loyalty, will and must eventually be crowned with success, when taking up the gauntlet of defiance, thrown down by the hand of imperious tyranny and base perfidy,

Chapter 14

The Congress at Vienna

The 31st of March 1814, was a proud day for the Allied monarchs, as it exhibited a gallant army of faithful Confederates defiling in splendid triumph through the gates of Paris: a triumph which has not only given an additional lustre to the patriotism and loyalty of their brave subjects, but conferred an everlasting honour on the countries over which they preside.

The banners of Prussia, Russia, and Austria, attended by victory, waved in the haughty city of Paris; which, for nearly four centuries, had not seen a foreign enemy before its walls.

Dire revenge might now be taken for the burning of Moscow; heavy contributions imposed for the pillage of Vienna and Berlin; and Paris stripped of those choice works of art and science, which had been her boast and ornaments.

But the generous conquerors, full of noble sentiments, here displayed those virtues and traits which always distinguish their characters, never, in any relations, to be perverted by the foul example of the chief of a system that aimed at the overthrow of all moral principle.

It may be said that Napoleon's greatness was at its zenith in Moscow, and that the goal of all his glory was at Paris. The man, who for so many years together had brought down upon the world unutterable miseries, was banished the continent.

★★★★★★

The life of Napoleon Buonaparte has displayed a variety of extraordinary incidents. His career of empire has been short, but it is nevertheless wonderful and astonishing.

It is but the other day, that this singular man was only a lieutenant in a company of artillery, and, after overturning thrones, and founding a stratocratic empire, upon bases formed of perfidy and impiety, we have lived to witness him an exile from the continent of Europe. Under the influence of his dazzling system, the French nation have displayed a gigantic strength, and made conquests that baffled all calculation. But the hostilities of Europe took a very different form to those of ancient times; they did not, as then, aim at the possession of some trifling slip of territory, or the obtaining of some petty right or privilege; but were openly avowed by Napoleon Buonaparte, as the main springs of action, to obtain universal, dominion, and, upon the ruins of his conquests, to erect an empire governed by laws that held revealed religion and social order in utter scorn and contempt, and that merged all power, all influence over the human mind, into that of the sword alone.

On closely examining results, we are not much inclined to admit that Napoleon Buonaparte showed, upon all occasions, in the various turns of fortune he has experienced, and the critical relations between himself and the belligerent powers of Europe, those stupendous talents which have so long afforded a theme for wonder and for praise. He attempted to force the suggestions of reason and sound policy to bend to his own imaginary infallible will. An unrelenting stubbornness marks the course of all his actions, which led him to commit the most absurd errors. He is a fellow of no principle, and the whole of his conduct and career exhibits a most flagrant and sinistrous aspect.

Can a man make a proper use of his talents without moral principles to curb the ebullitions of his passions, when tending to crime? Impossible! The smiles of fortune seduce him, his passions gain the ascendancy, and such a man proves the most accursed scourge to humanity, when power to do evil is thrown into the scale of unusual and splendid abilities.

★★★★★★

Legitimate governments were restored, the thrones of ancient dynasties secured from perfidious attacks, and the suffering world tranquillized with the consoling prospect of a durable and general peace.

The Confederate sovereigns, in testimony of their very honourable motives, during a period of warfare which had acquired an energy unknown in modern times, naturally contemplated the giving peace to the world, and to France, not by humiliating the nation itself, and making it suffer For the bloody deeds of the odious tyrant, but by hurling him for ever from his usurped seat on the throne of the

Bourbons. These generous intentions were universally known and acknowledged in France, and particularly in Paris, whose inhabitants greeted the illustrious personages with every mark of enthusiasm and gratitude. "Alexander the deliverer!"—"Frederick the harbinger of peace!" was shouted from all sides.

The taking of Paris gave peace to Europe.

Napoleon Buonaparte signed, on the 11th of April 1814, in the most formal manner, an act of abdication; adding, that, "there was no sacrifice which he was not ready to make, even that of his life, for the welfare of France:" and he arrived at the island of Elba on the 4th of May.

This singular personage thus closed a career which, since 1797, had excited the wonder and astonishment of the world, filled every one with fear and doubt, and been the cause that millions of the bravest warriors of Europe were sacrificed, and the treasures of France squandered in Spain and Russia. He had overturned several thrones, and erected others; but, by the downfall of his own usurped dominion, an end was put to the ephemeral existence of those to which he alone had given stability.

There was a time, when, in every corner of Europe, the words that dropped from his mouth were held of importance, and esteemed as oracles; and now he owed his life to the consideration of one of his marshals, and the noble generosity of those whose thrones he had once shaken to their very foundations. Instead, like a man of sound wisdom, of fixing the happiness of France upon the firmest basis, when he had destroyed the hydra of anarchy, he imposed upon her the more intolerable chains of tyranny and despotism.

This man was, in a manner, worshipped till the year 1813; but, from this period, he became the scorn and abhorrence of the world. The charm of his infallibility had been broken; and the triumph of revealed religion over gloomy atheism, moral rectitude over the iron hand of power, and virtue over vice, was complete. The utter worthlessness of all Napoleon's satellites, the monstrous progeny of the revolution, was now open to the comprehension of every individual in every station. Napoleon Buonaparte did not realise the summit of his ambition. His mortification was, however, commensurate with his former hopes, when he found himself exiled to the island of Elba.

In military affairs Napoleon had no doubt enjoyed a spring-tide of fame, and first appeared on the theatre of war replete with fair promise of future greatness. Various causes aided his attainment of glory; but let it be remembered, that none could ever make him the tyrant he was: the qualities of that monster amongst civilized nations were inherent in the man, and they gradually expanded themselves as he rose in power and authority. No one can deny that Buonaparte possesses a decision of character and energy of mind, combined with a pre-eminent genius for military command, that place him on a footing with the first generals of the present and former ages. It does not, however, follow, that he was faultless, or incapable of error. The events of this campaign, as well as of former ones, present numerous instances of his stubbornness of character, of his committing great mistakes in military calculations, accompanied by an unpardonable temerity, that seemed to defy both fate, possibility, and the elements.

In his former campaigns he had led on to victory files of revolutionary enthusiasts, and had to contend with the automatons of military discipline. His last campaign was singularly marked by the contrary; the mantling spirit of the revolution had evaporated; he had to combat with troops inspired with loyalty and a just sense of national honour—and Paris was occupied by the Allies.

England was the only state in Europe that had uniformly refused to acknowledge the dynasty of Napoleon Buonaparte.

The congress at Chatillon was dissolved on the 20th of March, and the Senate of France solemnly called Louis Stanislaus Xavier, the brother of Louis XVI. to the throne of that kingdom, and drew up a constitution, which he was to swear to observe before he was to be proclaimed. His Majesty made his public entry into Paris on the 3rd of May.

Towards the middle of May the Confederate Armies broke up from their cantonments to leave the soil of France, and to repass the Rhine on their return to their several countries.

Peace was signed between France, Austria, Russia, Great Britain, and Prussia, on the 30th of May.

The frontiers of France were nearly those of 1792. Swisserland remained an independent state; Austria received back her territories in Upper Italy; England kept possession of Malta; and to France were restored the whole of her colonies, except Tobago, St. Lucia, and the Isle of France. All claims were given up respecting the heavy contributions formerly imposed by France, on other countries.

The victors returned not evil for evil, but left France, though conquered, both great and powerful, Germany, if unanimous, could have nothing to fear from France; and of all the potentates that returned home, crowned with the laurels of victory and clemency, none could be more gratified than the Sovereign of Prussia.

Deeply sensible of the debt of gratitude this monarch owed to his faithful subjects, he issued the following proclamation to his people on the 3rd of June 1813, previous to his leaving Paris for England:

> That combat is now ended for which my people and myself sprung to arms; and most happily so, by the help of God, the faithful assistance of our Allies, and the energy, courage, perseverance, and privations, which everyone who calls himself a Prussian has conspicuously shown and endured in this severe struggle. Accept, for it, my thanks. Your efforts and your sacrifices have been great; I know and acknowledge them; and God, who watches over us, has likewise acknowledged them. We have acquired what we fought for.
>
> Prussia now stands before the present age crowned with glory, and independent by her own energies, existing both in success and in misfortune. All as one, one for all, you hastened to arms, only one sentiment pervading my people throughout! And such was the combat!—Such sentiments, I then exclaimed, God alone can reward. He will now reward them by the peace which he has given us. Better times will return through this peace. The industrious farmer will no longer sow for strangers, but will reap for himself. Commerce, trade, and the arts, will once more flourish; opulence throughout all ranks will again take root; and under a new order of things, those wounds will be healed which your long sufferings have inflicted.
>
> Frederick.
>
> Paris, June 3, 1814.

The Prussian monarchy regained its influence on the continent, as one of the first powers of Europe, not merely by increase of territory, but by the heroic efforts of her army, and by a pure national spirit, which has shown itself on many. memorable occasions.

His Majesty the King of Prussia now hastened to reward his brave generals and commanders in the field. Our veteran hero was raised to the dignity of prince; General von York was created Count York of Wartenberg; General von Kleist, Count Kleist of Nollendorf; General von Bülow, Count Bülow of Dennewitz; General Tauenzien, Count Tauenzien of Wittenberg; and the Quartermaster-General von Gneisenau, Count Gneisenau. The monarch accompanied these marks of his gratitude with presents of domains equal to the elevated rank of his intrepid and skilful commanders, and honourable to the munificence of Frederick the Beloved.

General Count Kleist was appointed to the command of the troops stationed on the Lower Rhine. General Count York was made Governor of Liège. Colonel von Kraussenbeck was stationed in Mentz, as *commandant*. Between the Moselle and the Meuse, a Prussian Army went into cantonments.

The King of Prussia returned to Paris from his visit to England on the 29th of June 1814, and arrived at Berlin on the 4th of August.

Prince Blücher of Wahlstatt, accompanied by the Crown Prince of Prussia and Prince William, His Majesty's nephew, reached Magdeburgh on their return to Berlin, from the most glorious and bloody campaign recorded in history, on the 24th of July 1814. And the flower of the Prussian Army, 66,000 men strong, under the command of Count Tauenzien-Wittenberg, made their triumphal entry into Magdeburgh on the 4th of July.

In the interim, a Prussian corps under General Count Kleist of Nollendorf, was stationed on the Middle Rhine; another, under Count Bülow of Dennewitz, near Coblentz; and on the banks of the Meuse stood the troops under the command of General Thielman. The headquarters of all these corps were at Aix-la-Chapelle, General von Müffling being appointed Quartermaster-general.

An army of British, Hanoverian, Dutch, and Belgic troops, was cantoned in Belgium, from Namur to Nieuport, and from the Meuse to the North Sea.

We must now call the attention of our readers towards the Congress at Vienna, which, according to the Convention of Paris of the 30th of May 1814, was to deliberate upon the future welfare of Europe, and on the issue of whose consultations the peace and happiness of so many millions of human beings were to depend. This illustrious assemblage of European princes and experienced statesmen seeks in vain for a parallel in history. Their avowed principle, into which all others merged more or less, of fixing the balance of power in Europe upon the firmest basis human foresight was capable of forming, caused this grand council of state to become the most dignified in regard to its object, and the most splendid in respect to its members; and, no doubt, it will prove for a long period, the most glorious memorial of unanimity and wisdom the Christian world may have to offer. The deliberations of this august assembly commenced on the 1st of November 1814.

Whatever the opinions of politicians might be, or the hopes that were entertained, throughout the states of Europe, yet no one was found hardy enough to oppose that system with which the happiness of all was so closely interwoven. The object was not to serve *one*, but to serve *all*. Virtue and morality, long since banished from one corner of Europe, were to be reintroduced under the auspices of a legitimate sovereign, and the pleasure-yielding paths of honour and esteem were again opened to those that had been led astray.

This dream of future happiness kept up its delusive powers but a few short months. The sittings of Congress were not even ended, when Buonaparte, the scourge of mankind, banishing truth as well as virtue from his conduct, and leaguing with duplicity and cunning, set at nought his oath and his declaration to all the kings he had warred with, again stepped forth on the theatre of carnage, equally perfidious, equally unjust and faithless to his engagements as ever he had been heretofore.

CHAPTER 15

Napoleon Buonaparte's Escape from Elba

In detailing the particulars of Napoleon Buonaparte's escape from the island of Elba, we present a picture of perfidy and perjury on the part of this usurper, of a most striking and impressive nature.

On the 26th of February 1814, Napoleon seized some vessels in the harbour of Porto-Ferrajo, and embarked with about 400 infantry and 100 Polish lancers of his guard. He landed with his troops on the 1st of March in the gulf of Juan, in France. On the 7th he reached Grenoble, and entered Lyons on the 10th. He slept at Fontainbleau on the 19th, and made his public entry into Paris on the 20th of March 1814.

Thus, terminated this momentous enterprise. It caused, in the interval of its execution, no blood to be shed, proving, however, but a deceitful calm, as a prelude to the avenging storm that was to burst over the abettors of this base act of treason and impious arrogance. A most profound emotion and sentiment of depression were felt by everyone at seeing France once again fallen under the yoke of a military despot, supported by a perjured army. The constitution which the generosity of the Allied Monarchs had permitted France to form and to swear to support, was here at one blow subverted.

Prince Talleyrand communicated to the Allied sovereigns at Vienna, in the name of the King of France, the landing of Buonaparte in France, adding, that the kingdom was threatened with a civil war. The sovereigns having assembled, gave on this occasion a new mark of that magnanimity, of that chivalrous spirit which animates them. They unanimously resolved not to separate till Europe should be restored to a state of tranquillity, and, weary of the agitations and misfortunes which had so long oppressed their people, would not lay down their arms till order should be everywhere restored. Measures dictated by prudence were immediately resorted to with energy. Several Prussian corps on the Oder, in Silesia, and on the Elbe, received orders to march to the Lower Rhine.

The Russian Army, under General Bennigsen, left Posen, their headquarters, for Germany; and the Austrian and Bavarian troops put themselves in motion towards the Upper Rhine. The Prussian Army under General Count Kleist proceeded from their cantonments on the Rhine to the French frontiers, and the British Army in the Netherlands received considerable reinforcements.

Those criminals who for twenty years have been employed in daily crimes, and their chief, who had acted as if there were nothing sacred upon earth, but what he pleased to term his will, hastened, by their perfidious acts, to receive that ample punishment for which their treasons and their treachery so loudly called, but from which the noble generosity of the Allied monarchs had hitherto suffered them to escape.

The nations of Europe were driven to arms by the fearful apprehension of again seeing despotism and the sword extinguishing the rights of humanity. Their princes and their leaders had felt the direful consequences of the want of unanimity amongst themselves in former times; and with an unexampled coalescence of interests they once more took the field against the common enemy of mankind. Their efforts have been crowned with victory, and the ruthless subverter of peace and tranquillity, of civic independence and religion, has been stripped of all his meretricious military fame, and expelled society.

His Majesty the King of Prussia adopted the most prompt measures to bring an active and efficient army into the field, accompanied by the following proclamation to his people, which was received with enthusiasm. In fact, the people of Prussia, always distinguished for their patriotism, never gave more striking proofs of it than at this moment. Citizens of all ranks and ages crowded to enrol themselves, and more eager to depart.

Vienna, April 7, 1815.

> When, in the time of danger, I called my people to arms, to combat for the freedom and independence of the country, the whole mass of the youth, glowing with emulation, thronged round the standards, to bear with joyful self-denial unusual hardships, and resolved to brave death itself. Then the best strength of the people intrepidly joined the ranks of my brave

soldiers, and my generals led with me into battle a host of heroes, who have shown themselves worthy of the name of Prussians. Thus, we and our Allies, attended by victory, conquered the capital of our enemy. Napoleon abdicated his authority: liberty was restored to Germany, security to thrones, and to the world the hope of a durable peace.

This hope is vanished. We must again march to the combat! A perfidious conspiracy has brought back to France the man who, for ten years together, has filled the world with sorrow. The people, confounded, have not been able to oppose his armed adherents. Though he himself, while still at the head of a considerable military force, declared his abdication to be a voluntary sacrifice to the happiness and repose of France, he now regards this, like every other convention, as nothing. He is at the head of perjured soldiers, who desire to render war eternal; Europe again is threatened: it cannot suffer the man to remain on the throne of France, who loudly proclaimed universal empire to be the object of his continually renewed wars; who confounded all moral principle, by his repeated breach of faith, and who can, therefore, give the world no security for his peaceful intentions.

Again, therefore, arise to the combat! France itself wants our aid, and all Europe is Allied with us. United with your ancient companions in victory, reinforced by the accession of new brethren in arms, you, brave Prussians, go to a just war with me, with the princes of my family, with the generals who have led you to conquest. The justice of the cause we defend will ensure us victory.

Thus united, with all Europe in arms, we again enter the lists against Napoleon Buonaparte and his adherents. Arise then, with God for your support, for the repose of the world, for order, for morality, for your king and country.

Frederick William.

The King of Prussia gave Prince Blücher the command-in-chief over the Prussian Armies. General Count Gneisenau was at the same time appointed quartermaster-general to the Army of the Lower Rhine, the staff of which was composed of General von Müffling, Colonels Pfühl, Grollmann, &c. &c. &c.

The Prussian Army that was now preparing to take the field,

amounted to about 230,000 men. It was divided into seven corps.

The 1st corps, under the command of Lieutenant-General von Ziethen; the 2nd corps, under the command of Lieutenant-General Count Bülow von Dennewitz; the 3rd corps, under the command of Lieutenant-General von Borstel; the 4th corps, under the command of Lieutenant-General von Thielman; composed the army of the Lower Rhine, under Marshal Prince Blücher, having its headquarters at Liège. Never did a finer and more enthusiastic army form under the banners of a more distinguished leader, and never had an army a more righteous cause to maintain.

Our illustrious veteran Blücher took leave of his sovereign, and departed from Berlin for the Prussian Army in the Netherlands, on the 10th of April 1815. On his arrival at Liège, he addressed the following proclamation to his army:

> Comrades! His Majesty the King has been pleased to confide to me the chief command of the army. I receive this favour with most lively gratitude. I am rejoiced to see you again—to find you on the field of honour, prepared for a new contest, full of new hopes. It is given to us again to combat for the great cause—for general peace! I congratulate you upon it. The course of glory is again opened to you. An opportunity offers to increase, by new deeds, the military renown which you have already acquired! Placed at your head, I doubt not of certain and glorious success! Show me, in this new struggle, the confidence you have placed in me during the last, and I am convinced that you will gloriously extend the fame of your brilliant deeds in arms.
>
> Blücher.

A declaration of the Allied powers, dated from Vienna, pronounced in a solemn and decisive manner, "That there is no peace with Buonaparte." This great sentence loudly proclaimed the desire of the belligerent Sovereigns to procure themselves a sure and durable peace, and that they will never recognise a military despotism with the means of incessantly threatening its neighbours, and which would force other powers continually to make efforts and new sacrifices.

The Duke of Wellington arrived at Brussels on the 4th of April, as commander-in-chief of the grand Allied Army of British, Dutch, and Hanoverians, collecting in the Netherlands, and had several interviews with General Count Kleist of Nollendorf, then commanding the Prussian forces, concerning the intended operations.

Field-Marshal Prince Blücher was at Brussels on the 28th of April, to be present at a grand review of the British cavalry, and had a long conference with England's hero.

The Prussian Army was cantoned in the neighbourhood of Liège, Namur, and Hannut; General von Ziethen's headquarters were at Jemappe, General von Borstel's at Binch, and General von Bülow's at Hannut.

Hostilities first commenced between the Prussians and the French on the 25th of April, near Falmignoul, two leagues from Givet, the French outposts being driven back, with some loss, upon the latter place.

It was for the common interests of Europe that this grand assemblage of gallant warriors, under Blücher and Wellington, was formed, mutually inclined to respect and regard each other. United by one sentiment, as well as by the general danger, standing in need of reciprocal aid, and breathing alike the same lofty spirit of honour and independence, the two armies never ceased to cultivate those ties that bound them closer together, and thus promoted an uninterrupted harmony in the councils of their illustrious chiefs.

Proudly conscious of the glory they had acquired in the last struggle, and full of confidence in themselves, the two armies awaited with manifest impatience the orders for marching beyond the frontiers of France to meet their enemy in the field.

The other Confederate powers were, meanwhile, not less intent upon completing their armies, and preparing them for an eventful campaign, and hostile entry into France, from the most vulnerable points.

The necessity of waiting till the whole of these mighty preparations were fully completed, caused at this period the armies of the Allies in the Netherlands to remain inactive.

Napoleon Buonaparte, at the head of the military power of France, adopted in the interim every coercive measure within his grasp, to reorganise his army, and to increase and consolidate his means of aggression. The time that now elapsed in a state of suspense, presented an awful interval full of hope, doubt, and fear to men's minds. It agitated the whole of Europe, set the theories of politicians at nought, and left little to console the heart of man but confidence and trust in Divine Providence. It seemed to be the miserable fate reserved for mankind, that a state of society in which all are soldiers—in which a military code was to predominate over civil institutions, and a new situation affecting the political relations of every power and the private condition of every individual, was going to be once more realised.

The month of May passed without any event taking place worthy of record. It was the interest of the Confederates to gain time, and to permit Buonaparte to be the first aggressor. They were not to risk the danger of exciting the popular feeling of France herself against their honourable views. It was the man, and not the nation, they warred with; and a material point was gained, if the nation remained convinced that Buonaparte and his adherents alone were to be chastised, on the Allies again entering their country as victors. England, Prussia, Russia, and Austria, therefore, avowed and declared their sole object to be the destruction and subjection of a nest of thieves, that preferred a life of rapine and plunder to the peaceful occupations of husbandry and civic independence.

Nothing that sprung from moral rectitude had been able to control the perfidious despot; and it was resolved, that the fetters of penal restraint should now bind him fast, and disable him from all commission of further evil.

The flower of the British, Prussian, Dutch, and Hanoverian Armies, concentrated themselves in the Netherlands; reinforcements daily joined, offering a pledge for a proportionate increase of energy to their exertions, when the campaign should open.

The French Army now assembled on the frontiers towards the Netherlands, might be computed at little short of 140,000 men. Every nerve had been exerted, and all physical powers stretched to their extreme tension, to bring it to a state of high organisation, and to improve its discipline. In the stupendous attempt of Buonaparte, both daring and important, of again rendering his seat firm on his usurped throne, it is to be supposed that he would not leave a single soldier in his rear, as reserve, that was fit to take the field; and consequently the whole efficient military strength of France might be considered as concentrated at this point.

In the early part of June 1815, Napoleon Buonaparte left Paris, and put himself at the head of five corps of the French Army, exclusive of the imperial guards and cavalry, taking up a position between Maubeuge and Beaumont. He commenced hostilities on the 15th of June, by driving in the Prussian videttes and outposts, and advancing on the right and left bank of the Sambre, by Thuin, against Charleroi, which, after a trifling affair, was occupied by the French.

The points of concentration of the Prussian Army of the Lower Rhine, under our veteran Prince Blücher, were at Fleurus and Namur. General von Ziethen had collected his corps near the former place, and after a very warm action with the enemy, on the 15th, maintained himself there in his position. The terrain of Sombref, about a league and a half from Fleurus, being chosen by Field-Marshal Blücher, on which to meet the enemy, the three other corps of the Prussian Army were consequently directed upon that place, where the 2nd and 3rd corps were to arrive on the 15th, and the 4th corps on the 16th.

In the morning of the 16th, the Prussian Army was posted on the heights between Bry and Sombref (see Map of the Battles of Waterloo and Ligny), and beyond the latter place, and occupied, with a large force, the villages of St. Amand and Ligny, situated in a ravine, on its front. Meantime only three corps of the army had joined; the fourth, under General Count Bülow, was stationed between Liège and Hannut, had been delayed in its march by several circumstances, and was not yet come up.

The French Army occupied the following positions: the left wing, under Marshal Ney, was posted at Frasne; the right wing, under Marshal Grouchy, in the rear of Fleurus. But, on Napoleon having reconnoitred the strength and positions of Marshal Blücher's army, he, about noon, changed front, and marched his left wing upon Les Quatre Bras, and his right and centre upon St. Amand and Ligny.

In the meantime the Duke of Wellington had collected his troops near Soignies and Brendleçon; and, on the 16th, Prince William of Orange, by order of the duke, took post with his corps at Les Quatre Bras, to be nearer the Prussian Army; and, by dividing the attention and forces of Napoleon, prevent his pressing with too great a superiority of numbers on Marshal Blücher's line of operations. The Prince of Orange was supported by the Duke of Brunswick's division, and a division of British troops, under Lieutenant-General Sir Thomas Picton; his left wing leaning on Sart à Maveline, and his right on the former place.

The Duke of Wellington directed the whole English Army to march upon Les Quatre Bras. Marshal Ney, with the 1st and 2nd corps, and the 2nd of cavalry, commenced the attack at about three o'clock, p.m. A wood, to the right of Les Quatre Bras, was several times taken and retaken; and the village of Pierremont, on the left, was carried at the point of the bayonet. And, after a sanguinary conflict, the array of the Allies maintained its position, and completely defeated

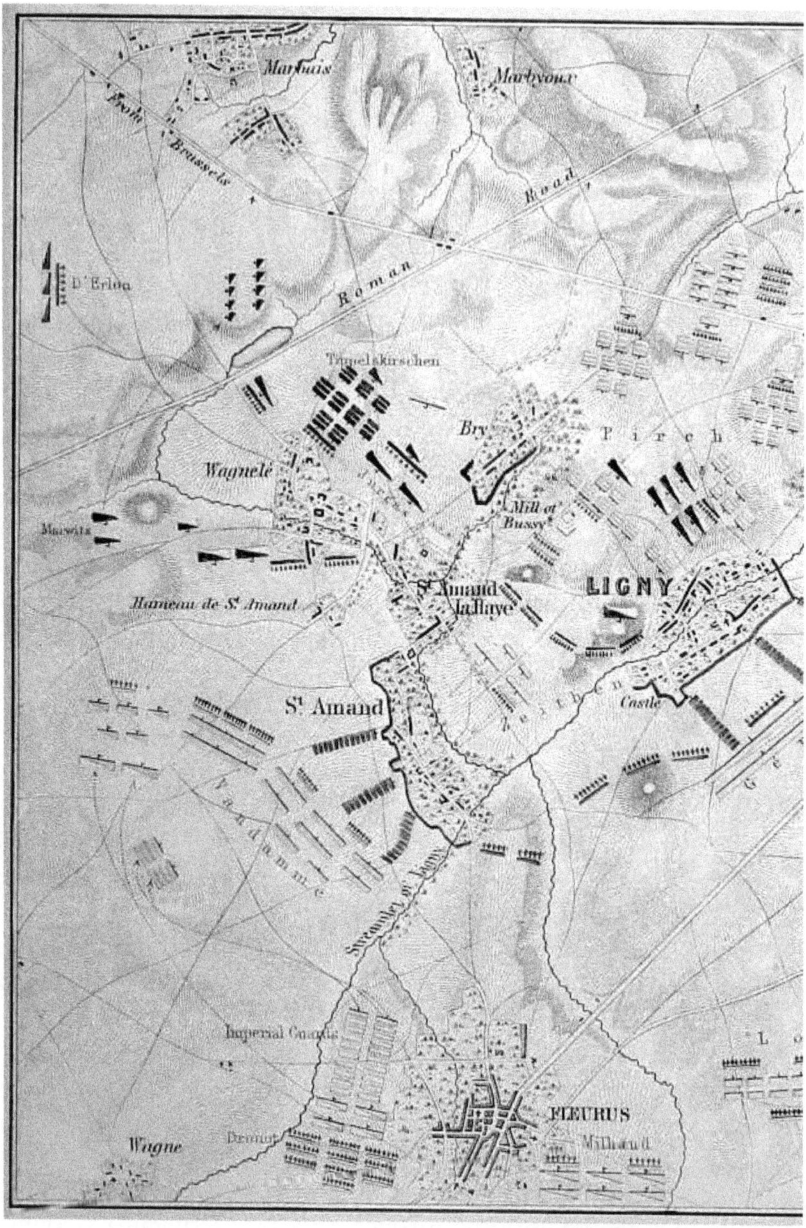

Marbais
Marbyoux
From Brussels
Roman Road
D'Erlon
Tangelskirschen
Bry
Pirch
Wagnelé
Mill of Bussy
St Amand la Haye
LIGNY
Hameau de St Amand
St Amand
Castle
Vandamme
Imperial Guards
FLEURUS
Milhaud
Wagne

BATTLE
OF
LIGNY
16th June 1815.
French
Prussians
Cavalry
Infantry
Artillery
SCALES
1 English Mile
Pontorieux
Vieille Maison
Hamre
Sombreffe
Point du Jour
To Namur
Tongrinne
Mt. Potriaux
Thielmann
Boignée
Balatre
Excelmans
Fay
Velaine
Wanfersee

and repulsed every attempt against it, though repeatedly assaulted by large bodies of infantry and cavalry, supported by a numerous and powerful artillery.

Our veteran Prince Blücher still resolved to give battle in his position at Sombref, although his 4th corps was not yet in line, and his army, in point of numbers, was much inferior to that of the French; but, notwithstanding, every foot of ground was obstinately contested, and the position maintained with unparalleled bravery and resolution.

At about three o'clock, p.m. great masses of the enemy, under Marshal Grouchy, attacked the village of St. Amand; it was defended with intrepidity, and its transient occupation cost the French an enormous number of men; the Prussians rallied, and it was again carried after a sanguinary conflict; again lost; then stormed, for a third time, by a gallant battalion with our veteran hero at its head, and the heights of La Haye and Little St. Amand were at last regained, and occupied by the Prussian Army.

It was near five o'clock, p.m. and the enemy now directed his efforts against Ligny: this is a large village, solidly built, situated on a rivulet of the same name. It was here that a contest began, which may be considered as the most sanguinary in history. The terrain of action was confined to a very narrow space, fresh troops were, on both sides, continually brought into fire, and the combat was maintained about Ligny with unexampled fury. By regaining the height of La Haye, affairs seemed to take a favourable turn for the Prussian arms. The issue, however, seemed to depend on the arrival of the English troops, or on that of the 4th corps of the Prussian Army.

In fact, the co-operation of this last division would have afforded the field-marshal the means of making immediately, with the right wing, an attack, from which great success might be expected; but news was brought that the English division, destined to support Prince Blücher, was violently attacked by the French Army, under Marshal Ney, and it was with great difficulty it had maintained itself in its position at Les Quatre Bras. The 4th corps of the army did not appear; so that our veteran marshal was forced to maintain alone the contest with an enemy greatly superior in numbers.

For four hours the combat about Ligny continued with the same fury, and the same equality of success; the danger became every hour more and more urgent, our dauntless hero, sword in hand, repeatedly led his divisions into fire; the arrival of the succours so necessary was in vain invoked, and there was not any corps in reserve to support the

BLÜCHER FALLS FROM HIS HORSE AT LIGNY

prodigious efforts of the troops, and the personal bravery and example of our intrepid Blücher.

It proved, however, a drawn battle, as no ground was lost or won on either side. Towards nine in the evening, Napoleon attempted, with his masses of cavalry, to attain his object of interrupting the communication between the armies of Marshal Prince Blücher and the Duke of Wellington. The attacks of the French cavalry were coolly repulsed by the Prussian infantry, which now retreated in good order upon the heights, whence the Prussian Army continued its retrograde movement upon Tilly. The villages of Bry and Sombref were kept occupied during the night, and the corps under General Thielman began slowly, at daybreak, to retreat towards Gembloux, where the 4th corps, under General Count Bülow, had now arrived.

The 1st and 2nd corps proceeded, in the morning, behind the defile of Mount St. Guibert. Marshal Prince Blücher held it advisable to take up a position, on the evening of the 17th, near Wavre, that he might be nearer his reinforcements, and be able to form a complete junction with the army of the Allies, under the Duke of Wellington.

The loss of the Prussians at the Battle of Ligny, on the 16th, was great; but no prisoners were taken by the enemy, except a part of the wounded. The troops fought with a bravery which equalled every expectation; their fortitude remained unshaken, because everyone retained his confidence in his own strength. On this memorable day, however, Field-Marshal Blücher had encountered the greatest dangers. A charge of cavalry led on by himself, had failed; while that of the enemy was vigorously pursuing, a musket-shot struck the field-marshal's horse; the animal, far from being stopped in his career by this wound, began to gallop more furiously, till it dropped down dead.

The field-marshal, stunned by the violent fall, lay entangled under the horse. The enemy's *cuirassiers*, following up their advantage, advanced; the last Prussian horseman had already passed by the field-marshal; an adjutant alone remained with him, and had just alighted to share his fate. The danger was great, but Heaven watched over him. The enemy, pursuing their charge, passed rapidly by the field-marshal without seeing him; the next moment, a second charge of cavalry having repelled them, they again passed by him, with the same precipitation, not perceiving him any more than they had done the first time. Then, but not without difficulty, the field-marshal was disengaged from under the dead animal, and he immediately mounted a dragoon. horse.

The Prussian Army had concentrated itself on advantageous ground, in the environs of Wavre. The Duke of Wellington issued the necessary orders to form a junction with Marshal Blücher; the English Army, in consequence, made a corresponding movement with that of Blücher's, and fell back upon Genappe, and then on Waterloo, on the morning of the 17th, at ten o'clock. The enemy did not attack Blücher or the English Army in their march, but only followed with his cavalry.

The Battle of Ligny was marked by the peculiar fury and hatred with which the Prussians fought the French. Their mutual animosity was beyond conception. The slaughter made by the Prussians was immense; they refused to take quarter, as much as the French refused to give it; and it may be easily supposed that there never was such havoc made as here, for, where men fight with equal desperation, the loss on both sides is always terrible. It was evident, from the tardiness of the pursuit, that the French felt but little confidence of success from any further efforts.

The loss of the Prussians may be estimated at about 10,000 men, killed and wounded.

The Duke of Wellington, after the action of Les Quatre Bras, had taken up a position with the army of the Allies, on the road to Brussels (see Map of the Battles of Waterloo and Ligny), having his right wing leaning upon Braine la Leu, the centre near Mont St. Jean, and the left wing against Ter la Haye. The duke wrote to the field-marshal, that he was resolved to accept battle in this position, if the field-marshal would support him with two corps of his army. Our veteran hero promised to come with his whole army. He even proposed, in case Napoleon should not attack, that the Allies themselves, with their whole united force, should attack him the next day. This may serve to show how little the battle of the 16th had disorganised the Prussian Army, or weakened its moral strength. Thus, ended the day of the 17th.'

On the 18th, Napoleon had detached his right wing, under Marshal Grouchy, in pursuit of the Prussians towards Wavre; he himself fixed his headquarters at Planchenoit, and, with his left wing and centre under Marshal Ney and Jerome Buonaparte, took up a position, with his right on the heights in front of Planchenoit, his centre at La Belle Alliance, and his left leaning on the road to Brussels, and nearly opposite the village of Mont St. Jean. The *cuirassiers* and the guards were posted in reserve on the heights behind.—(See Map of the Battles of Waterloo and Ligny.)

The movement of Prince Blücher to Wavre, on the 17th, had, as already mentioned, induced the Duke of Wellington to remove his headquarters to Waterloo.

The position of Waterloo is in advance of that place, where the high road from Brussels to Namur crosses that which leads to Braine la Leu. Though this ground is open and without any remarkable feature, it rises almost suddenly upon this point, to the distance of half a league. There is at the right extremity of the front of this elevation, a farm, consisting of a stone house, a wall round the premises, and a wood, intersected by natural hedges and ditches.

It was upon this ground that the Duke of Wellington resolved to wait for the enemy. He placed his batteries, occupied the farm and the garden, and ranged his army along the eminence, protected by its heights from the enemy's fire. The army being composed of troops of different nations, he took the precaution to support each of them by English infantry, all dispersed in such a manner as to be able to succour the point that was threatened.

On the 18th, at noon, the French Army, commanded by Buonaparte, commenced the attack; his first efforts were against the farm of which we have spoken. After several attempts he succeeded, about half past one o'clock, p. m. in dislodging some part of the troops. The duke hastened to the spot, and ordered two battalions to retake it, and to defend themselves there to the last extremity. His orders were punctually obeyed.

The enemy then directed two strong columns against the centre. The duke in person led some battalions of infantry against these columns, and Lord Uxbridge the cavalry. They charged with the bayonet; the French were overpowered, and their cavalry broken. In this charge were taken an eagle, a standard, and 1,200 prisoners. The victorious troops instantly returned to their place, and again formed.

The attack on the farm continued; the enemy penetrated to it, but could never establish a footing there.

Buonaparte, seeing that he could not obtain any advantage, manoeuvred, with all his cavalry, and a part of his infantry, against the right of the Allies, attempted to outflank it with 17,000 cavalry, and began a most vigorous attack. The duke made his arrangements accordingly: the cavalry of the two armies charged; the squares of infantry remained immovable, and repulsed every attack. This attempt of the enemy was baffled. At last, about six o'clock, he made another attack upon the centre, and reached the eminence. The duke attacked him, overthrew and pursued him, and the rout soon became general.

The army of the Duke of Wellington did not exceed 50,000 men, actually engaged. The enemy was very superior, particularly in cavalry.

The headquarters of the Duke of Wellington were removed to Nivelles after the battle.

Meanwhile the army under the command of Marshal Prince Blücher began again to move from the environs of Wavre at break of day on the 18th. The 4th and 2nd corps marched by St. Lambert, where they were to occupy a position, covered by the forest, near Frichemont, to take the enemy in the rear when the moment should appear favourable. The 1st corps was to operate by Ohain, on the right flank of the enemy; the 3rd corps was to follow slowly, in order to afford succour in case of need. The conflict began about ten, a. m. In a short time, the battle became general along the whole line.

It seems that Napoleon had the design to throw the left wing upon the centre, and thus to effect the separation of the English Army from the Prussian, which he believed to be retreating upon Maestricht. For this purpose, he had placed the greater part of his reserve in the centre, against his right wing; and upon this point he attacked with fury. The English Army fought with a valour which could not be surpassed. The repeated charges of the old guard were baffled by the intrepidity of the Scotch regiments; and at every charge the French cavalry was overthrown by the English cavalry. But the superiority in numbers of the enemy was too great; Napoleon continually brought forward considerable masses, and with whatever firmness the English troops maintained themselves in their position, it was not possible but that such heroic exertions must have a limit.

It was half past four o'clock. The excessive difficulties of the passage by the defile of St. Lambert, had greatly retarded the march of the Prussian columns, so that only two brigades of the 4th corps had arrived at the covered position which was assigned them. The decisive moment was come; there was not a moment to be lost. The Generals did not suffer it to escape. They resolved immediately to begin the attack with the troops which they had at hand. General Count Bülow, therefore, with two brigades and a corps of cavalry, advanced rapidly along the rear of the enemy's right wing. The enemy did not lose his presence of mind; he instantly returned his reserve against the Prussians, and a murderous conflict began on that side. The combat remained long uncertain, while the battle with the English Army still continued with the same violence.

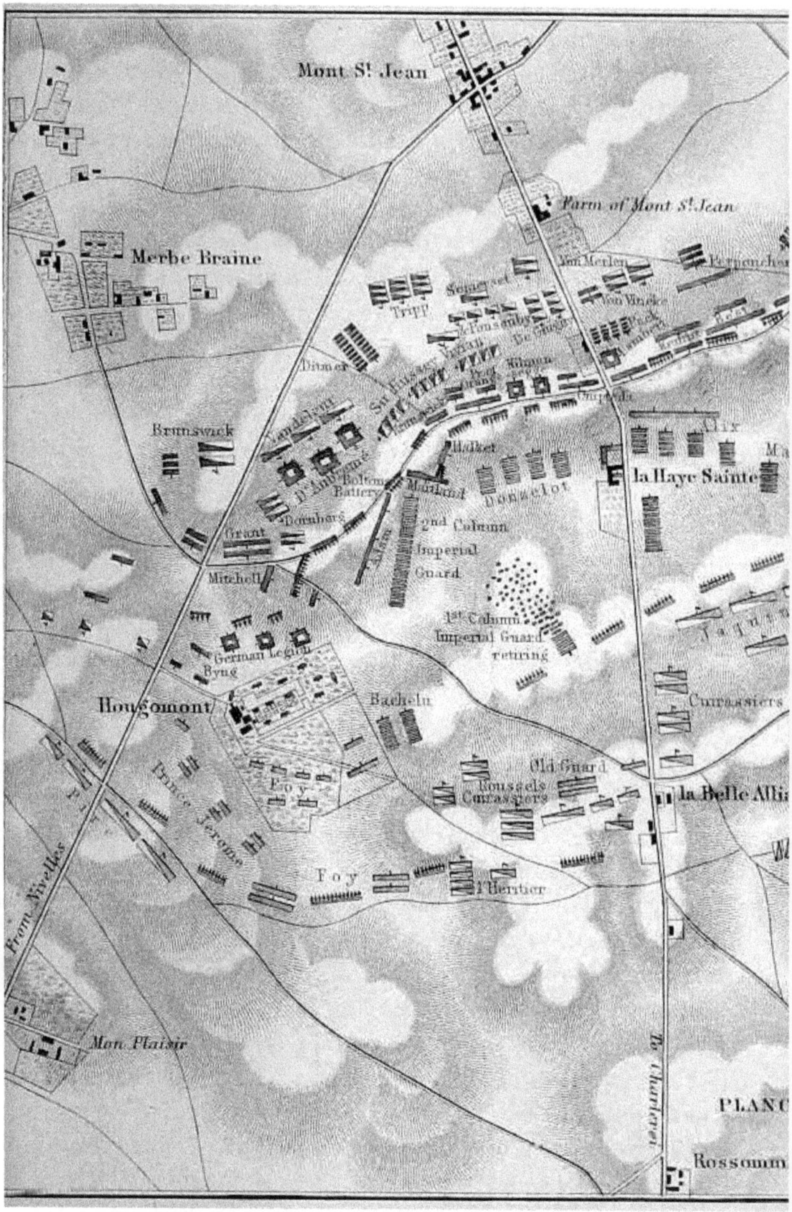
Mont St. Jean
Farm of Mont St. Jean
Merbe Braine
Somerset
Brunswick
Grant
Mitchell
German Legion
Byng
Hougomont
Bachelu
Prince Jerome
Foy
Foy
l'Heritier
Old Guard
Roussels Curassiers
Curassiers
la Haye Sainte
Donzelot
Halket
Maitland
Bolton's Battery
2nd Column Imperial Guard
1st Column Imperial Guard retiring
Mon Plaisir
From Nivelles
To Charleroi

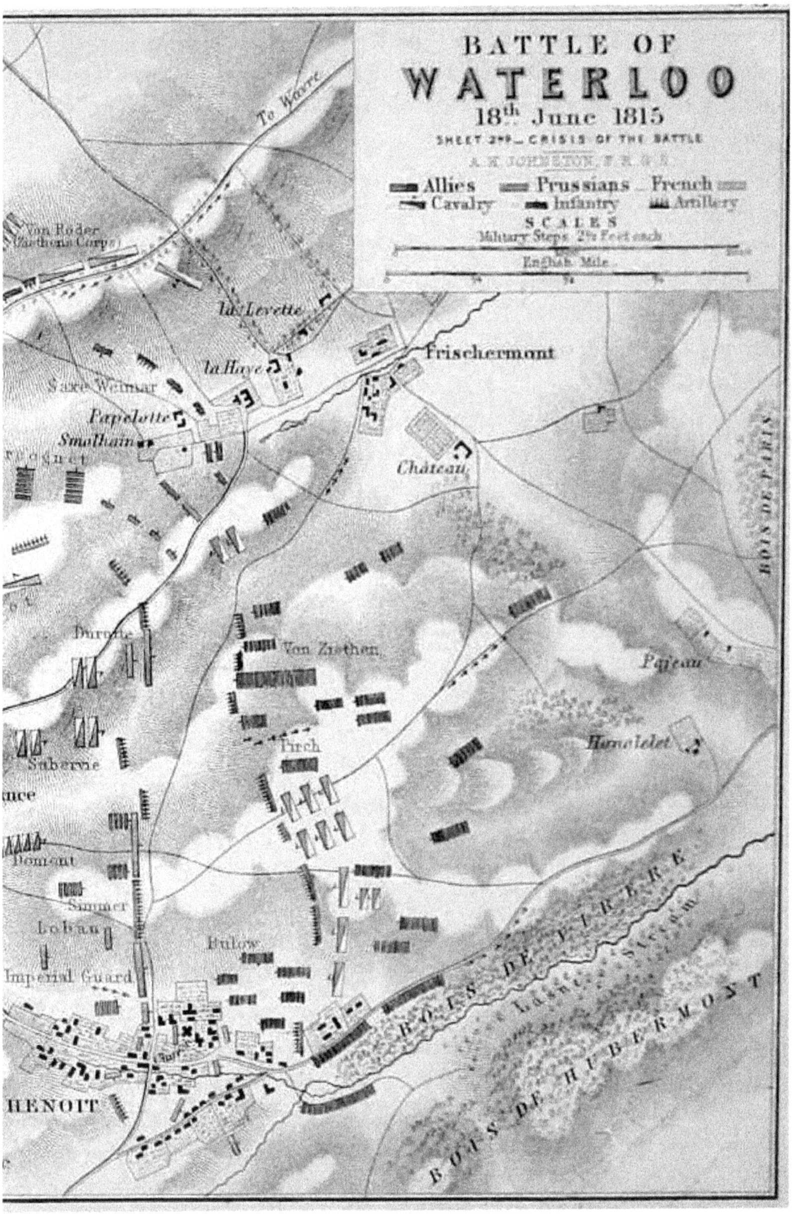
BATTLE OF
WATERLOO
18th June 1815
SHEET 2ND _ CRISIS OF THE BATTLE
Allies
Prussians
French
Cavalry
Infantry
Artillery
SCALES
English Mile
To Wavre
Von Röder
la Haye
Frischermont
Saxe Weimar
Papelotte
Château
BOIS DE PARIS
Durutte
Von Ziethen
Pajeau
Pirch
Subervie
Domont
Lobau
Bulow
Imperial Guard
HENOIT
BOIS DE VIRERE
BOIS DE HUBERMONT

Towards six p. m. news was received that General Thielman, with the 3rd corps, was attacked near Wavre by a very considerable corps of the enemy, and that they were already disputing the possession of the town. The field-marshal, however, did not suffer himself to be disturbed by this intelligence; it was on the spot where he was, and nowhere else, that the affair was to be decided. A conflict, continually supported with the same obstinacy, and kept up by fresh troops, could alone ensure the victory; and if it was obtained here, any reverse sustained near Wavre was of little consequence. The columns, therefore, continued their movements.

It was half past seven—and the issue of the battle was still uncertain. The whole of the 4th corps, and a part of the 2nd under General Pirch, had successively come up. The French fought with a desperate fury; however, some uncertainty was perceived in their movements, and it was observed that some pieces of cannon were retreating. At this moment the first column of General von Ziethen arrived on the points of attack, near the village of Smouhen, on the enemy's right flank, and instantly charged. This movement decided the defeat of the enemy. His right wing was broken in three places; he abandoned his positions. The troops rushed forwards at the *pas de charge*, and attacked him on all sides, while, at the same time, the whole English line advanced.

Circumstances were entirely favourable to the attack formed by the Prussian Army: the ground rose in an amphitheatre, so that their artillery could freely open its fire from the summit of several heights, which rose gradually above each other, and in the intervals of which the troops descended into the plain, formed into brigades, in the most perfect order, while fresh corps continually unfolded themselves, issuing from the forest on the height behind. The enemy, however, still preserved means to retreat, till the village of Planchenoit, which he had on his rear, and which was defended by the Old Guard, was, after several bloody attacks, carried by storm.

★★★★★★

Napoleon's corps of Old Guards was posted at Planchenoit as reserve. It was the 15th regiment of Prussian Infantry, led on by Major von Keller, and supported by some battalions of Prussian *landwehr*, that stormed their position, and completely put them to the rout. The greater part of them were bayoneted—no prisoners were made, and no quarter was given.

★★★★★★

From this time the retreat became a rout, that quickly spread throughout the whole French Army, which, in its dreadful confusion, hurrying away everything that attempted to stop it, soon assumed the appearance of the flight of an army of barbarians. It was half past nine: the field-marshal assembled all the superior officers, and gave orders to send the last horse and the last man in pursuit of the enemy. The van of the Prussian Army accelerated its march. The French Army, pursued without intermission, was absolutely disorganised. The cause way presented the appearance of an immense shipwreck; it was covered with an innumerable quantity of cannon, caissons, carriages, baggage, arms, and wrecks of every kind.

Those of the enemy who had attempted to repose for a time, and had not expected to be so quickly pursued, were driven from more than nine bivouacs. In some villages they attempted to maintain themselves; but as soon as they heard the beating of the Prussian drums, or the sound of the trumpet, they either fled or threw themselves into the houses, where they were cut down or made prisoners. It was moonlight, which greatly favoured the pursuit; for the whole march was hbt a continued chase, either in cornfields or the houses.

At Genappe the enemy had intrenched himself with cannon and overturned carriages, at the approach of the Prussians. Suddenly they heard in the town a great noise and a motion of carriages; at the entrance they were exposed to a brisk fire of musketry, which was replied to by some cannon-shot, followed by a hurrah; and an instant after the town was theirs.

✶✶✶✶✶✶

It was Major von Keller, at the head of the advance, that charged into Genappe at the time that Napoleon was driving through the place in his carriage, attended by his suite in several other vehicles: the major's movement was so sudden, that Napoleon had only time to mount a horse to escape falling into his hands. His hat and sword were found in the carriage. His treasures, his jewels, his imperial mantle, and the whole of his baggage, fell into the hands of the Prussians, besides maps, charts, and military plans, without number; and, above all, his personal *portefeuille*, containing the whole of his private and secret correspondence.

✶✶✶✶✶✶

Thus, the affair continued till break of day. About 40,000 men in the most complete disorder, the remains of the whole army, saved themselves by retreating through Charleroi, partly without arms, and carrying with them only twenty-seven pieces of their numerous artillery.

Few victories have been so complete, and there is certainly no example that an army, two days after losing a battle, engaged in such an action, and so gloriously maintained it. Honour be to the troops capable of so much firmness and valour! In the middle of the position occupied by the French Army, and exactly upon the height, is a farm called La Belle Alliance. The march of all the Prussian columns was directed towards this farm, which was visible from every side. It was there that Napoleon was during the battle—it was there that he gave his orders, that he flattered himself with the hopes of victory—and it was there that his ruin was decided. There, too, it was, that, by a happy chance, Field-Marshal Blücher and the Duke of Wellington met in the dark, and mutually saluted each other as victors.

The Allied Army under the duke pursued the flying French, till, overcome with fatigue, the troops could follow them no further. But Buonaparte was not suffered to rest; the Prussians, under General Count Gneisenau, started afresh in the pursuit, where the British Army and the Allies stopped, and hung on the rear of the fugitives for the whole night, avenging, amply, the fate of 10,000 of their brave countrymen, who had so nobly spilt their blood in the battles of the 15th and 16th.

Marshal Prince Blücher's headquarters were at Genappe on the morning of the 19th, from whence he dated the following autograph letter to the Governor of Berlin, General von Kalkreuth;

> I have to inform Your Excellency, that, in conjunction with the British Army under the Duke of Wellington, I yesterday gained the most complete victory over Napoleon Buonaparte, that ever was obtained. The battle took place in the neighbourhood of a few houses, situated on the road from hence to Brussels, called La Belle Alliance; and a better name cannot well be given to this important day. The whole French Army is in a state of perfect dissolution, and an extraordinary number of guns have been taken. Time will not permit me to state more particulars to Your Excellency. The details shall follow; and I only beg you to impart this news immediately to the loyal citizens of Berlin.
>
> Blücher
>
> Headquarters, Genappe, June 19,
> Half past Five o Clock, a.m.

★★★★★★

At the conclusion of the battle the marshal also wrote the following letter to his lady:

My Dear Wife,

You well know what I promised you, and I have kept my word. Superiority of numbers forced me to give way on the 17th; but, on the 18th, in conjunction with my friend Wellington, I put an end at once to Buonaparte's dancing. His army is completely routed, and the whole of his artillery, baggage, tumbrils, and equipages are in my hands. The insignia of all the orders he had worn are just brought me, having been found in his carriage in a casket. I had two horses killed under me yesterday. Buonaparte's affair will now soon be terminated.

Blücher.

P. S. (*Written by his son on the road to Genappe.*) Father Blücher embraced Wellington in so hearty a manner, that everyone present said it was the most touching scene that could be imagined.

★★★★★★

The Battle of Waterloo was fought by Buonaparte with every power called into action; he knew that he must infallibly lose all if victory did not overawe his foes and encourage his well-wishers. He made one desperate, bloody struggle, and—he failed.

The immediate fruits of this victory were between 20,000 and 30,000 prisoners, with more than 250 pieces of cannon, and the almost complete destruction of the only French force which could properly be called an army.

The following proclamation was addressed by Field-Marshal Prince Blücher to the army of the Lower Rhine, to be read at the head of every battalion, after the victory of Waterloo, on the 18th of June 1815.

Brave Officers and Soldiers of the Army of the Lower Rhine! You have done great things, brave companions in arms—you have fought two battles in three days. The first was unfortunate, and yet your courage was not broken. You have had to struggle with privations, but you have borne them with fortitude. Immovable in adverse fortune, after the loss of a bloody battle, you marched with firmness to fight another, relying on the God of Battles, and full of confidence in your commanders, as well as of

BATTLE OF
WAVRE
18th & 19th June 1815.

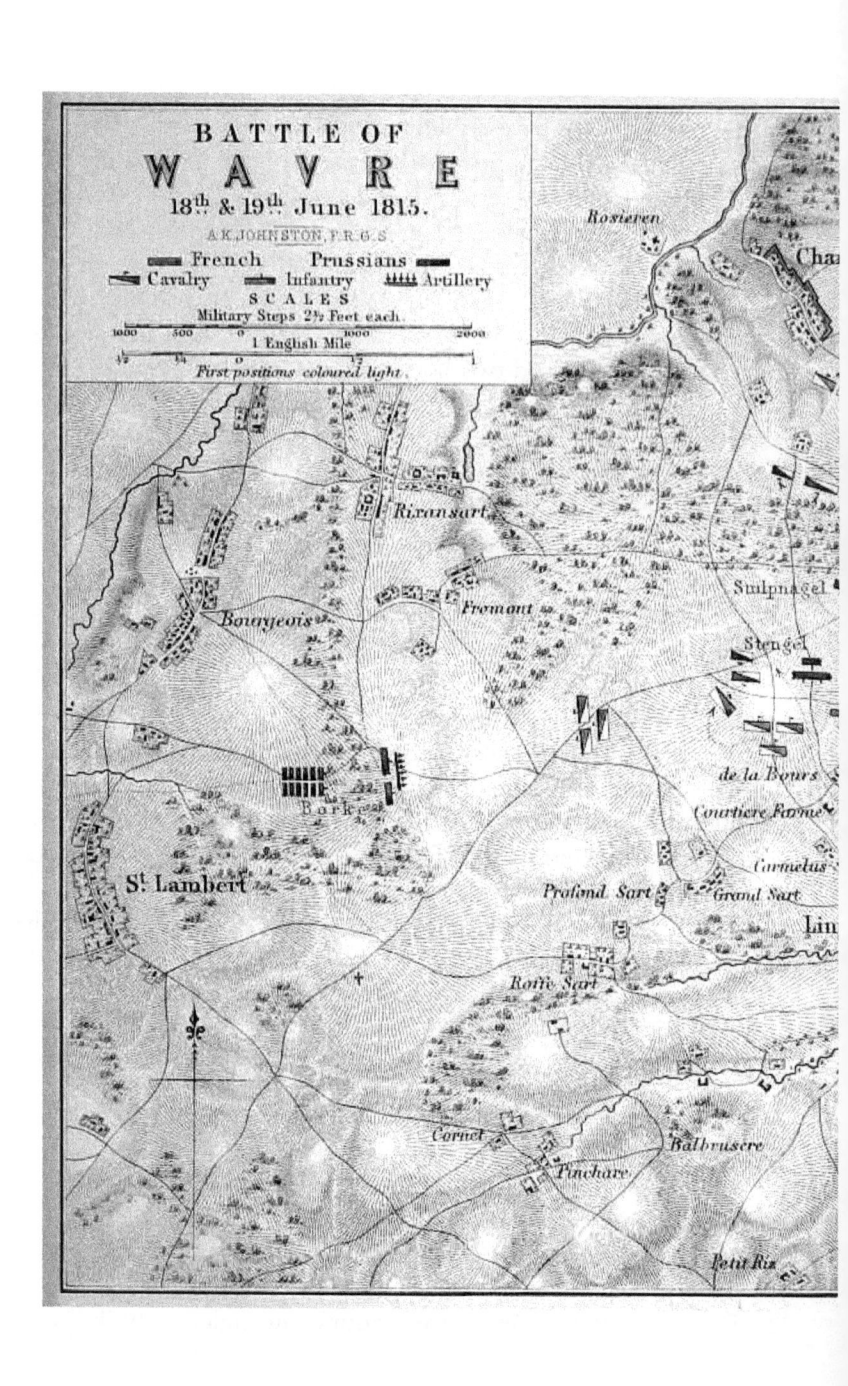

A.K. JOHNSTON, F.R.G.S.

French ——— Prussians ———
Cavalry — Infantry ⋈⋈⋈ Artillery

SCALES
Military Steps 2½ Feet each.
1 English Mile

First positions coloured light.

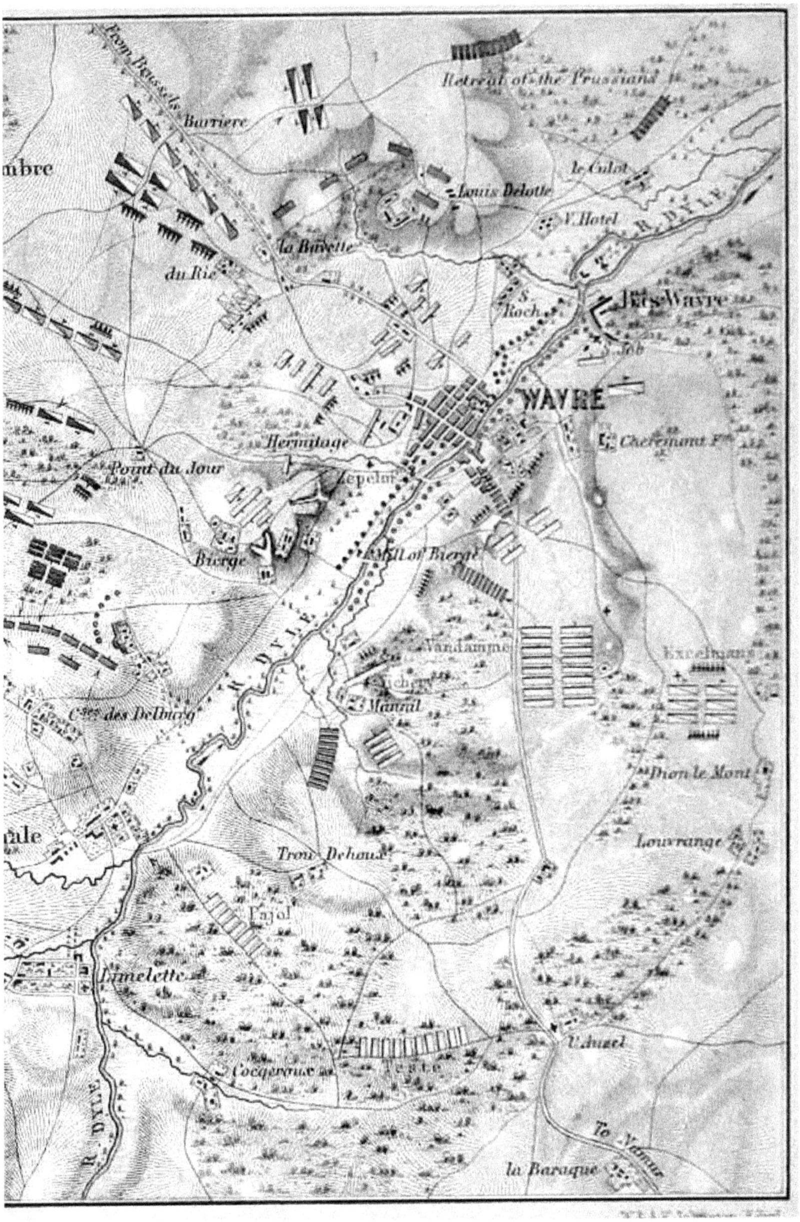

From Brussels
Barriere
Retreat of the Prussians
mbre
le Culot
Louis Delotte
V. Hotel
R. DYLE
la Buvette
du Rie
S. Roch
Bas Wavre
Job
WAVRE
Chermont Fe.
Hermitage
Point du Jour
Bierge
Mill of Bierge
R. DYLE
Vandamme
Exelmans
Manial
Dion le Mont
Lourange
Trou Dehaut
Pajol
Limelette
l'Auzel
Cocgeroux
Teste
R. DYLE
To Namur
la Baraque

perseverance in your efforts against presumptuous and perjured enemies, intoxicated with their victory. It was with these sentiments you marched to support the brave English, who were maintaining the most arduous contest with unparalleled resolution. But the hour which was to decide this great struggle has struck, and has shown who was to give the law—whether an adventurer, or governments who are the friends of order.

Destiny was still undecided, when you appeared, issuing from the forest which had concealed you from the enemy, to attack his rear with that coolness, that intrepidity, that confidence, which characterizes experienced soldiers, resolved to avenge the reverses they had experienced two days before. There, rapid as lightning, you penetrated his already shaken columns. Nothing could stop you in the career of victory. The enemy, in his despair, turned his artillery upon you but you poured death into his ranks, and your progress caused in them disorder, dispersion, and at last a complete rout. He found himself obliged to abandon to you several hundreds of cannon—and his army is dissolved!

A few days will suffice to annihilate those perjured legions who were coming to consummate the slavery and the spoliation of the universe. All great commanders have regarded it as impossible immediately to renew the combat with a beaten army: you have proved that this opinion is ill-founded; you have proved that resolute warriors may be vanquished, but that their valour is not shaken. Receive, then, my thanks, incomparable soldiers, objects of my esteem! You have acquired a great reputation. The annals of Europe will eternise your triumphs. It is on you, immovable columns of the Prussian monarchy! that the destinies of the king and his august house will for ever repose. Never will Prussia cease to exist, while your sons and your grandsons resemble you.

Blücher.

Marshal Prince Blücher continued in march on the left of the Sambre, and crossed that river on the 19th, in pursuit of the enemy; and his army entered the French territory on the 21st, by Beaumont.

★★★★★★

The Allied forces which were on their march into France at this period, have been estimated as follow:

	Men
The Russian Army	225,000
The Austrian army	250,000
The Prussian Army	150,000
The British, Dutch, and Hanoverian Army	100,000
The Saxons	15,000
The Bavarian Army	40,000
The Würtemberg Army	12,000
The contingents of the German Princes	20,000
The troops of Baden	10,000
Total	822,000

Our gallant veteran issued, at this time, the following proclamation:

      Marshal Prince Blücher to the brave Belgians.

My army being on the point of entering the French territory, we cannot leave you, brave Belgians! without bidding you farewell, and without expressing our lively gratitude for the hospitality you have shown to our soldiers. We have had an opportunity of appreciating your virtues—you are a brave, a loyal, and a noble people. At the moment when danger seemed to threaten you, we were called to give you aid: we hastened to come, and it was much against our will that we found ourselves compelled, by circumstances, to await so long the commencement of the contest, which we should have been glad to see begin sooner. The presence of our troops has been burdensome to your country, but we have paid with our blood the debt of gratitude which we owe you; and a benevolent government will find means to indemnify such of you as have suffered the most by the quartering of the troops.

Adieu, brave Belgians! The remembrance of the hospitable reception which you have afforded us, as well as the recollection of your virtues, will be eternally engraven on our hearts. May the God of peace protect your fine country— may he remove from it, for a long period, the troubles of war —may you be as happy as you deserve to be!

    Headquarters, Merbeu-le-Château,   Farewell.
    June 21, 1815.   Blücher.

★★★★★★

The wrecks of Buonaparte's army retired upon Laon in the most wretched state; and, in addition to its losses in battle, vast numbers deserted continually. On the 24th Marshal Blücher took possession of St. Quintin, after it had been abandoned by the enemy; and, by the little resistance that was everywhere made, it was found that it had been impossible for the enemy to collect an army to make head against the Allies, and obstruct their direct march on Paris. The spirit of the French soldiers was broken, the infallibility and invincibility of their General was no more, and the chase of glory was given up at once as an idle dream.

The Prussians, flushed with victory, pursued their rapid march on Paris; their van-guard was attacked at Villars Coterets on the 28th; but Marshal Prince Blücher coming up with the main body, the enemy were repulsed with the loss of 6 pieces of cannon and about 1,000 prisoners. This small body of the enemy, on being forced from off the high road from Soissons to Paris, got upon that of Meaux. General Count Bülow fell in with them on this road—he briskly attacked them, took 500 prisoners, and drove the rest across the Marne. Their shattered remains afterwards got into Paris.

On the 30th, Marshal Blücher passed the village of Vertus, and, moving to his right, crossed the Seine at St. Germain; continuing his march, he posted his right, on the 2nd of July, near Plessis Pique, his left at St. Cloud, and his reserves at Versailles. The enemy had strongly fortified the heights of Montmartre and the town of St. Denys; and, by means of the little rivers Rouillon and La Vielle Mar, they inundated the ground on the north side of that town.

The heights of Belleville were likewise well fortified. Our veteran hero was powerfully opposed by the enemy in taking the position on the left of the Seine, particularly on the heights of St. Cloud and Meudon; but the gallantry of the Prussian troops under General Ziethen, surmounted every obstacle, and they succeeded, finally, in establishing themselves on the heights of Meudon, and in the village of Issy. The French attacked them again in Issy, at three o'clock in the morning of the 3rd, but were repulsed with considerable loss; and, finding that Paris was then open on its vulnerable side, the enemy sent to desire that all firing might cease on both banks of the Seine, with a view to the negotiation, at the palace of St. Cloud, of a military convention between the armies, under which the French Army should evacuate Paris.

Officers accordingly met at St. Cloud, and a military convention was agreed to and ratified on the night of the 3rd of July 1815, by the Duke of Wellington and Marshal Prince Blücher, and, on the part of the French Army, by the Minister at War. This convention decided, that the wrecks of the French Army were to evacuate Paris, to retire to the banks of the Loire, and the consequent surrender of Paris a second time to the Allies. Louis XVIII. entered the capital of his kingdom on the 8th of July, the same day with the British and Prussian forces.

Their Majesties the Emperor of Russia and the King of Prussia arrived on the 10th of July at Paris.

The three corps of Marshal Blücher's army, under the command of Generals Count Bülow and Kleist, and General von Ziethen, now took up their quarters in the city.

The most extraordinary feature in this occurrence, of the entry of the august Allies into Paris for the second time as victors, was, that the national guards, formed of the mass of citizens, showed so very little enthusiasm and loyal feeling.

If the restoration of the Bourbons is to produce peace between France and Europe, what other pledge can be desired than the unanimity and good faith of the French themselves? and what better proof could they produce of their sincerity, repentance, and return to civic order and domestic virtue, than their standing up, one and all, and hailing their king as their deliverer? But they received their sovereign and legitimate prince as tranquilly as if it were a spectacle or a procession, they were daily accustomed to.

The occupation of Paris by the Allies must strengthen the general and sanguine opinion, that war and bloodshed are to cease, and that the restoration of the Bourbons is the prelude to a durable state of tranquillity amongst the nations of Europe.

Field-Marshal Prince Blücher traversed the capital of France, at the head of his victorious troops once more as conqueror. His military glory had now reached its acme.

Our hero's life, as it can be viewed by a distant observer, appears to have been an uninterrupted series of uncommon events. Distinguished in the army at a late period in life, called afterwards to the command of that army, advancing in promotion and reputation, until he was made a general field-marshal, and selected for a post, with the due execution of which, the future existence and happiness of his country were intimately connected; subsequently rewarded by the second dignity of the Prussian realm, the father of gallant sons, and, in a vigorous old age, still able to feel all the honour and glory of his situation, what has he not experienced of those things which are supposed to constitute the splendid or the solid satisfactions of life? That he may long continue to enjoy them, to be the first support of the Prussian monarchy—the terror of its enemies—the pride of his sovereign—and the idol of his brave troops, is most devoutly to be wished and desired.

Ingram Content Group UK Ltd.
Milton Keynes UK
UKHW011923070623
423060UK00001B/14